Jean Primrose
Whyte

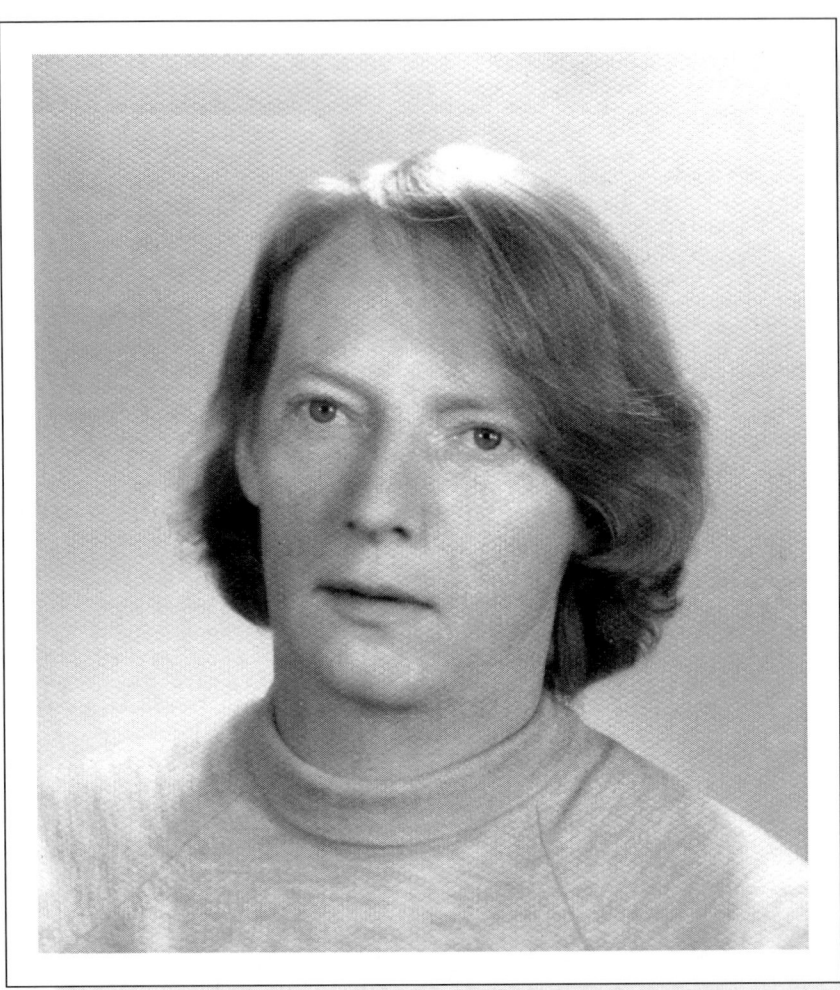

Jean Primrose Whyte

A PROFESSIONAL BIOGRAPHY

CORALIE ELSENORE JANIS JENKIN

Produced by Monash University Custom Publishing Services on behalf of the Faculty of Information Technology, Monash University.

Monash University Custom Publishing Services
Matheson Library
Building 4, Monash University
Clayton, Victoria 3800, Australia

www.epress.monash.edu.au/mucps.html

First published 2010

Copyright © 2010

All rights reserved. Apart from any uses permitted by Australia's Copyright Act 1968, no part of this book may be reproduced by any process without prior written permission from the copyright owners. Inquiries should be directed to Monash University Custom Publishing Services.

PRINTER

Sydney University Publishing Service

DESIGN

AK Design (*www.akdesign.com.au*)

COVER IMAGE

Portrait of Professor Jean Primrose Whyte
Courtesy of Monash University Archives: IN 808.

QUOTES FROM FACING PAGE

1. By strength and courage.
2. Jean Whyte's description of herself:
    Jean Whyte to Andrew Osborn, February 21st 1959. SU: M 465.

This book is available online at www.epress.monash.edu/mucps.html

ISBN 978-0-9805108-4-3 (pb)
ISBN 978-0-9805108-5-0 (web)

Pages: 164

Vi et Animo

I've got gingery hair, a grumpy expression & am above average height.

For Brian McMullin,
with thanks.

JEAN PRIMROSE WHYTE
A PROFESSIONAL BIOGRAPHY

CONTENTS

ix	List of illustrations	
x	Acknowledgements	
xi	Abbreviations	
xii	Foreword by Neil Radford	

Chapter No.

00	Prologue	
01	**Jean Primrose Whyte** Jean's childhood and schooling	
02	**Miss Jean Whyte, BA (Hons) (Adelaide), AM (Chicago)** Jean at the Public Library of South Australia and her study in Chicago	
03	**Miss Jean Whyte, BA (Hons) (Adelaide), AM (Chicago), FLAA** Jean at the University of Sydney and at the University of Western Ontario	
04	**Interlude** The *Australian Library Journal*	
05	**Miss Jean Whyte, BA (Hons) (Adelaide), AM (Chicago), FLAA, 2nd division APS** Jean's short stay at the National Library of Australia	
06	**Professor Jean Whyte, AM, BA (Hons) (Adelaide), AM (Chicago), FLAA** Jean becomes the Foundation Professor of the Graduate School of Librarianship, Monash University	
07	**Emeritus Professor Jean Whyte, AM, BA (Hons) (Adelaide), AM (Chicago), Hon DLitt (Monash), FLAA** 1. Themes from Jean's work 2. Themes from Jean's life	
08	Epilogue	
09	Appendix 1: A word from Callimachus	
10	Appendix 2: 'Such a mixture of contradictions': Alexander Macully	
11	Appendix 3: Letter from K.A. (Axel) Lodewycks to R. Selby Smith, June 15th, 1967	
12	Appendix 4: Brief history of the Graduate School of Librarianship, Monash University	
13	Appendix 5: Jean Primrose Whyte: a bibliography	
14	Bibliography	
15	Index	

A note about pagination and chapter identification

Page numbers in this book do not run consecutively across chapters. Instead, the page numbering restarts on the first page of each chapter and is prefaced by the chapter number. Thus 01.1 is chapter 1, page 1; 01.2 is chapter 1, page 2; 02.1 is chapter 2, page 1; 02.2 is chapter 2, page 2; and so on.

This system, in which page numbering is self-contained within each chapter, allows the publisher, Monash University Custom Publishing Services, to publish individual chapters online.

LIST OF ILLUSTRATIONS

Portrait page. Jean at the University of Sydney Library, 1968.
Courtesy of the University of Sydney Archives: J.P. Whyte 1968. SU: G3/224/0423.

Figure 1. Jean and her sister Billie, c.1926.
Courtesy of the State Library of South Australia: SLSA: PRG 1335.

Figure 2. Jean at Yadlamalka.
Courtesy of the State Library of South Australia: SLSA: PRG 1335.

Figure 3. Jean's graduation, 1952.
Courtesy of the National Library of Australia.

Figure 4. Alexander Macully.
Private collection.

Figure 5. Kitty Whyte.
Courtesy of the State Library of South Australia: SLSA: PRG 1335.

Figure 6. Prim Whyte.
Courtesy of the State Library of South Australia: SLSA: PRG 1335.

Figure 7. Portrait of George Chandler, Alan Fleming, Kenneth Myer, Harrison Bryan and Harold White at the farewell ceremony [for Ken Myer], Canberra, 5 February 1982.
Courtesy of the National Library of Australia. Photographer: Henk Brusse. PIC NL35646/4 LOC Cabinet NLA-Council.

Figure 8. Hector Monro.
Courtesy of John Crossley.

Figure 9. Dame Roma Mitchell at the launch of the Barbara Hanrahan Exhibition, Adelaide, 21.4.1994.
Courtesy of the State Library of South Australia. SLSA: B 58940.

Figure 10. Andrew Osborn receiving the Margaret Mann Citation, June 24th, 1959.
Courtesy of the University of Sydney Archives. SU: G3/224/2759.

○ ACKNOWLEDGEMENTS

I am grateful to the many people who helped me with this book.

Thank you to Neil Radford who wrote the Foreword.

Thank you to the staff of the following:

> Deakin University Library
> Geelong Regional Library
> Monash University Library
> Monash University Archives
> National Library of Australia
> State Library of South Australia
> State Records Office of South Australia
> State Library of Victoria
> University of Sydney Library
> University of Sydney Archives.

Thank you to Monash University staff – past and present – including John N. Crossley, who represented the Jean Whyte Fund Advisory Committee.

Thank you to those who provided advice and information, including Peter Adamson, Ross Harvey, David Jones, John Lowe, Graeme Powell, Rachel Salmond, and Michael Talbot.

Thank you to those people who allowed me to interview them and granted me permission to quote them. Thank you to the families who allowed me to stay with them during interstate visits: Le/Nguyen family in Sydney, the Veitch/Fellner family in Adelaide, and the Fox family in Canberra.

And thank you to my friends Zorro, Aria, Mister Bones, Clancy and Lucia who kept me company.

> Coralie Jenkin
> June 27th, 2009.

ABBREVIATIONS

ABC	Australian Broadcasting Corporation
ALJ	*Australian Library Journal*
ALS	Adelaide Lending Service
AM (Chicago)	Master of Arts
AM	Member of the Order of Australia
AUC	Australian Universities Commission
Auntie	Eileen Whyte
Billie	Phyllis Whyte
COPQ	Committee on Overseas Professional Qualifications
FLAA	Fellow of the Library Association of Australia
GLS	Graduate Library School (University of Chicago)
GSL	Graduate School of Librarianship (Monash University)
Hon DLitt	Honorary Doctor of Letters
Institute	Australian Institute of Librarians
Kitty	Kathleen Whyte
LAA	Library Association of Australia
LAC	Library Advisory Committee
MLib	Master of Librarianship
MON	Monash University Archives
NLA	National Library of Australia
PLSA	Public Library of South Australia
Prim	Ernest Primrose Whyte
RMIT	Royal Melbourne Institute of Technology
SLIS	School of Library and Information Science (University of Western Ontario, London, Canada)
SLSA	State Library of South Australia
St Peter's	St Peter's Collegiate Girls' School
SU	University of Sydney Archives

FOREWORD

Any list of Australian librarians who made a truly significant and lasting contribution to the profession in the second half of the twentieth century would have to include (in alphabetical order) Harrison Bryan, John Metcalfe and Jean Whyte. The first two named have not yet received the biographical recognition and analysis which they deserve, but that will surely come. For Jean Whyte we can be grateful that, after five years of painstaking research, Dr Coralie Jenkin, one of Jean's students at Monash University, has written a very fitting professional biography.

I should state my interest from the outset. I am one of hundreds of Australian librarians whom she infected with what she called 'library mania' and who owe much of the success they achieved in their careers to Jean's example, support and encouragement. We first met in 1959 when she became Public Services Librarian at the University of Sydney, where I was a Junior Library Assistant. She quickly identified me as someone who had potential, and then made sure that I didn't let her down. In 1966 she was responsible for my enrolment at her *alma mater*, the Graduate Library School at the University of Chicago, an experience which changed my life both professionally and personally. She was a member of the selection committee which appointed me to succeed Harrison Bryan as Librarian of the University of Sydney in 1980. And I am just one of hundreds who benefitted from her influence.

In the introductory chapter of her history of the Australian Institute of Librarians (left unfinished at her death and superbly completed by Dr David Jones) Jean repeated the standard warning of historians: 'if we write to praise heroes and achievements we shall not create an enduring work'. In this biography its subject is a hero and her achievements are legion. Any Australian librarian could tell you that, if you mentioned the name of Jean Whyte. But neither she nor her achievements were perfect and complete, and that is where Dr Jenkin's analysis and assessment are valuable. Jean's career had its share of disappointments and frustrations and she often wished she had done more or had done differently. Her unbounded enthusiasm sometimes led her astray, and, in particular, several of her most important mentors and supporters disappointed her on closer inspection. But her essential commonsense soon put things right, and her talent for seizing the opportunity and turning it to her (and the profession's) advantage overcame these setbacks.

At the Public Library of South Australia, then the University of Sydney, and later at the National Library of Australia Jean turned problems into challenges and inspired her staff to set their sights higher and achieve more. Any spare time or energy they had left over was expected to be channeled into the Library Association of Australia, and it usually was. In the last phase of her career, as founding Head of the pioneering Graduate School of Librarianship at Monash University, Jean had, and exploited, the opportunity to mould bright young minds and to encourage her students to perform better than they thought they could. She just assumed that you were as competent and dedicated as she was, and treated you accordingly. So you found yourself expected to perform better, and you somehow did. We are all better librarians, and better people, for having fallen under her influence. It is a debt we can repay only by trying to do the same for the next generation of librarians who work for us or study under us.

Jean was a modest and self-effacing person. If she read Coralie Jenkin's book she would probably be both delighted and embarrassed, which shows what a good and balanced professional biography Dr. Jenkin has produced.

Neil A Radford

PROLOGUE

> *The chronology – the 'when?' – is not difficult, but when we start to ask the more interesting questions of 'why?' and 'who?' and 'how?' the answers are not so readily found. Those which are readily found are not always convincing.*[1]

I met Jean Whyte at Monash University in 1986. The Graduate School of Librarianship at Monash had been recommended to me as the best library school in Australia. At the time I was accepted as a student by the School I was living far from Monash (Clayton, Victoria), in Orroroo (east of Port Augusta, South Australia), a town of about 600 people, where some households had wood stoves, manual telephones and electricity generators; where there were thousands of sheep, kangaroos and emus; where children on stations were students of the School of the Air; where we drove on dirt roads and lived in the quiet beauty of the bush.

My first day at Monash. Concrete and bitumen. People everywhere. The modern, multi-storied Menzies Building. Electricity humming. Escalators. Corridors with dead walls. Graffiti. Rubbish. Computers. I found the School. Fourth Floor South. I went into Professor Whyte's office. I met the formidable Professor Whyte.

I spoke of the contrast between Monash and Orroroo. Professor Whyte replied 'I'm from north of Augusta …'

Oh take me back
Where the dust blows thick
Please take me back
For I'm home sick.[2]

ENDNOTES

1. Jean Whyte and David J. Jones. *Uniting a Profession*, 2007, 3.
2. Brian McMullin. 'Yadlamalka girl shaped Australian librarianship'. *The Age*, April 18th–19th, 2003, 19.

Figure 1: Jean and her sister Billie, c.1926

Figure 2: Jean at Yadlamalka

Figure 3: Jean's graduation, 1952

Figure 4: Alexander Macully

Figure 5: Kitty Whyte

Figure 6: Prim Whyte

CHAPTER 1

○ JEAN PRIMROSE WHYTE
JEAN'S CHILDHOOD AND SCHOOLING

> *showed enthusiasm and zeal, carrying out her duties with much ability and faithfulness*[1]

Jean's earliest memory was seeing her mother killed by a shark.[2]

Jean, two and a half years old, sitting on the Brighton (Adelaide) Jetty with her younger sister, watched as their mother, Kitty, was attacked and killed by a shark. Also watching from the jetty were Kitty's swimming students, one of whom was Roma Mitchell, who would become Jean's lifelong friend. In the family album is a photograph of Kitty, standing in the shallows with her two children, perhaps her last photograph. A memorial to her stands near the Brighton Jetty.

Kitty – Kathleen Duncan Campbell Macully[3] – was a swimming teacher and a lifesaver who had saved a number of lives and earned the Royal Lifesaving Society's Grand Diploma.[4] She

> was well known to swimming and Life Saving enthusiasts. The [Royal Lifesaving] Society regarded her as one of their most valued supporters, and she was second to none in her methods of teaching and instilling confidence in her pupils; she was especially interested in teaching swimming to children, who worshipped her, and her kind and gentle disposition made her beloved and respected by all.
>
> In 1913 Mrs. Whyte gained the Proficiency Certificate and Bronze Medallion, and from that time she took a keen interest in the work, passing in turn for the Teacher's Certificate, the Hon. Instructor's Certificate, and the Award of Merit. And on April 8th, 1919, she gained, with honors, the highest award issued by the Society, the Diploma, being the first swimmer in South Australia to gain this distinction.[5]

When Kitty married Prim Whyte in 1920 she moved from Brighton to the Outback. Perhaps missing the beach, her family and her friends, she returned to Brighton for holidays. She was buried there, in the cemetery at St Jude's Church of England, where her father, Alexander Macully, had been the incumbent.

Alexander Macully was an interesting character with a varied career, as we read in his obituary:

> Mr. Macully was widely known. He was born in the cathedral city of Armagh, Ireland. When he was a child his parents emigrated to Melbourne, and there his father occupied an important position in the Civil Service for about 35 years. He was educated at Scotch College, Melbourne, and distinguished himself in English literature, and obtained the first prize in elocution. He played cricket well, and occupied a place in the college eleven. Desiring to read for holy orders, he entered the famous Irish University, Trinity College, Dublin, and gained honours and took the degrees of M.A. and LL.B. During his college course he gained a host of friends, and was acknowledged as the first interpreter of

literature, particularly Shakespeare, in Dublin. He gave several recitals in the hall of Trinity College ... 'His naturally fine gifts of voice and expression were united with the gains which come from careful study ... ' In 1880, at Meath, Mr. Macully was ordained [Church of England] deacon ... he married a daughter of the Hon. Alexander Campbell, of Rosemont, Sydney. For some years Mr. Macully took up the role of teaching in the colleges. In 1897 he returned to his work as a clergyman ... Bendigo ... Brisbane ... Hindmarsh and Bowden ... Penola ... Semaphore. From 1905 until 1908 he was in charge of St. Jude's, Brighton ... [6]

I began looking for, but was unable to trace, Macully's birth record. He may have been born in Ireland, but, as his obituaries are selective in the material they use – perhaps because Macully was likewise selective – and his Irish connections important to him, I wondered whether the Irish birthplace may have been a romantic fabrication. This concern led eventually to the discovery of early newspaper articles which referred to Macully being 'an Australian native', who, after studying in Ireland, returned to Australia 'the land of his birth'.[7]

Alexander was an Honorary Fellow of The Society of Science, Letters, and Art in London. He taught the culture of the speaking voice and the art of reading at Trinity College, Dublin, and then in studios first in Melbourne and subsequently in Brisbane and Adelaide, and he spoke at recitals and lectured in poetry. Early in his career he was given the title 'Professor' when he taught 'Elocution and Aesthetics of English Literature' at Alexandra College and the Rutland Square Institute, Dublin. His obituary does not mention his temporary departure from the Anglican Church, when, for three years, he was minister at the Unitarian Church, East Melbourne, perhaps because his 'aspirations toward religious freedom were not supported by any very strong convictions ... he was only an enquirer in theological matters, and hence was not enthusiastically followed as a leader ... Within a year a very serious falling off in attendance was manifested and before the term of his engagement was completed the congregation was fast approaching vanishing point'.[8]

The Macullys were wealthy, their home 'Cullymont' in Melbourne, built in 1889, now listed by the National Trust, is possibly Victoria's largest semi-detached pair of mansions, bearing the Macully coat of arms with the motto 'Vi et Animo' (by strength and courage)[9] and featuring 'intricately detailed stained glass roundels in the sidelights and transom of the front door depicting Shakespearian characters ... one of the finest grand family residences'.[10]

Alexander married Maria Julia (Minnie) Campbell, the daughter of the Hon. Alexander Campbell, MLC, JP, born in Scotland, who sailed to Sydney 'to seek his fortune'. He found it. He became a director and, several times, the Chairman, of the Sydney Stock Exchange and a director of the Australian Mutual Provident Society, founded the Mercantile Bank of Sydney, was manager of Agra and Masterman's Bank, was a member of the Chamber of Commerce, and had various pastoral interests. He was a member of the Legislative Assembly of New South Wales and later of the Legislative Council, Postmaster-General and associate of Sir Henry Parkes. Campbell 'was prepared to give the working classes such liberties as did not affect the revenue. He was a vital member of Sydney's mercantile world and a shrewd businessman whose main concern both in private and in public was the advancement of the colony's commerce and trade'[11]

(Jean avoided staying with her Sydney relatives: 'they are just so bloody "upper-class" that I should have to live on alka-seltzer').[12]

Alexander and Minnie had another mansion built, in Brighton, Adelaide, which they named 'Dunluce' after the Northern Irish castle on which it was modelled. The Brighton 'Dunluce', built on twelve acres, looked like a castle, with coach house and stables – it still looks grand but now has little land. It is difficult to single out the grandest mansion: the Campbells' 'Rosemont' (which later became the home of Sir Charles and Lady Lloyd Jones), 'Cullymont' or 'Dunluce'.

The Macully family moved to Brighton in 1905 when Alexander took up the incumbency of St Jude's Church of England (built in 1855 but not consecrated until over a century later, in 1977, because £100 was owed to the builders),[13] while continuing to teach elocution and to lecture at the South Australian Institutes. He later developed dementia and became a 'wanderer', shouting 'Macully's lost! Macully's lost!' until rescued.[14] He died in 1921 – 'so dear old Professor Macully has joined the angels! A most lovable man, and such a mixture of contradictions! Believed all things, hoped all things; to him nothing was impossible but what was impracticable'.[15]

Alexander and Minnie had three daughters, of whom Kitty was the youngest, and a younger son, Arnold, who died in France in World War I.[16] Dunluce was not far from a mansion owned by the wealthy and childless John and Louisa Whyte, so it is likely that their proximity resulted in Kitty meeting her future husband, their nephew, Ernest Primrose (Prim) Whyte.

A question often asked about Jean was the origin of her name 'Primrose': Primrose was a name from Kinross, Scotland,[17] which Prim's father, William Whyte, left for the Victorian gold diggings, arriving in 1852, followed by his brother John a year later. They soon moved to Adelaide, where John found work in a draper's shop and married the shop's widowed owner Louisa Heath. William, John and Louisa, together with Louisa's brother, James Counsell, set up the very successful grocery firm Whyte, Counsell and Company, which also had a large interest in the paddle steamers which transported their goods along the Murray River. They also owned land in the dry north of South Australia – John Whyte held 21 pastoral leases totalling 3,343 square miles in 1877, which led to a number of places being named in his honour.[18]

William married Sarah Hodge, who died giving birth to their first child, Frank. William then married Eleanor May McDonald, with whom he had at least twelve children, Prim being one of the youngest. An undated newspaper clipping about Prim is entitled 'Our great northerner' – there is a handwritten note at the top 'exaggerated' (no doubt about that, and a lot of mistakes as well):

> Picture a man of about five feet ten inches in height, with a figure that might easily be the envy of a Greek God, who walks with the lithe springy stride of youth ... Less than 40 years ago he was christened Ernest Primrose Whyte ... He first made his infantile voice heard at North Adelaide ... received his education at ... Prince Alfred College ... On leaving school 'Prim' went to Mundowdna Station, near Hergott Springs ... owned by Mr. John Whyte ... moved on to Lake Torrens ... remained there for ten years ... 'Prim' was among the first to enlist in the A.I.F. 1914 ... He was on active service for four years, attaining the rank of Warrant Officer ... when feed was very scarce he ... [drove] sheep in search of scant herbage ... During the twelve months that the sheep were on the road 'Prim' did not once sleep under a roof. 'Prim' Whyte is typical

of your true Northerner ... strong, self-reliant, courageous almost to the point of foolhardiness in time of danger, hospitable, and – a fine sportsman ... 'Prim' Whyte is a superb horseman and, as a younger man, he rode many winners round the North.[19]

Prim's war service records show that, at the time of his enlistment in January 1915, he was 33 years old, 5 feet 10½ inches tall, had fair hair, grey eyes and a ruddy complexion, was a member of the Congregational Church, had never married, and his rank was Sergeant. He left Adelaide on HMAT *Afric*, in 1915. He joined the 4th Light Horse Brigade and, like most members of the Brigade, he had worked with horses.[20] He served in various Australian Army Service Corps known as 'the train', transporting food and supplies to soldiers, serving in the main theatres of war – mostly in France – for more than three years without injury (he did have the mumps). He was discharged as medically unfit (peritoneal adhesions) and returned to Australia in August 1918.[21]

Prim returned from the War to manage Wirraminna Station (which he part-owned) on the East-West railway line in Outback South Australia. He married Kitty at St Jude's Church of England, Brighton, on November 30th, 1920, when he was thirty-nine years old and Kitty was twenty-nine. Their first child was Jean Primrose, born in the MacDowell Ward of Quambi Nursing Home, South Terrace, Adelaide, on June 27th, 1923, who was followed by Phyllis Primrose (Billie) on May 6th, 1925. Following Kitty's death in 1926 Prim sold Wirraminna and moved to Yadlamalka Station, where he was Manager for the rest of his working life.[22]

Yadlamalka was the first home Jean could remember, a three-hundred-and-thirty-square-mile sheep station, carrying about 10,000 sheep, forty miles north of Port Augusta in South Australia, fifteen miles from the nearest neighbour and with few roads and few people, but in good spells there were kangaroos, emus, horses, foxes and camels. It was hot, dry, dusty, flat country, which relied on rainfall, but Prim's reports to the station owners, T.H. Doman & Co. Ltd, tell of drought years, with an average annual rainfall of only five inches, not enough workers during World War II, and the need for more land to keep Yadlamalka viable – nearby stations Marachowie, Kalliota and Lake Hut were added during Prim's time. Yadlamalka appears to have been relatively successful – Prim, in encouraging Domans to buy nearby Wilkatana station to increase the holding, said that it would make Yadlamalka 'second to none'.[23] One visitor to the station was Bejah Dervish, a famous South Australian camel-train driver, the 'grand old man of the desert', whose life is commemorated with a plaque in North Terrace, Adelaide. Kitty wrote of a 'lovely moonlight night & camel bells are tinkling', and she was photographed seated on a camel, holding Jean, then only a few months old.

Although Kitty's sisters offered to care for the girls following her death, Jean and Billie returned to live at Yadlamalka with their father. Prim later married Kitty's older sister Eileen (Jean and Billie called her 'Auntie'). Eileen and Prim remained at Yadlamalka until Prim's retirement, then they moved to 'Wintabatinyana', a house in exclusive Unley Park, Adelaide.[24]

Jean and Billie were educated at home by correspondence courses and a series of eight governesses – 'for whom one must confess a sneaking sympathy';[25] Jean said that 'as the governesses were the only women on the property most of my early years were spent in the company of men'.[26] Then Jean left Yadlamalka, aged 11, to board at St Peter's Collegiate Girls'

School, Adelaide. Apart from holidays she was never to return to the Outback, but yearned for it for the rest of her life. She wrote of its influence on her life:

> it taught me to ride a horse, to class merino wool, to follow tracks, to fix almost anything with a piece of wire and a rusty nail, and to be content with my own company and a book. Perhaps too some of my patience with slow students was learnt when drafting sheep or coaxing young lambs and kangaroos to drink![27]

That Jean's move from the Outback to boarding school was not easy is not surprising: 'at first I was a rebel against the unaccustomed discipline, and I found it difficult to adjust myself to life among other children, who played what I considered foolish games; but I soon learnt to like it and to share all their activities'.[28] Jean did very well at St Peter's: she was Captain of the debating team, Chair of the Literary and Dramatic Society, an actor in school plays, a member of the Music Club (she gave a paper on 'Romantic Music'), a member of the Library Committee, a boarders' prefect for her house, Kennion, Vice-Captain of Kennion, then Captain in her final year; she captained both the first hockey team and the second tennis team, edited the annual *Chronicles of St Peter's Girls*, wrote the Old Scholars Association Essay in her final year and published her poems in the *Chronicles*.[29] She wrote: 'School for me meant debating, writing poetry, tennis and hockey'[30] (sporting ability may have been aided by her height).

Of her academic work Jean wrote: 'As a scholar I was not outstanding. I usually topped the class in English and History and came close to bottom in Latin and Mathematics'.[31] She gained her Intermediate Certificate with passes in English Literature and Botany and credits in History and Physiology (only one other student gained a single credit). In her Leaving examination Jean passed English Literature, Economics, Modern History and Physiology, and in Leaving Honours she passed English, Modern History and Economics, but she did not complete her Leaving Honours Certificate until she passed her Latin examination in 1946,[32] five years after she left school. She won South Australia's Tennyson Medal for Matriculation English and left St Peter's with a glowing reference from the Principal, Sister Persis.

Jean and Billie (also a student at St Peter's) returned to Yadlamalka for holidays, sometimes taking school friends with them, one of whom was Mavis Crawford, who became Jean's lifelong friend and mother of Jean's godson, Bruce. Mavis told of gracious standards being kept at Yadlamalka: in the Outback, listening to the dingoes howl at night, the Whyte family dressed for dinner in formal clothes, the girls usually wearing their black velvet boarding school dinner dresses. The cook prepared meals for the staff in the men's quarters and, wearing a chef's hat, would carry the evening meal into the house on a tray held high. He prepared the main course, Auntie the dessert.[33]

At the end of Jean's schooling comes a curious episode. The school's records show that, in Jean's final year, she was a prefect, but the Head Prefect was Christobel Williams.[34] Jean, in her 1952 scholarship application, wrote: 'In my last year at school I was Head Prefect (that is Captain of the school)'. And, in his speech at her retirement, Harrison Bryan referred to her as having been Head Girl at St Peter's.[35]

ENDNOTES

1. Sister Persis. [Reference for Jean Whyte], 1942. NLA: MS 9616.
2. 'there are sharks … my earliest memory is watching my mother being attacked and killed by one here at Brighton. I was on the jetty'. Jean Whyte to Andrew Osborn, January 2nd, 1959. SU: M 465.
3. The surname is variously spelled M'Cully, McCully or Macully. Campbell was Kitty's mother's birth name.
4. *Brighton: a walk through history,* 2001.
5. ['It is with sincere regret']. [Newspaper clipping], [1926]. SLSA: PRG 1335/1.
6. 'Obituaries. Rev. Alexander Macully, M.A., LL.B.'. *The Observer* [SA], January 15th, 1921, 34b.
7. Joseph Fraser. 'Pen and ink sketches of prominent persons'. [Newspaper clipping], [1888?]. SLSA: PRG1288.
8. Quoted in Dorothy Scott. *The Halfway House to Infidelity,* 1980, 38.
9. The coat of arms can still be seen from the street.
10. [Estate agent's promotional pamphlet], [1999?]. SLSA: PRG 1335/10/2-9.
11. Douglas Pike, ed. *Australian Dictionary of Biography. Volume 3: 1851–1890,* 1969, 341–342.
12. Jean Whyte to Andrew Osborn, February 5th, 1959. SU: M 465. I assume that she was referring to the Campbell family, as I have not found references to other Sydney relatives.
13. *Brighton: A walk through history,* 2001.
14. Interview: Douglas Muecke, 2005.
15. ['From "One of his many friends"']. [Newspaper clipping], [1921]. SLSA: PRG 1335/10.
16. *Pioneer Index. Victoria 1836–1888* records the death of an Oscar Campbell Macully, aged 7 months, son of 'AlexR' and 'Minnie' Campbell Macully in 1887. Although this name does not appear in family records I assume that Oscar was Minnie and Alexander's child (could 'Oscar' have been in honour of Oscar Wilde, the Irish writer who was a contemporary of Macully at Trinity College, Dublin?). Minnie and Alexander appear not to have registered the births of any of their children except Arnold.

    The Macully daughters were born between 1885 and 1891; the explorer Sir Douglas Mawson was born in 1882 and lived nearby in Brighton from 1904. I wonder whether the Misses Macully in the 'castle' were friendly with Mawson? The handsome Mawson was 'being pursued by Adelaide's society matrons' (Nancy Robinson Flannery, ed. *This everlasting silence,* 2000, 2). The woman Mawson was to marry, Paquita, was born in the same year as Kitty Macully and, like Kitty, had wealthy parents who lived in Brighton (on a five-acre estate). Mawson is buried in St Jude's Cemetery, Brighton.
17. Whyte was a common surname in Kinross, with William, John, Primrose, Jean, etc. being common forenames. Many Kinross villagers with similar names migrated to Australia in the nineteenth century, which has led to confusion in the records. Although the name Primrose was given to both daughters, there was no-one else of that name in his family in Australia, so the name may have been given in memory of a Primrose in Kinross.
18. *Pastoral Pioneers of South Australia,* 1925–1927, 150–151.

    'John Whyte (c.1825–1902) pastoralist and a member of the grocery firm, Whyte, Counsell & Co … is remembered by the **Hundred of Whyte**, County of Victoria, proclaimed on 18 February 1869 … **Mount Whyte**, east of Lake Torrens – he held pastoral lease no. 96 from 1880 and **Whyte Well**, on section 121, Hundred of Marmon Jabuk … The town of **Whyte-Yarcowie**, 32 km south of Peterborough, was proclaimed on 28 May 1874 as "Yarcowie", [but] was altered to "Whyte-Yarcowie" on 5 September 1929, so as to conform with the name of the local railway station. The prefix "Whyte"

19 alludes to the same gentleman, while *yarcowie* is Aboriginal for "flood" or "great waters".' (Geoffrey H. Manning. *Manning's place names of South Australia*, 2006, 455).

Whackers Up. 'Our great northerner', n.d. SLSA: PRG 1335/1. The article is difficult to date, as it contains so many mistakes. It must have been written after 1918, as it refers to Prim's return to civilian life. But there is not enough time for the five years at Wirraminna between the end of the war in 1918 and Prim's fortieth birthday in 1921 (assuming that 'christened' refers to the year of his birth).

The collection of Jean Whyte material held in the State Library of South Australia (PRG 1335) includes many undated cuttings written in the same tone (errors and hyperbole). They tell of Prim and his family's activities, including visits to Adelaide and Sydney, and a few references to Jean's activities such as 'I also saw a pretty picture of Prim's daughter, Jean, shepherding rams on Yadlamalka on her grey pony "Tiny"'. And 'The eldest girl is making quite a name for herself as a juvenile poetess. The jovial Primrose himself assists ... what Prim doesn't know about "metre," "rhythm" and such things that are bothersome but so necessary for the poetically-minded isn't worth knowing'.

20 'Australian Imperial Force. Nominal Roll. 4th Light Horse Brigade Train, 14th A.S.C.'. National Archives of Australia. Defence Service Records. [NAA:B2455, Whyte, Ernest Primrose].

21 Prim's Defence Service Records were provided by the Department of Veterans Affairs and the National Archives of Australia. Peter Adamson, an historian with an interest in the Great War, conjectured that, although Prim enlisted in 1915, the records may have been compiled later, based on the evidence that Prim's war service number changed from 5835 to 8782 in early 1918 yet 8782 appears earlier than that in the handwritten copy, and that notes up to August 1917 are all in the same handwriting. It is possible that the original or first page is missing, and that the record was rewritten, perhaps in 1917 (Interview: Peter Adamson, 2005).

22 Prim's occupation is given as 'Pastoralist' on Jean's birth certificate and as 'squatter' in 'Woman killed by shark'. *The Register* [SA], March 19th, 1926, 9.

'Prim part-owned Wirraminna with Mr. Lillecrap and G.F. and R.K. Jenkins. Lillecrap is likely to have been Horace G. Lillecrap; G.F. and R.K. Jenkins to have been George Frederick (1878–1957) and his half-brother Richard Kirkhouse (1889–1950), sons of George Kirkhouse Jenkins' (Jill Statton, ed. *Biographical Index of South Australians 1836–1885*, 1986, Vol. II, 838).

Yadlamalka was an Aboriginal name; spellings include Yadlumulka, Yedlamulka, Yudamulka. The name comes from an Aboriginal language, 'mulka' meaning 'to talk'.

'Yadlamalka [is] the limit of rains from the south and very rarely gets anything but a flying shower from that quarter, though the rains extend for some 20 miles further north in the ranges ... Its only chance of grass for the summer is from September thunder showers which are the exception, not the rule. The rains it depends on to fill its tanks, fall in January, February and March and are the tails of tropical rains ... what makes Yadlamalka pay well is that after heavy summer rains the proprietor is able to buy store sheep and fatten them quickly, having his dams to fall back on when the claypans dry up'. (Geoffrey H. Manning. *Manning's place names of South Australia*, 2006, 471).

23 E.P. Whyte to Messrs T.H. Doman & Co. Ltd, November 9th, 1943. SLSA: PRG 1335/8.

24 Wintabatinyana, built in 1922, has had two owners in its more than 80 years – Kitty and Prim bought the house soon after it was built; Auntie and Jean sold it to Joan and Rudi Lange, the current owners, in 1962. Joan Lange, at home when I called looking for Jean's former home, showed me around. In a quiet court, Wintabatinyana is a gracious and lovely house with an impressive recessed ceiling in the lounge room (Interview: Joan Lange, 2005).

25 Harrison Bryan. 'Jean Primrose Whyte'. *ALJ* 38 (1) 1989, 6.

26 Jean Whyte to the Secretary, American Association of University Women, 1952. NLA: MS 9616.

27 Ibid.

28 Ibid.
29 Jean Whyte. 'The greater things'. *Chronicles of St Peter's Girls,* 54, 1941, 23–24.
30 Jean Whyte to the Secretary, American Association of University Women, 1952. NLA: MS 9616.
31 Ibid.
32 H.R. Othams to Jean Whyte, October 28th, 1952. SLSA: PRG 1335.
33 Interview: Mavis Crawford, 2008. The current manager of Yadlamalka lives in the same house.
34 'School officers'. *Chronicles of St Peter's Girls,* 54, 1941, [1]; *St Peter's Collegiate Girls' School 1894–1968,* 1972, 207.
35 Jean Whyte to the Secretary, American Association of University Women, 1952. NLA: MS 9616; Harrison Bryan. 'Jean Primrose Whyte'. *ALJ* 38 (1) 1989, 6.

CHAPTER 2

○ MISS JEAN WHYTE, BA (HONS) (ADELAIDE), AM (CHICAGO)
JEAN AT THE PUBLIC LIBRARY OF SOUTH AUSTRALIA AND HER STUDY IN CHICAGO

is endowed with a great strength of character and possesses outstanding qualities of leadership[1]

Now began Jean's distinguished career in librarianship, but, as Jean said, 'I was a librarian by accident simply because I couldn't afford to go to the university, so I went into the library in order to sneak down to the university at night and do my degree'.[2] There were several 'accidents' which led to, and subsequently punctuated, Jean's early career in librarianship. Throughout the chapter I will refer to these as 'accidents', although in some places 'opportunity', 'serendipity', or 'fortunate combinations of circumstances' would be closer to the mark. These fortunate accidents led to a lifelong syndrome that Jean referred to as 'library mania'.[3]

Jean's first fortunate accident was that her father and step-mother wanted her to return to Yadlamalka, whereas Jean wanted to go to University so that she could 'reform the world (in my last year at school I had become an ardent supporter of World Federal Union) but the family could not afford to send me, nor did they believe in university careers for girls, besides I was a useful stockman'.[4] So, needing to support herself while she studied, Jean looked for a job in Adelaide, preferring to work close to the University so that she did not need to travel far between work and study.

Another fortunate accident: 'after weeks of fruitless searching',[5] Jean found work at the Public Library of South Australia (PLSA) in North Terrace, near the University of Adelaide, where she wanted to study.[6] The Colony of South Australia was established in August 1834, and in the same month books were collected for the Colony by the South Australian Literary and Scientific Association. The first collection of books was sent to South Australia in 1836, and a library was set up in Adelaide. Various locations and names followed until the PLSA (later renamed the State Library of South Australia) was formed in 1884. When Jean arrived the PLSA was South Australia's only free library service, as the government used the existence of South Australian Institutes' libraries – which required paid membership but could not cater for the growing need for library services – as an excuse for not creating suburban and regional free library services (these were the libraries of the same South Australian Institutes in which Alexander Macully had lectured). The PLSA had a Reference Library, Children's Library, Country Lending Service, the Adelaide Lending Service, Research Service, a Youth Lending Service and Archives. It was under-staffed and under-resourced, and its collections were too small for the number of users – for example the Children's Library had 14,000 'specially selected volumes' to lend to 15,000 borrowers, issuing almost 200,000 items annually.[7] Within weeks of beginning her first library job Jean had made up her mind to be a librarian.[8]

Jean made the most of the proximity of the PLSA to the University of Adelaide. After years of part-time study she graduated Bachelor of Arts with first-class honours in English Language and Literature in 1952 and was awarded the John Howard Clarke prize for first place in English

Literature – 'I think that I have made amends for an unimpressive scholastic record as a school-girl' she said.[9] Jean's graduation ceremony was held in Bonython Hall at the University of Adelaide, on Wednesday, April 2nd, 1952 at 3 pm. Jean is listed under 'Scholars and prizemen for 1951'.[10] It was reported that

> Wide interest will be taken in the announcement that Miss Jean P. Whyte has gained a BA honors degree in English Language and Literature at the University of Adelaide and has been recommended for the John Howard Clark [sic] prize.
>
> His [sic] sister Phyllis was second in the same examination.
>
> They are daughters of Mr. Prim Whyte, ex-manager of Yadlamalka station Port Augusta, now of Unley Park. Their mother was a daughter of Professor Macully, formerly of Brighton; their step-mother is too.
>
> Miss Jean Whyte is a member of the Public Library staff.[11]

In commenting on Jean's achievement Harrison Bryan wrote that 'honours degrees are difficult enough to secure with full-time study, that only workaholics can manage them part-time and that only brilliant workaholics can collect first class honours under such conditions'.[12]

At the same time as she studied for her degree Jean studied for her librarianship qualifications, being one of the first group of candidates to sit for the Australian Institute of Librarians' Preliminary Examinations in 1944.[13] She completed the Qualifying Certificate in Librarianship (later renamed 'Registration Examinations') in 1946. Jean wrote that these examinations were not easy, which convinced her 'that it is a professional examination of a high standard – which is as it should be'.[14] The subjects which Jean passed were:[15]

> Preliminary Examination, 1944
> 5.1.11 The Catalogue, shelf list and accession record. Elementary cataloguing excluding subject cataloguing.
> 5.1.12 Elementary shelf classification, subject cataloguing and book numbers.
> 5.1.13 Library routine, order work, circulation and reference work.
> 5.1.14 The Book, the library and the reader.
>
> Qualifying Examination
> Section 1, 1945:
> 5.1.15 Advanced cataloguing, excluding subject cataloguing: theoretical.
> 5.1.16 Advanced cataloguing, excluding subject cataloguing: practical.
> 5.1.17 Classification and subject cataloguing: theoretical.
> 5.1.18 Classification and subject cataloguing: practical.
> Section II, 1946:
> 5.1.19 Book selection, reference work, relations with readers, readers' advising.
> 5.1.20 Organisation of knowledge and aids to research.

Jean was soon working back after 'normal' hours, four or five nights each week,[16] her usual hours being from 9.15 a.m. to 9.30 p.m., as well as Saturday mornings, and she prepared lectures in her own time.[17] Jean noted that 'My university work, like my study for the library examinations, was mostly done between 8.00 p.m. and 1.00 a.m. There is no surer way of learning to concentrate than the knowledge that there will be no time for re-reading'.[18]

Another fortunate accident: women had been discouraged from being cadet librarians at the PLSA, but as so many young men were away at World War II the PLSA changed its policy in order to employ women (in some departments the head was the sole male employee), in the process saving money by employing women at the lower rate of clerk rather than that of library assistant.[19] One of these clerks was Jean, who began work in June 1942 in the Country Lending Service, which sent boxes of books to rural areas,[20] to schools, and, during the War, to soldiers stationed in South Australia and the Northern Territory. The Service grew quickly and was too successful for the 'temporary' accommodation (which they occupied for 20 years), for the budget, for staff and for the available resources.[21] Jean's work included 'typing labels for book-parcels, sorting cards and putting away books'.[22]

During her years at the PLSA Jean was to move to the Reference Library, where she began by reshelving used materials and staffing the information desk; to the Adelaide Lending Service, where she was second in charge; to two branch libraries – she catalogued both the South Australian Department of Mines Library[23] (where she became Officer in Charge in 1949) and the Botanic Gardens Library (in 1952); then to librarian in charge of Government Departmental Libraries. She returned to the Reference Department, where she became a Senior Assistant before becoming Staff Training Officer in 1955.[24] Jean said: 'I started wrapping up parcels of books for the country service and progressed to choosing them. In the 15 years I was there I did just about everything and caught library mania well before finishing my degree'.[25]

One of the happiest accidents during Jean's time at the PLSA was the presence there of George Pitt, who inspired Jean in her career. Their friendship, which was to continue until the end of Pitt's life, was based on 'our love of our work, especially what we have helped to create together'.[26] Pitt had begun his career at the PLSA in 1906, when he was 15 years old, and stayed for his working life. He became the state's first Archivist and later Principal Librarian (the equivalent of the modern State Librarian), and soon after beginning the latter appointment went to look at libraries in Great Britain and the United States, writing to Jean throughout this tour, addressing her as 'Miss Whyte' and signing as 'The Boss'. The letters were predominantly about library matters, and many threads which can be traced through the rest of Jean's life first appear here: her interest in all aspects of librarianship and archives, concerns about her health, involvement with the Institute, followed by its successor, the Library Association of Australia (LAA), long working hours, and more and more work.

Pitt had taken charge of the Adelaide Lending Service when it opened in 1946. The two friends prepared for the opening by spending their evenings together cataloguing after Jean 'discovered' cataloguing and studied it after work.[27] The timing of the Lending Service's opening was also serendipitous: Jean had had three years' experience at the PLSA, had worked with Pitt in the preparation and had taken up the number three position (which was actually second in charge, as that position was unfilled), and, on Pitt's recommendation, she was formally appointed to second in charge of the Adelaide Lending Service in 1948,[28] a notable step, as the two top positions were reserved for men.

The Service occupied much of their correspondence during Pitt's overseas trip: 'What an exacting mistress the ALS has been, and how much pleasure she has given us!'[29] He praised Jean:

> I shall always remember your enthusiasm, your wish to understand everything and to have a hand in it, your wonderfully quiet insight in to the heart of problems, and above all your strong loyalty. It always did me good to see you – intelligent, quick, and alive to what was best for the Service.[30]

The Adelaide Lending Service grew so quickly it was 'the young giant in a strait jacket',[31] its lunch-hour rush like 'Woolworth's on a bargain day'.[32] This led to the publication of a newspaper article which was possibly the first public recognition of Jean's work:

> New Australians are showing keen interest in the recent establishment of the foreign library in the lending section of the Public Library, North Terrace, where Miss Jean Whyte an Honors English student at the Adelaide University, is in charge.
>
> Miss Whyte, who is buyer of literature for the lending library, will begin her leave today and while in Melbourne will seek sources for further purchases of foreign books to suit the many New Australians who call at the library daily. There were eight borrowers last September compared with 446 last month.
>
> The lending section had about 300 books in foreign languages covering German, Russian, Finnish, French, Lithuanian, Estonian and Ukrainian, with more to come, Miss Wyte [sic] said.[33]

Another fortunate accident: being asked to teach librarianship. Pitt, recognizing Jean's talent, asked her to teach PLSA cadet librarians (librarianship at this time was usually taught in the workplace, and Pitt himself had taught Jean). Jean began teaching in 1948: 'After my first lecture I realized that I had found the work that I wanted to do. I was not a good lecturer or teacher – but I wanted to be a good teacher more than anything else'.[34]

There is a description of her role in the PLSA's staff journal, unsigned but without doubt written by Jean herself, in which the Staff Training Officer's job of selecting and inducting staff is compared with that of overseer on a sheep station drafting sheep. The Staff Training Officer had to choose the best potential librarians (or lambs), then put them through a Basic Training Program; the survivors were sent to different departments (paddocks), and they later returned to the Staff Training Officer, who introduced them to 'the routines, responsibilities and ideals of librarianship'.[35]

Jean described her duties as

> Giving lectures and conducting seminars covering the following subjects as set out in Syllabus of the Library Association of Australia: Preliminary Course on Books & Libraries. Preliminary Course on Acquisition & Preparation of Books. Registration courses on Cataloguing and Classification; theory & practise. Registration courses on the administration, provision, processes and services of Reference Libraries and of Lending Libraries, and of Special Libraries.

> Registration course on the History and Purposes of Libraries. Registration course on the production, publication, history and care of books. Registration course on Library Work with Children [i.e. all subjects except Archives].
>
> Planning and conducting a Basic training Course for new members of staff. Interviewing applicants for positions in the library and recommending appointments. Advising on, and checking on, in-service training in the departments. Selecting books in the field of Literature and Librarianship for reference and lending services.
>
> Preparation of administrative reports on the organization of the library and the establishment of local public libraries.[36]

Jean taught an introductory course for cadet librarians, which she saw as a way to select people who would become 'real librarians' and to give them 'basic skills, understandings, and attitudes'.[37] She taught all courses for the Institute's Preliminary Examinations and Qualifying Certificate in Librarianship,[38] her favourite subjects being 'Book production, publication, history & care' and 'History & purposes of libraries'.[39] She considered that keeping up with and teaching so many subjects was 'an almost incredible load'.[40] She was thorough, preparing new lectures even in subjects she had taught many times. An undated newspaper clipping says that she had 93 students,[41] which would have included all the PLSA recruits, as well as most librarians preparing for Registration Examinations in South Australia with the exception of teacher librarians. She was pleased with her students: 'I doubt that they can be a better bunch than the 1958 and 1959 group here',[42] and librarians Jean had trained were sought by other libraries.[43] One of Jean's innovations was to set up an exhibition – one of a number she organized at the PLSA – of developments in librarianship, as an aid to her teaching.

In contrast to her high opinion of the standard of examinations at the time, she was worried about the standard of teaching, and when she was leaving the PLSA she thought that she was deserting teaching when she was needed – the examination papers she was working on 'are a constant reminder that it may be wrong to run out on teaching when the Australian standard is so very low'.[44]

Teaching librarianship was the subject of one of Jean's earliest published essays: 'In-service training or library schools'. In this article she described in-service training as 'a programme of training determined and controlled by a specific library to train its own staff', whereas 'library schools' taught librarianship, whether they were independent, attached to libraries or in universities, usually preparing students for qualifications awarded by a national association. She was already an advocate for librarianship to be taught in universities, arguing that students would be independent of their teachers, that the teachers would be set apart to be thinkers who would advance librarianship, and that the school would be part of the wider academic world of universities. She also considered a question which is now far removed from twenty-first-century academia:

> the pertinent question is not, 'if we put faculties of librarianship into our universities, will they harm the English department, or the Engineering school?' The pertinent question is 'Will they benefit the practice and the profession of

> librarianship?' ... My ideal system for the education of librarians is graduation
> from a university graduate course in librarianship ... but we are a long way
> from realizing such a system.[45]

Jean was twenty-one years from realizing that dream. The other part of Jean's position as Staff Training Officer was staff selection, and her ability to select staff became one of her most admired qualities, but, she said,

> I'm a bad selector of staff – one of the young female graduates who I thought
> that I'd recruited to start next Tuesday has just walked in to announce that she
> is going into the convent instead. The worst of it is that I've often said that the
> best cure for our staff turnover problems would be to turn the library into a
> convent & have all the girls dedicated to a single life: Grrrrr.[46]

Following Pitt's retirement in 1955 Hedley Brideson became Principal Librarian. Brideson had been head of the PLSA's successful Research Service. Jean did not like 'Heddles' (a view shared by many of the staff):[47] 'no morals, only politics'.[48] Carl Bridge, author of the history of the PLSA – while noting the singlemindedness which later would lead Brideson to his downfall – is kinder, writing of Brideson's energy, entrepreneurship and enthusiasm.[49] Jean, by now a senior staff member, considered that everything that she accomplished was against what he wanted and loathed defending his views – which she did not agree with – to the staff.

An example of their conflict was in Jean's role of staff selection: Brideson, a social climber, wanted the daughters of wealthy parents, privately educated young women wanting to fill in time between school and marriage, on the staff. Jean, wanting to create a balance, deliberately chose staff who were male, state-school educated and/or working class. It is ironic that Brideson wanted women of Jean's social standing despite Jean being such an irritant, but although she may have irritated him she was very useful for doing such distasteful work as sackings, and he would have respected her intellect, her many abilities and her management of her huge workload.[50]

Brideson took the 'no morals, only politics' line when the South Australian government, under pressure to establish local public libraries, legislated to develop regional public libraries. Jean was given the task of setting up the first, in suburban Elizabeth, in 1957, and the experience was clearly important to her, as she was to recall this event in her retirement speech 30 years later.[51] When the library was ready to be opened Brideson made his first visit 'to say that he had seen it'.[52] Brideson was also the recipient of a cautionary message from the then Premier of South Australia, Sir Thomas Playford, advising him that a member of the PLSA staff, George Buick, was in the Public Gallery of Parliament during discussion of the first Act to subsidize public libraries. Brideson cautioned the male staff against attending the parliamentary sessions, because it might ruin their careers. Jean said 'isn't it a good thing I don't have a career to think of'.[53]

Both Brideson and Jean were involved with the Institute, which was to become a dominant factor in Jean's career – she was to say the most important factor – as membership gave her the opportunity to discuss professional issues.[54] She attended her first Institute meeting on October 8th, 1942[55] and continued to attend meetings of both the Institute and its successor, the LAA, throughout her career. She described being one of four library assistants who went to see Pitt, then the State Archivist, to complain about the local Branch, which the four thought spent too much time discussing or going on library visits and not enough on what they considered to be the 'serious' issues of librarianship, such as cataloguing and classification. They wanted a new association. Pitt, instead of rejecting them, suggested that they take over running the Branch themselves, as the current members had been running it since 1937.[56] By 1948 Jean was President of the South Australian Branch and the other three were committee members. Jean climbed the Institute ladder in two-year steps: 1942, she joined the PLSA; 1944, she passed her Preliminary Examinations; 1946, she completed her Qualifying Certificate in Librarianship; and by 1948 she was South Australian President. By this time she was second in charge at the Adelaide Lending Service, lecturing in librarianship and 25 years old.

Jean joined her first Institute committee (in 1946)[57] and various LAA sections, such as the Children's Libraries Section (SA), the Special Libraries Section (SA) and the SA Branch Library Promotion Committee.[58] She was on a committee to promote setting up a public library in Nuriootpa[59] (which was part of the push to develop free libraries in South Australia)[60] and chaired a sub-committee set up 'to investigate problems of professional education ... the acquisition and circulation of information on librarianship; the compilation of bibliographies on specific library problems; and what help can be given to students studying for the L.A.A. examinations'.[61] She chaired a discussion group for students preparing for the Qualifying Examination,[62] began her long membership of the Board of Examination and Certification (and its successors)[63] and became an examiner.

Jean became a member of the LAA Committee on Cataloguing, Classification and Bibliography, set up to consider and improve procedures.[64] She also joined the Committee on Publications (and was Chairman 1956–1958), which was set up to advise the LAA on publication matters. These committees gave her a national profile, which would have been important to Jean, as she wanted to move from the PLSA.

Jean joined the Institute's SA Branch Committee in 1951 (Cynthia Paltridge, who studied with Jean and was top student in the state,[65] was elected president;[66] she was also at Jean's retirement party) and represented South Australia on the LAA Federal Council.[67] Her presidency of the Branch came in 1948, after she had been Vice-President in 1947. She was again Branch President in 1956 and 1957 (by now the Institute had become the LAA). During her presidency speakers at Branch meetings included her friends and her interests, such as poetry and censorship.[68] Her 1949 Presidential message quite remarkably sets out aims and themes which continued throughout her career: education for librarianship, the Board of Examination and Certification, the importance of libraries in providing information to the community, and freedom of information (as the reverse of censorship).[69]

Jean attended Institute and LAA Conferences, beginning with the Institute's Hobart Conference in 1946. She also gave papers and workshops, appeared in the newspapers on behalf of the LAA and the PLSA and was interviewed on ABC radio.[70] She was Chair of the 1957 Adelaide LAA Conference Committee (her friend Ray Olding was Secretary). The Conference included a reception for about 250 people,[71] where Jean's interest in wine makes its first appearance: 'Dine with fine wines in Adelaide in August' beckons the conference advertisement.[72] At the conference Jean presented a paper on recruitment and a seminar on 'Education for librarianship'.[73] The *Australian Library Journal (ALJ)* reported that it was 'one of the best attended sessions of the Conference ... It would perhaps be not unfair to say that a number of people who attended did so because of a misunderstanding as to the subject of the seminar'; then the report congratulated two men on their method of catalogue-card reproduction.[74]

Jean also contributed much to *ALJ*, including articles, book reviews and poetry. I suspect, too, that Jean was Branch correspondent for *ALJ*, as there is a great deal more news while Jean was active in the Branch (perhaps the Branch was more active?) than there was while she was away. So it probably surprised no-one when in October 1958 she was appointed Honorary Editor of the *ALJ*, to assume her position in January 1959.[75] And, by this time, no-one was surprised that Jean would take up such a time-consuming position in addition to her already heavy workload.

Jean's interest in, and output of, writing on librarianship had now taken off. It included an interest in library history, and, during her second term as President, Jean composed the remarkable 'A word from Callimachus', written in verse, which was both her first published article on library history and her second presidential address.[76]

Another fortunate accident came in the form of Professor E.H. Behymer of Bethany College, West Virginia, who visited Australia to conduct a series of seminars for the LAA and who encouraged Jean to study in the United States.[77] Jean thanked Behymer, saying that without his help she would never have left Australia.[78] She said that she wanted to study so that she could teach librarianship, as she believed that Australia needed 'more professionally trained people'.[79] Jean studied at the Graduate Library School (GLS) at the University of Chicago – then the most distinguished school of librarianship in the United States – believing that the United States provided the best form of education for librarianship and that the best school was the GLS, a view she held throughout her career.[80] Her study was made possible by a Travel Grant which included her airfares to and from the United States, a University of Chicago Fellowship, and an American Association of University Women Fellowship, which was awarded 'to help women of outstanding ability who may be expected to do constructive work on returning to their own country', providing for expenses, living costs, university fees, some travel and a stipend of US$600 (it appears that Jean was the only Fellow appointed to the school that year),[81] which meant that she did not need to work, although 'as I have done both my University course and my LAA course in my spare time after working at least forty hours per week I am quite accustomed to doing both things'.[82]

Jean's referees included Roma Mitchell, who said that Jean 'is endowed with a great strength of character and possesses outstanding qualities of leadership';[83] Alec Ramsay, General Manager of the South Australian Housing Trust, who said that Jean's determination and energy for librarianship were tempered by outside interests, making her a more rounded personality;[84] and George Pitt, who said that

> Miss Whyte is outstanding as the most brilliant and versatile officer on the staff of this library. She is alert, intelligent and impressionable. She has independence of character, thinks clearly, and has the power of penetrating quickly to the core of problems ...[85]

Jean's thesis for the AM (Master of Arts) was entitled 'Education for librarianship in the United States and in Australia: a comparison', which was designed to make a comparative study of the organization and content of education for librarianship in Australia and the United States in terms of some of the major factors which may be assumed to influence the organization and content of such education, with the purpose of providing data pertinent to the following question:- 'can Australian education for librarianship benefit from the lessons learned in the United States during seventy-five years of education for librarianship; or are conditions in Australia sufficiently different from those in the United States to make the transfer of American methods inapplicable?'[86]

Jean studied both countries' approach to education for librarianship, relating the ways the programs differed to the structure of education and of librarianship in the two countries. She looked at the two countries' different structures of tertiary education, the types of libraries students were preparing to work in, the influence of professional organizations on library education, and the structure and content of education for librarianship, concluding with an evaluation of the possibility of adapting American methods of education for librarianship to Australian conditions.[87]

Jean visited 14 library schools in the United States, where she found that their students were graduates, that many schools specialized in teaching different librarianship for specific types of libraries, and that schools had high academic standards. She was impressed similarly by their teaching methods, which concentrated on seminars and discussions, with the approach 'general rather than specific'. This was in marked contrast to what she considered to be the low standard of education for librarianship in Australia, where few librarians were university graduates, where there was no 'real library school',[88] and where the standards in most areas of librarianship were low. She praised the GLS: the availability of appropriate courses, good teachers and teaching methods, high standards and professional approach, saying that 'I have complete confidence in the content of the curriculum, in the methods of teaching and in the faculty who teach both as teachers and as librarians'.[89] She was impressed by the libraries she used, the accessibility of the materials, the emphasis on research, the interest in student work shown by the University and the hospitality she received.[90] Her findings were to influence her views for the rest of her career.

Not surprisingly, Jean was a 'star student'.[91] Her subjects were Academic library (Fussler); Library work with children and young people (Hayes); Library surveys and library planning (Carnovsky); Library history (Winger); Problems in the bibliographical organization of knowledge (Egan); Communication and libraries (Asheim); Survey of library literature (Carnovsky); and Organization and administration of technical services (Dawson).[92] She received A's in all subjects except for a B in Library history – remarkable, because Jean was so interested in library history (perhaps the subject was library history in general and the history of American libraries,[93] whereas Jean's interest was specifically Australian library history). She audited another eight courses,[94] visited many branches of the American Association of University Women, attended the meetings of various library associations and other groups, and travelled in the United States. She also attended an American Library Association Convention, with 5,000 participants – enormous by Australian standards (would there have been 5000 librarians in Australia in 1955?).

Jean graduated in absentia, as the graduation ceremony followed her return to Australia.[95] She had spent 20 months in the United States,[96] returning via England and Switzerland – 'I've always been keen on alps, any alp, it doesn't matter how big or small', she said[97] (it begs the question where she might have seen alps before leaving Australia, certainly not in South Australia, although she enjoyed visits to the Flinders Ranges).[98]

Jean returned from Chicago to resume her usual activities: her busyness with the LAA, a second term as President of the South Australian Branch of the LAA, the development of regional public libraries in South Australia, the exasperating Brideson. But she was unsettled: 'the problem that I have been acutely aware of since I returned home is professional loneliness. For this reason the idea of going back to U.S.A. has been very attractive and it's taken all the toughness of my grim Scotch Presbyterian ancestors to keep a conscience about working for Australian librarianship. Also of course it's only too easy to develop a swollen head'.[99] And 'Almost everything that I've accomplished here, since I returned from U.S.A. & found the new robes didn't sit as comfortably as the old, I've managed to do in spite of the whole senior staff. And I've <u>had</u> having to defend him [Brideson] & approve his policies in staff-room and social gatherings'.[100] After her return from the United States, Jean stayed another three years at the PLSA.

Then came the fortunate accident which would lead Jean to the next step in her life: Hedley Brideson chose not to attend a seminar (Jean claimed that Brideson did not want to interrupt his summer holidays),[101] and so sent Jean in his stead: the seminar became known as the Metcalf Seminar after the guest speaker, Dr Keyes D. Metcalf, who had recently retired from his position as Director of Harvard University Libraries. The seminar was organized by Harold White, Librarian of the Commonwealth National Library (now the National Library of Australia (NLA), Canberra), and held at that institution. The 28 seminarians were the leading librarians from all Australian states; five were women, and five were from New Zealand. Harrison Bryan, a fellow seminarian, wrote later that the membership looked like a *Who was who* of Australian librarianship.[102]

Metcalf's letter – which begins 'Dear Seminarians' – sets out the aims of the seminar as discussing objectives, administration and policies rather than 'techniques'. The ambitious outline of the seminar looks like a library degree in nine days. The main subjects were:

i. The Building of Library Collections and Problems relating to their use

    a. Acquisition problems
    b. Cataloguing problems [including 'Work that doesn't stay done']
    c. The use of collections

ii. Library personnel
iii. Space problems
iv. Planning for the future.[103]

Jean, in hindsight, saw the seminar as a milestone in Australian librarianship, the first meeting of librarians of major libraries in Australia 'sitting down talking about common problems without arguing with each other too much', resulting in improvements to the development of librarianship in Australia and a proposal that a study of Australia's library resources be undertaken – a study subsequently published as the Tauber Report in 1961.[104]

Whereas the other seminarians were leaders in the profession Jean saw herself as an observer, the only person who had no power to make changes.[105] But she was an active participant, with Metcalf (whom she had met in the United States) commenting: 'well I always enjoy having an argument with you, Jean'.[106] The seminar gave her an opportunity to discuss the big issues with leaders of the profession and, more importantly, for them to see her.[107]

The importance of the Metcalf Seminar for Jean was that it was there that she met Andrew Osborn and so moved to the next stage of her career. And perhaps the last of the fortunate accidents at the PLSA – Jean's dislike of 'Heddles' – made it easier for her to leave (I wonder whether Brideson's decision to send Jean to the seminar and the glowing reference he wrote for her were signs that he wanted to be rid of her).

Yes, these were accidents – serendipity may be a better description – but Jean took advantage of each one.

Acknowledging Jean's accidental entry into the librarianship profession Neil Radford said:

> How fortunate we as a profession are that, back in 1941 [sic], when looking for work close to the University of Adelaide, she sought a job in the Public Library of SA and not in the adjacent art gallery or the museum! She would have been a great success in those institutions, too, but Australian librarianship would have been much the poorer.[108]

ENDNOTES

1. Roma Mitchell to American Association of University Women, October 31st, 1952. NLA: MS 9616.
2. Transcript of a conversation between Jean Whyte and Geoffrey Alley, 1981. MON 1059: 2000/68/5. The transcript has been written with little regard for punctuation, and is quoted as is.
3. 'Doubling the number'. *Canberra Times*, September 28th, 1972.
4. Jean Whyte to the Secretary, American Association of University Women, 1952. NLA: MS 9616.
5. Ibid.
6. A fortunate accident for Jean, but good planning had made the two institutions neighbours.
7. H.C. Brideson. 'The Public Library of South Australia', 1957, 62.
8. Jean Whyte to the Secretary, American Association of University Women, 1952. NLA: MS 9616.
9. Ibid.
10. 'The University of Adelaide'. [Newspaper clipping], n.d. NLA: MS 9616.
11. 'Clever woman'. [Newspaper clipping], n.d. SLSA: PRG 1335/1.
12. Harrison Bryan. 'Jean Primrose Whyte'. *ALJ* 38 (1) 1989, 7.
13. Australian Institute of Librarians. South Australian Branch. *Quarterly Bulletin* 1, 1944, [14]. The Australian Institute of Librarians, which I refer to as 'The Institute', should not be confused with the South Australian Institutes.
14. Jean Whyte to the Secretary, American Association of University Women, 1952. NLA: MS 9616. Jean still held this view in 'The Accreditation of Courses in Librarianship', 1974, 593–608.
15. [LAA Certificate], September 17th, 1952. NLA: MS 9616.
16. Interview: Ray Olding, 2008.

17 Jean Whyte to Andrew Osborn, January 27th, 1959. SU: M 465; Jean Whyte to Andrew Osborn, January 14th, 1959. SU: M 465.
18 Jean Whyte to the Secretary, American Association of University Women, 1952. NLA: MS 9616.
19 Carl Bridge. *A Trunk Full of Books*, 1986, 156.
20 'Rural' meant more than seven miles from the Adelaide Post Office (Carl Bridge. *A Trunk Full of Books*, 1986, 153).
21 The Lending Service, 'a deliberate move against the subscription-based Adelaide Circulation Library[,] was a great success' (Harrison Bryan. 'Jean Primrose Whyte'. *ALJ* 38 (1) 1989, 8).
22 Jean Whyte to the Secretary, American Association of University Women, 1952. NLA: MS 9616.
23 Referred to variously as the Department of Mines and Geology, the Department of Mines and Industry and the South Australian Mines Department.
24 Jean Whyte. 'Position application and curriculum vitae', 1959. NLA: MS 9616; Jean Whyte. 'Curriculum vitae', 1974. NLA: MS 9616.
25 'Doubling the number'. *Canberra Times*, September 28th, 1972.
26 G. H. Pitt to Jean Whyte, April 20th, 1948. SLSA: PRG 1335/3-4.
27 Jean Whyte to the Secretary, American Association of University Women, 1952 NLA: MS 9616.
28 Ibid. Jean said that she was 'Second-in-charge' from 1946 (Jean Whyte. 'Curriculum vitae', [1972?]. NLA: MS 9616), which is correct in that there was no-one in that position, so she was effectively second in charge, but the appointment was not formalized until 1948.
29 G. H. Pitt to Jean Whyte, April 20th, 1948. SLSA: PRG 1335/3-4.
30 Ibid.
31 Carl Bridge. *A Trunk Full of Books*, 1986, 174.
32 South Australia. State Records Office. Page 34/79 GRG 26 Series List 10/11 page 25. *Monthly and annual reports of Adelaide Lending Service 1946–69*. Series 11, No. 9.
33 'To help New Australians'. [Newspaper clipping], n.d. SLSA: PRG 1335/1.
34 Jean Whyte to the Secretary, American Association of University Women, 1952. NLA: MS 9616.
35 [Jean Whyte?] 'Know your department – Staff Training Officer'. *Foggy Dew* 2 (3) 1957, 8.
36 Jean Whyte. 'Position application and curriculum vitae', 1959. NLA: MS 9616.
37 [Jean Whyte?]. 'Know your department – Staff Training Officer'. *Foggy Dew* 2 (3) 1957, 8.
38 Libraries Board of South Australia. 'Annual Report of the Libraries Board of South Australia, 1st July, 1957, to 30th June, 1958', 1958, 9.
39 Jean Whyte to Andrew Osborn, January 17th, 1959. SU: M 465.
40 [Jean Whyte?]. 'Know your department – Staff Training Officer'. *Foggy Dew* 2 (3) 1957, 8.
41 'Books – all types – are exhibits at show'. [Newspaper clipping], n.d. SLSA: PRG 1335/2.
42 Jean Whyte to Andrew Osborn, January 2nd, 1959. SU: M 465.
43 Interview: Michael Talbot, 2008.
44 Jean Whyte to Andrew Osborn, January 2nd, 1959. SU: M 465.
45 Jean Whyte. 'In-service training or library schools'. *ALJ* 5 (1) 1956, 3–4.
46 Jean Whyte to Andrew Osborn, January 21st, 1959. SU: M 465.
47 Interview: Ray Olding, 2008.
48 Jean Whyte to Andrew Osborn, January 14th, 1959. SU: M 465.

49 Carl Bridge. *A Trunk Full of Books*, 1986, 200.
50 Interview: Ray Olding, 2008.
51 Jean Whyte. 'Retirement Reminiscences', 1988. NLA: MS 9616.
52 Jean Whyte to Andrew Osborn, February 8th, 1959. SU: M 465.
53 A story handed down by State Library of South Australia staff, parts of which were related by different interviewees (Interview: Michael Talbot, 2005; Interview: Ray Olding, 2008).
54 Jean Whyte and David J. Jones. *Uniting a Profession*, 2007, 2.
55 Australian Institute of Librarians. South Australian Branch. *Minute Book*. October 8, 1937–December 17, 1952. SLSA: SRG 109 Series 2, Vols. 1–7.
56 Jean Whyte and David J. Jones. *Uniting a Profession*, 2007, 2.
57 Australian Institute of Librarians. South Australian Branch. *Quarterly Bulletin* 7, 1946, [1].
58 Jean Whyte. 'Positive application and curriculum vitae', 1959. NLA: MS 9616.
59 'Branches'. *ALJ* 2 (2) 1953, 38–42.
60 'Branches'. *ALJ* 2 (3) 1953, 72.
61 'Branches'. *ALJ* 1 (6) 1952, 139.
62 'Officers and councillors, 1953'. *ALJ* 2 (1) 1953, 2.
63 [Board of Examination]. 'Executive Officers, representative councillors, Board of Examination'. *ALJ* 5 (1) 1956, 22. I use 'Board of Examination' regardless of the precise title at any particular time during Jean's membership.
64 Jean Whyte. 'Position application and curriculum vitae', 1959. NLA: MS 9616.
65 Australian Institute of Librarians. South Australian Branch. 'Congratulations'. *Quarterly Bulletin* 1, 1944, [14].
66 'Branches'. *ALJ* 1 (4) 1952, 90–92.
67 Jean Whyte. 'Curriculum vitae', [1972?]. NLA: MS 9616.
68 Australian Institute of Librarians. South Australian Branch. *Minute Book*. October 8, 1937–December 17, 1952. SLSA: SRG 109 Series 2, Vols. 1–7.
69 Jean Whyte. 'Presidential message'. Australian Institute of Librarians. South Australian Branch. *Quarterly Bulletin*, 10, 1949.
70 'Branches'. *ALJ* 2 (2) 1953, 38–42; 'Branches'. *ALJ* 2 (3) 1953, 72; 'Branches'. *ALJ* 2 (4) 1953, 107.
71 '250 at library party'. [Newspaper clipping], n.d. SLSA: PRG 1335/1.
72 [Advertisement]. *ALJ* 6 (1) 1957, 11.
73 Jean Whyte. *The Recruitment of Librarians*, [1959?].
74 'Library Association of Australia. Ninth Annual Conference'. *ALJ* 6 (4) 1957, 150.
75 'Editorship of the journal'. *ALJ* 7 (4) 1958, 118.
76 Jean Whyte. 'A word from Callimachus'. *ALJ* 6 (3) 1957, 95–100. Reproduced in Appendix 1.
77 My finances did not stretch to overseas visits, so the Chicago and, later, Canada sections are written from information available in Australia.
78 Jean Whyte. 'Education for Librarianship in the United States and in Australia, 1956'. NLA: MS 9616.
79 Jean Whyte to the Secretary, American Association of University Women, 1952. NLA: MS 9616.
80 'Late start, but Jean Whyte has the last word'. *Monash Reporter*, 9-88, 1988.

81 'Valuable grant for study in U.S.'. *Advertiser* [SA], March 18th, 1953, 11; University of Chicago. *Fellowship appointments for the academic year 1954–55*. NLA: MS 9616.

82 Jean Whyte to the Dean, Graduate Library School, University of Chicago, Illinois, June 18th, 1952. NLA: MS 9616.

83 Roma Mitchell to American Association of University Women, October 31st, 1952. NLA: MS 9616.

84 A.M. Ramsay to American Association of University Women, November 3rd, 1952. NLA: MS 9616.

85 G.H. Pitt to Committee on Fellowships and Scholarships, University of Chicago. September 5th, 1952. NLA: MS 9616. 'Impressionable' appears to have had a positive meaning.

86 Jean Whyte. 'A Proposal for a Master's Thesis', 1954. NLA: MS 9616.

87 Ibid.

88 Transcript of a conversation between Jean Whyte and Geoffrey Alley, 1981. MON 1059: 2000/68/5.

89 Jean Whyte. 'Second Report to American Association of University Women', 1954. NLA: MS 9616.

90 'SA librarian studies training in American library schools'. *Advertiser* [SA], May 31st, 1955, 16.

91 Harrison Bryan. 'Jean Primrose Whyte'. *ALJ* 38 (1) 1989, 8.

92 Jean Whyte. 'Position application and curriculum vitae', 1959. NLA: MS 9616.

93 Jean Whyte. 'Making history', 1985, 135.

94 Jean Whyte. 'Position application and curriculum vitae', 1959. NLA: MS 9616.

95 Jean Whyte to Lester Asheim, August 9th, 1956. NLA: MS 9616.

96 'Branches and Sections'. *ALJ* 4 (3) 1955, 115.

97 'Books – all types – are exhibits at show'. [Newspaper clipping], n.d. SLSA: PRG 1335/2.

98 Interview: Ray Olding, 2008.

99 Jean Whyte to Andrew Osborn, January 2nd, 1959. SU: M 465. One of the GLS staff, Ruth Strout, offered to look for a teaching position for Jean in the United States: 'certainly before Dec. 1958 I should have answered "yes – I want to come back to U.S." – but now the answer is unhesitatingly "No". I've found the job I want' (Jean Whyte to Andrew Osborn, February 14th, 1959. SU: M 465).

100 Jean Whyte to Andrew Osborn, January 14th, 1959. SU: M 465.

101 Transcript of a conversation between Jean Whyte and Geoffrey Alley, 1981. MON 1059: 2000/68/5.

102 Harrison Bryan. 'The Metcalf seminar – 25 years on'. *ALJ* 33 (1) 1984, 32.

103 Commonwealth National Library. 'Advanced Library Seminar. Papers', 1958. NLA: MS 9616.

104 Transcript of a conversation between Jean Whyte and Geoffrey Alley, 1981. MON 1059: 2000/68/5; Harrison Bryan. 'The Metcalf seminar – 25 years on'. *ALJ* 33 (1) 1984, 32–35.

105 Transcript of a conversation between Jean Whyte and Geoffrey Alley, 1981. MON 1059: 2000/68/5.

106 Harrison Bryan. 'Jean Primrose Whyte'. *ALJ* 38 (1) 1989, 9.

107 Transcript of a conversation between Jean Whyte and Geoffrey Alley, 1981. MON 1059: 2000/68/5.

108 Neil A. Radford. 'Obituaries. Jean Primrose Whyte AM', [2003].

MISS JEAN WHYTE, BA (HONS) (ADELAIDE), AM (CHICAGO), FLAA
JEAN AT THE UNIVERSITY OF SYDNEY AND AT THE UNIVERSITY OF WESTERN ONTARIO

> *I know of no woman in Australia who could a fill a high administrative position in a library with such ability and distinction as Miss Whyte*[1]

In 1959 Miss Jean Whyte, BA (Hons), AM (Chicago), moved to the position of Assistant Librarian in charge of Public Services at the University of Sydney Library. At the same time she became Editor of *ALJ*.[2] Each position was demanding.

Jean's move to University of Sydney Library, known as the Fisher,[3] was a career change from public to academic libraries. Jean said:

> I changed my career, or my professional direction a bit at the Metcalf Seminar mostly because I met Andrew Osborn and realised that Sydney University would be a good place to go to. It certainly sounded interesting ... [4]

The months after the Metcalf Seminar were a rollercoaster ride for Jean – high-speed, emotional, exhilarating: she moved to Sydney less than ten weeks after meeting Osborn, the University of Sydney Librarian, who had wanted her to work with him immediately. They corresponded frequently during this period, but whereas Osborn's letters to Jean were enthusiastic but formal, such as 'I am tremendously keen on getting you here',[5] Jean was besotted with Osborn:

> I don't know that I have ever wanted to do anything as much as I want to go to Fisher. I'm half afraid to be as happy as I am.

> I only hope that I don't let you down, Andrew. Please remember that I really don't know so much about librarianship – but that I care a great deal about it and that I want to learn and that I don't mind how long or how hard I work.[6]

And

> I seem to be living on your letters at present – & they make me very certain of two things. Firstly that if you were running a library in Greenland I would want to go there (& I hate the cold) & secondly that I'll have to go like hell if I'm not to disappoint you.[7]

Jean's letters were long and effusive, including poetry and personal details, and ending with 'goodnight'. She was full of evangelical zeal for her new position and the future of the Fisher – as I read her letters I was listening to the radio and heard, appropriately,

> I will not cease from mental fight,
> Nor shall my sword sleep in my hand,

Till we have built Jerusalem
In England's green and pleasant land.

(The frenetic activity of Jean and Osborn was more like building the Tower of Babel).

Jean had met Andrew Osborn, then aged 56, soon after he took up his appointment as Librarian of the University of Sydney, having returned to Australia after thirty years in the United States. They shared 'library mania' with a United States bias, which both linked and isolated them – Jean called it 'professional loneliness',[8] a feeling shared by Osborn, who, finding Australian libraries far below the standard of university libraries in the United States, was full of energy and new ideas. Harrison Bryan referred to Osborn as 'the man for the hour',[9] 'dragging the country's largest and oldest university library firmly into the 20th century'[10] (in 1959).

Osborn had recruited Jean because he needed new staff who shared his enthusiasm, in order to implement his ideas and to help overcome the resistance to change shown by the Library's many long-term staff members. He created a new staff structure, 'giving the place a face lifting before term time next year' (i.e. 1959).[11] The position of Assistant Librarian in charge of Public Services (later to be renamed Readers' Services Librarian), one of five Assistant Librarians, on the third tier of the library hierarchy, reported to be 'the third highest job open to librarians in Australia',[12] was advertised, but no interviews were held: four people looked at the applicants' names and 'unanimously and without hesitation passed [Jean's] name on to the Senate [of the University of Sydney]'.[13] They would have been foolish not to. Jean's references were glowing, including Hedley Brideson's 'I consider Miss Whyte to be the most versatile and brilliant officer on my staff … I know of no woman in Australia who could fill a high administrative position in a library with such ability and distinction'.[14]

Not just the references, but also the referees were impressive: Mr. W.A. Cowan, Librarian, Barr Smith Library, University of Adelaide; Professor W.G.K. Duncan, Department of History and Political Science, University of Adelaide, past President of the LAA in South Australia; and two state librarians, her friend George Pitt (now retired) and Hedley Brideson.

Jean's main worry was the medical examination which was required before she could take up the new position: 'I hate, fear, and generally disapprove of medical examinations. It isn't made any better by the fact that the Dr. can't see me until February 18th – which means that I have time to develop some incurable disease between now and then'.[15] The medical check calmed her fears (but only her immediate fears – she always worried about her health). Jean then moved to Sydney in February 1959, flying there on the TAA cannon-ball.[16] She was excited by the move, wanted to begin work the day she arrived in Sydney, and wanted temporary accommodation while she looked for a flat so that she did not need to stay with her Sydney relatives (or buy Alka-Seltzer). Baggins the cat, who lived with Jean in Adelaide, moved to Sydney with her; otherwise this would have been a lonely time, her first move interstate, far from family and friends. Prim had died shortly before the Metcalf Seminar, trunk calls and air fares were more expensive than they are now, forty years later, she would have known few people in Sydney, and the friendship with Osborn quickly cooled.

Jean had moved to the oldest university in Australia, founded in 1850. Thomas Fisher, a bootmaker and property investor without formal education, left a bequest of £30,000 in his will in 1884 for a library. The Fisher Library, opened in 1909, was the first purpose-built university library in Australia.[17] Jean went to the University while this building was still being used:

> The main library, generally referred to as 'The Fisher', is housed in an extremely beautiful building in the middle period Gothic style which took six years to build and was finished in 1908.
>
> The present Fisher building consists of a Reading Room [now MacLaurin Hall] one hundred and twenty-two feet long with an open timbered roof of cedar, (its walls being covered to a height of seven feet with carved cedar panelling), a bookstack of glass and steel which is seven stories high, two smaller reading rooms, one again beautifully panelled and with a cedar roof, and various other rooms. The entrance stair case, which is of stone as is the whole building, is very handsome with elaborate carving and the roof is of fan tracery. The windows here are of stained glass. The whole exterior of the building is richly ornamented with carvings of gargoyles and other decorations. The main Reading Room was originally designed to accommodate two hundred and fifty readers and had no books in it, the library being set up as a closed access library ... The present Fisher building with many makeshifts of recent times, has served the University Library for fifty years, but it is now totally inadequate in accommodation for both books and readers ...[18]

Jean began work at the University of Sydney in February, 1959. Her work is a story of coping with 'books, buildings and bodies, or alternatively ... stock, stacks and staff'.[19] Jean's story is also the story of the Library, where she was at the forefront of coping with the demands of 'the great decade for Australian university libraries'.[20] Here she 'developed reader services to a level that set a new standard for Australian university libraries'.[21] As I read of Jean's work the words 'problem' and 'challenge' often appeared. I see the words as two different ways of dealing with issues – naming something as a 'problem' may be used as an excuse to leave it sitting in the 'too hard basket', whereas a 'challenge' points to the intention to deal with an issue. Jean saw challenges rather than insoluble problems: the changes in librarianship and technology, the changes in tertiary education and the library's buildings, all provided challenges; we will see how she dealt with them.

'The great decade for Australian university libraries':[22] Jean's time at Sydney University coincided with a time of enormous change and development in the Library, at the University and in tertiary education throughout Australia. Many of the changes were due to the increase in student numbers as post-war baby-boomers reached tertiary education – Sydney University's student population doubled in size between 1953 (7,366) and 1962 (14,907)[23] – leading to 'too few books and too few seats', a lack of post-graduate study materials, inadequate budgets, insufficient research collections, and further pressure on the libraries due to changing methods of undergraduate education which required more extensive use of libraries.[24] Jean wrote that

> At the end of the 1950s university libraries were in cramped buildings, their collections were growing and the readers were crowding in their doors. Ten years later most of these libraries were occupying new buildings or extensions,

their staffs in the reader services departments had grown far faster than anyone would have predicted a decade earlier, and they had a strong missionary belief that every student at the university needed to use the library. The 1960s were indeed the great decade for Australian university libraries.[25]

University libraries were much smaller than they are now, as Andrew Osborn wrote in 1959: 'if you were to take all the books and periodicals in all the universities and university colleges in Australia, you would be able to create just one large library and not a particularly large library at that'.[26] Some reminders of the differences in university libraries at this time come from Jean's article 'Direct service to readers', such as the 'tradition that for generations had regarded the use or non-use of the library by students as of little interest to librarians ... Before the Second World War Australian university libraries were relatively quiet places in which members of the academic staff expected and received preferential treatment, and where students queued up for the few books that were kept in reserve behind the desk ... After the Second World War when returned servicemen began to flood into the universities the pace of life in the libraries changed forever ... direct supervision could no longer be the first task of the librarians'! Jean summed up the situation at the University of Sydney: it 'was trying vainly to cope with a population explosion of undergraduates and the Library was hopelessly inadequate both in space and in collections'.[27]

Service to academics was seen to be the main role of the Library: academic staff were given preferential treatment and unlimited – and sometimes the only – access to materials, while students were supervised in their use of materials. At the Fisher Library a stack pass, available to academics and honours students, but not to undergraduate students, allowed the holder to enter the stacks, behind a large Queensland cedar desk, and get materials they needed. Osborn removed the desk to allow open access to the bookstack by undergraduates, which was seen as 'almost revolutionary'.[28] His egalitarianism, not surprisingly, worsened his relationship with academic staff, who wanted to retain their privileges.

Andrew Osborn left the University of Sydney in 1961. He had had problems with the University administration prior to Jean's appointment, when he had been at the University for just six months:[29] 'he had a profound conviction of his own infallibility and this led him, on the one hand, to an impatience with financial constraints and, on the other, to a reluctance to conciliate, in any way, those whom he was all too ready to identify as imposing bureaucratic obstructions in his way'.[30] He was replaced by another Metcalf seminarian, who became Jean's lifelong friend, Harrison Bryan – 'Congratulations and our sympathy' wrote Frank Rogers to Harrison Bryan.[31]

The new building was planned by Osborn, but it was during Bryan's term that it was opened. Bryan subtitled his essay on the 'new' Fisher Library 'an inheritor's impressions', perhaps a way of saying that he was not responsible for the building's design. Bryan began by referring to libraries being designed by librarians close to their retirement, thus bringing 'the perpetuation in concrete of prejudices accumulated in a lifetime of professional frustration and of an inflexible unreceptiveness to new ideas'. Although giving assurances that this was not the case with the Fisher, Bryan credited the building's planning to his predecessor, with some words on the 'general satisfaction' of the building, before launching into the building's faults and failures, ending ambiguously: 'The new Fisher is in a very real sense a librarian's library' (a reference to the librarian who designed it just before his retirement?).[32] Jean spoke of the new building at her retirement, remembering 'looking at the sap dripping from the dying trees that had been up-rooted to make way for the great new Fisher Library and thinking that we must see that our services are indeed worth this desecration'.[33]

As the 'new' Fisher opened in sections, Jean's staff faced the challenging and disruptive process of moving the collections. The entire collection was moved to the Undergraduate Wing during the 1962–1963 long vacation, and in 1966 and subsequent years the research collections were moved into the newly built Research Library wing, described as the largest single move by a library in Australia, with the exception of the NLA.[34]

Not only a new building but new technology was catching up with the Fisher. An example of the rapid changes in libraries which Jean was dealing with was the automation of library services, which began with the introduction of the first photocopying machines in an Australian university (1963 for staff, 1964 for students; more soon arrived). The arrival of the photocopier brought with it questions of copyright, which Jean wrote about in 'Copyright Law in Australia', including the legal history of copyright and its implications for librarians.[35]

Soon the photocopiers were joined by telex machines, punched cards, a mechanized loan system and a Xerox copier for reproducing catalogue cards (the first in Australia).[36] New forms of automation brought many challenges for Jean, such as the difficulties of introducing new technology to students and staff, resistance to automation, costs, training, repairs, copyright law, problematic 'advances' (and being watched by other librarians), and lack of dedicated technical support staff and systems librarians. Harrison Bryan described the changes as 'changing in mid-stream from what was the best horse available at the time to a completely untried animal, and only an imitation animal at that'.[37] In his report 'University of Sydney Library. Library Automation Programme' Bryan wrote that

> The Library pioneered in Australia the large scale use of unit-record equipment for routine library processes, with the installation of the modified Brooklyn College circulation system in 1964.
>
> In progressing towards actual computer application to library processes and services, the Library has displayed well justified caution ...
>
> In 1966 the Library produced the preliminary edition of a computer-printed catalogue of the Undergraduate library ... the first substantial computer-produced catalogue produced by an Australian library.[38]

Automation was used for the circulation system, and preliminary work on a Union List of Serials was undertaken, with automation providing printouts such as reference lists, bibliographies, catalogues, shelf-list updates, dissemination of information, accession lists, current awareness, etc. Staff tried different forms of automation to introduce students to the Library: 'tours are regarded as supplementing the library's television presentation ... the old picture of one soft-voiced librarian trailing around the building followed by a string of fifty to eighty students is avoided'.[39] Jean used old 'technology' – poetry and print – to air her thoughts on new technology:

'AND NOW THE VIDEOTAPE'

Once it was only words, in memory stored,
Recited and retold to younger men –
And so the legends and the poems lived.
Then on the sands of Asia, and the banks
Of Nile men learnt to write –
And so the record passed to men unborn.
The ages passed. Men made an alphabet,
And Chinese wood-blocks, and at last in Mainz
The type of Gutenberg meant books for all.
Five hundred years have added photographs,
And motion-pictures and recorded sound,
As mortals strive against oblivion.
And we, who keep those records from the dark,
Collect and catalogue, preserve, arrange
Their letters, poems, pictures, songs and books
To help their sons and grandsons understand –
At last can leave to them not just the words,
Not just the voice, but all the image of the man.
Turn the machine and watch your grandfather –
Or see the statesman speak and hear his words
Not just the poem, but the poet too.
And in a hundred years will all men leave
A videotape as record that they lived?
And will we class it genealogy?[40]

Jean recognized and employed new technology, seeing it as a natural development in librarianship and as a way of preserving the past: 'I think the computer is in libraries to stay and it's important and I think we take it over rather than it takes us over'.[41] The term 'a necessary evil' may have been appropriate, as Jean found it difficult to cope with herself, sometimes taking an administrative rather than 'hands-on' role, and often questioning:

> In the last few months a machine called the *document-shredder* has appeared on the market. The advertisements for this machine claimed that 'In go confidential papers. Out comes unreadable packing material. Just press the button and office records are instantly reduced to 1/16" strips'. This machine is an enemy. As librarians we must enlist the historians, the sociologists, the scholars and all who think that the true history of man's social, business and political activities should be recorded, in the army of those who seek to destroy the *document-shredder*.[42]

The new technology – audiovisual, microform, computers, hardware, materials and training – had to be paid for in a time of high inflation: the cost of books and periodicals was rising by about 10 per cent per year.[43] As the library grew more librarians were employed, including the first Systems Librarian (a woman):[44] recruiting and training new staff added to Jean's workload and to the Library budget. Not only the Library but the University itself in 1967 was in dire financial straits, but there were more and more students who made ever-increasing use of the Library, and although library use increased by approximately ten times in ten years there was an increase of only two and a quarter times in staff.[45] Jean was dealing with a massive increase in library use, but without sufficient staff and funds to match the increases.

Adding to Jean's workload was the frustration caused by decisions made by the Library Advisory Committee (LAC), which was, I think, more than a problem or a challenge, more like a chronic headache. The Librarian reported to the LAC, whose members included 'the Professors' as an entire body, as well as holders of academic administrative positions: the Chancellor, the Deputy Chancellor, the Vice-Chancellor, etc. It was a cumbersome committee, lacking knowledge of the rapidly changing world of librarianship and expertise in library management. The LAC resisted change and was unable to deal with library issues, so, while the LAC dithered, the Librarian managed the Library without reference to it.[46] The LAC endlessly deliberated the problem of staff overdue loans, without progress, at almost every meeting during the thirteen years Jean was at the University, and no action had been taken by the time she left. The problem was that some staff members 'borrowed' material permanently, as staff were not limited in the number of items which they could borrow or the length of time they could hold them, nor were they fined when they did not return materials.[47] The problem had existed for more than half a century: J. Le Gay Brereton, appointed as Assistant Librarian in 1902,

> was perfectly capable of drawing attention to the library sins of the very professors who had appointed him and who had indeed dominated the library for at least forty years ... a librarian attempting to establish himself and his library against the Divine Right of Professors ... [A report in 1935] showed 'at least 30,000 library books are at all times in their possession.[48]

Jean was involved in the issue, but there is no evidence that she was able to do anything contrary to the will of the LAC. Her department sent more than 1,300 overdue notices to staff in three months in 1969: growing numbers of students needed materials, and the library lacked funds to buy more resources. One of the staff members Jean 'spoke to' about this matter was Wallace Kirsop, who was to become Jean's friend at Monash. He said that he borrowed books in his own name because his students were unable to get the books they needed.[49] Some 'borrowed' materials were added to departmental collections, which proliferated in both size and number, bringing for Jean the usual problems associated with multiple collections such as distance from the Library (some off-campus), duplicate copies, access, costs, security, etc. The Library began to consolidate the departmental collections into branch libraries,[50] but there were still 55 departmental and branch libraries when they came under Jean's control in 1966.[51]

Not just staff: students too were not returning materials, though students could be fined, so, on Jean's recommendation, library fines for students were raised (according to a poem Jean raised the fines to fund the 'new' Fisher).[52] The students were riled, as they had not been consulted, so they conducted 'sit-ins' in the Library after closing hours. Discussions between staff and students resolved to continue the increased fines and increase student consultation, but unfortunately the LAC did not learn from this how to resolve the staff loans problem.[53]

The LAC sometimes discussed the problem of excess noise in the new building, a problem for them, a challenge for Jean: Professor Jocelyn said 'that the removal of the catalogue from the reference area would eliminate one source of disturbance. The Acting Librarian [Jean Whyte] said that she believed that it would not be a reference area if the catalogue were removed. She said that one difficulty was that the reference area was too small'.[54] Not surprisingly, Jean used to talk about the infuriating nature of academics in their dealings with Fisher.[55]

Some of Jean's biggest challenges came from the increase in the collection's size: the number of books in the catalogue almost doubled in Osborn's four years – from 400,000 volumes in 1958 to 776,548 in 1962[56] – causing substantial cataloguing arrears (some acquisitions from Osborn's time remain uncatalogued today).[57] Harrison Bryan became a 'closet cataloguer' – he was reported to have catalogued more than 4,000 items in 1969 – 'the price we paid for Andrew Osborn'.[58] The books included bequests which were often made through Osborn's personal contacts, including '36 volumes including autographed editions of the works of Charles R. Jury donated by Jean Whyte'.[59] In his last letter to Jean, Osborn wrote: 'I'm still buying books to give to Fisher Library. By now I've given 40,000 books to Fisher'.[60] Despite this growth and the introduction of purchasing multiple copies of required texts, undergraduates still lacked materials and so resorted to using the Public Library of New South Wales, creating problems between the two institutions.[61]

Much of Jean's workload was caused by the Library's success: in 1963 the 'new' Fisher was used four times as heavily in one term as Old Fisher had been in the corresponding period in the previous year;[62] in 1964 the daily attendance at the Library had risen to 13,000 (with only 16,000 students);[63] in 1965 attendances rose by 27 per cent and borrowing by 47 per cent;[64] in 1966 information searches rose by almost 50 per cent;[65] in 1967 the Library acquired its one millionth volume, the first university library in Australia to reach this figure; by 1969 borrowing had risen 248 per cent and library operations increased 45 per cent in five years.[66] By 1972 a report on the Reader Services Unit showed that the Fisher was the largest university library in Australia, with 1,325,411 volumes (the University of Adelaide was second with 471,457), and the highest lender, with 540,923 loans per annum (almost twice as many as the next highest, Macquarie University). These statistics do not include the branch libraries, numbers of which fluctuated.[67]

Harrison Bryan compared the University of Sydney statistics with those of the University of Michigan Undergraduate Library,

> which is generally regarded as the most conspicuously successful undergraduate library operation in the world ... on the face of it at least, a Sydney student body of something more than half of the size of that at Michigan borrowed more than 90% of the number of books borrowed at Michigan, from a collection only slightly more than half of the size of that at Michigan; and certainly used the Library much more intensively, both in terms of number of visits and, notably, in terms of book use therein; this despite the fact that the library at Sydney was open only 80 per cent of the time that Michigan's was open ... the

reader service area continued to provide the most dramatic demonstration of the mass of the Library's operations and of the degree to which improved facilities have wrought a revolution in student reading habits.[68]

In 1966 the staff structure was reorganized into two: Jean was appointed Librarian in Charge of Reader Services, and Owen Slight Librarian in Charge of Technical Services, a structure which was again changed in 1971, when Jean became Associate Librarian (Reader Services) and Owen Slight the Associate Librarian (Administrative and Technical Services).[69] Jean's responsibilities now included all reader services in the Fisher, Undergraduate, Research and Rare Book libraries.

Jean's rise to the second level hinged on transferring one of the long-term staff members, Beatrice Wines, to the position of Associate Librarian. Miss Wines 'largely personified the Fisher Library'[70] – an appropriate comment, as at the time of Jean's appointment Miss Wines and the Fisher Library had been around for a long time and now found themselves in outdated clothing which they had no desire to change.[71] Osborn moved Wines from Officer-in-Charge of Reference and Issue[72] to Associate Librarian, but Wines realized that her promotion was to make way for Jean, and she made life difficult for her. Not only Miss Wines: 'I fear that she [Jean] was not greatly beloved of the Fisher ladies. She was younger, she did not come from Sydney and she had … impatience with pretension – and perhaps with other things too', said Harrison Bryan.[73] Jean worked through the challenges imposed by Miss Wines and other staff as she worked through the other challenges of Sydney University.[74]

Jean was involved in work outside her given role at the Library, including setting up the Friends of Fisher Library, the Rare Book Collection and hand-printing at the Piscator Press. And she continued her involvement in the LAA. Although most of her time was taken up in editing *ALJ*, she also attended NSW branch meetings (and arranged dinners between work and the meetings to encourage others to attend), and she became a member of the NSW Branch Council.[75] She chaired a group to discuss the new Registration syllabus and the possibility of an LAA section for tutors and lecturers[76] and convened the Interlibrary Loans Committee, set up to revise and improve the loans procedures.[77] She attended LAA conferences, chaired sessions, presented papers, and was a member of the 1971 Conference Committee. At this conference three papers were given on the recent University of Sydney loans survey, including a paper given by Jean which was to become a classic in Australian library literature: 'Who uses a University Library – why and to what effect?'[78] Harrison Bryan described this Conference as the first opportunity 'to show off Fisher and its services and a series of papers organized (and contributed to) by Jean was an occasion to demonstrate the extent of the reader services revolution that had occurred'.[79]

Jean still lectured for the LAA, teaching cataloguing, reference work and the production publication, history & care of books, and she was an examiner for LAA Registration examinations in cataloguing & classification in theory & practice, History & purposes of libraries, and the History & comparative study of libraries & librarianship.[80] She also continued her membership of the Board of Examination. She and Harrison Bryan each chaired the Board at various times, which led to a curious incident. Bryan was the University Librarian, while Jean was a member of the Library staff at the time she was Chair, so that their place in the pecking order was reversed at Board meetings. Perhaps this niggled Bryan:

> The Librarian regrets that last week's LIB [Librarian's Information Bulletin] did not appear. If I have to have a scapegoat it is the Board of Examination of the Library Association of Australia which held an emergency meeting under Miss Whyte's chairmanship on Tuesday. Board members met again on Wednesday and the tumult and the shouting can hardly be held to have died yet.[81]

Another librarianship activity was an overseas trip, during which Jean presented a paper entitled 'The Availability of Scientific Information in Australia: working paper presented to the Conference of Directors of Scientific Information Centres in the Asian-Pacific Region, June 10–14, 1963, Hong Kong'.[82] We may pass this over quickly, as the practice of academics giving papers at overseas conferences is now not uncommon, but Harrison Bryan wrote at the time: 'I think I can speak for you all in offering our congratulations to Miss Whyte on being invited to address this conference. This is an honour which cannot but reflect favourably on the university'.[83]

Also during her time at the University of Sydney Jean spent a semester as Visiting Professor at the School of Library and Information Science (SLIS) at the University of Western Ontario, London, Canada. The invitation came from Andrew Osborn, who rang Jean at work in Sydney, inviting her to teach for a year, in 1968–1969, the year after the school opened. Jean accepted, but for one semester only, taking leave without pay from the University of Sydney.

Andrew Osborn had spent four years as Professor of Library Science at the School of Library Science at the University of Pittsburgh before moving to SLIS, where he was Foundation Dean. He invited international leaders in librarianship to teach, including another Metcalf seminarian and friend of Jean, Geoffrey Alley, who had recently retired from his position as New Zealand's National Librarian.

Jean thought SLIS one of the best library schools in North America,[84] and the best resourced school she had seen.[85] She became convinced that the best way to teach librarianship was through discussion in seminars, the method introduced at SLIS by Osborn. She thought it a good model but later said that 'I suspect that the model was Andrew's version of the one that he had experienced at the Harvard [Business] School, and that something had been left out'.[86] Jean was also influenced by what she saw was wrong with SLIS: the librarianship students did not mix with students from other faculties or use the university – it was 'a separate little island set up trying to have a university status' – although this problem was the same in about eighty per cent of library schools in universities.[87] She was also critical of the SLIS library. According to Jock McEldowney,

> With the advantage of 'the largest library school budget anywhere in the world', [Osborn] quickly built up a 'demonstration' library of some 40,000 volumes, which included not only the 'best' or accepted books in various fields but others which were not of the same standard, together with examples of poor printing, successive imprints to illustrate developments in production, and so on.[88]

For Jean the demonstration library was 'a bad idea I thought. It was also a very messy looking library';[89] and 'I think that it is very important that library school students learn to use the big library and that you don't have separate libraries'.[90] Jean worked hard at SLIS, enjoying the scenery, but not the cold weather.[91] She also spent three months visiting libraries in Canada, the United States and the United Kingdom, looking especially at the problems related to the development of reader services.

Osborn did not last long at SLIS. His appointment was not renewed: again he had given questionable leadership to an innovative program – 'Andrew madder than ever and I am now just amused by the folly and stupidity of it all', wrote Alley.[92]

Jean returned to library administration rather than to pursue a career in teaching, despite her interest in education for librarianship. She remained at the University of Sydney until 1972.

What more can we say of Jean's life during this time? Her life was devoted to the Fisher Library: 'JPW' expected everything to be sacrificed to the 'Holy Grail', said Joan Barry.[93] Jean worked long hours: she wrote that 'I always thought it unfair that at Sydney University he [Harrison Bryan] was considered efficient for arriving at 7.30 am whereas I was inefficient because I was still around at 7.30 pm'.[94] And she could see the Library from her flat on the other side of Sydney Harbour, so she would ring if the Library lights had not been extinguished when they should have been.[95]

As well as the huge workload at the University, as Editor of *ALJ*, and her involvement in the LAA, Jean passed the course-work examinations for Master of Arts (Honours) in English Literature in 1961 but did not write the thesis (in South Australia she had planned but not completed a Master of Arts). Although her interest in literature continued throughout her life, she did not attempt any further academic qualification (in literature or otherwise).

Jean had various relationships; her love of animals continued, with Jean writing to Osborn: 'I think I shall bring my blue-tongue lizard to Sydney. He's no trouble & just eats beef & eggs. He does look a bit like a tiger snake. (It's OK I won't keep him in your library)'.[96] The cat, Baggins, whose dinner often waited in the Library fridge, occasionally visited the Library; he would have done so more often except that Harrison Bryan was allergic to cats. She had moved to a series of flats in Kirribilli, North Sydney, and Hunters Hill,[97] the last of which, a flat she bought in 1969, was probably her first property purchase. She also bought her first car just before she left Sydney: until that time she had requested lifts, including sometimes thumbing a lift in the chauffeur-driven Mercedes of Bruce Williams, Vice Chancellor of the University of Sydney,[98] who had lectured in Economics at the University of Adelaide when she was a student.

The combined talents of Jean and Osborn had benefited Fisher: 'she was responsible for implementing Andrew Osborn's vision for a new standard of service for Australian undergraduate students, an innovation so successful that it is now the norm for the country'.[99] Jean left the University of Sydney to join the staff of the NLA. At the meeting of the Senate of the University of Sydney on August 8th, 1972, her resignation was accepted, and appreciation of her work minuted:

> In recent years the University of Sydney Library has emerged quite clearly as a leader among Australian libraries, in a number of areas. To its permanent pre-eminences of age and size, it has added notably the distinction of being the most heavily used of the Australian University libraries. It is not at all too much to say that in this, thanks in large part of the University's generous provision of accommodation, staff and funds, the Library has established a new standard for this part of the world and perhaps for other parts as well.

> Miss Whyte's contribution to what has been, in a real sense, a revolution in library use, has been quite central. By her own efforts and by the very enthusiasm she has engendered in her colleagues, she has raised the quantity and level of reader services to the point where, while still properly open to criticism, they are almost unbelievably in advance of any previous achievement in this country. It is very difficult to see how it could have been done without her.
>
> The Chancellor said that her departure was a great loss to the University and a great gain for the National Library of Australia.[100]

Four other resignations, all from academics, were accepted without comment.

ENDNOTES

1. H.C. Brideson. [Reference for Jean Whyte]. May 8th, 1956. NLA: MS 9616.
2. Although the editorship was entirely within the time she was at the University of Sydney, I have left the discussion of this until later so as not to interrupt the narrative of Jean's career.
3. Jean Whyte (and others) note that 'the University of Sydney Library is not officially the Fisher Library … Fisher is name of the central building' (Jean Whyte. [Memorandum]. January 7th, 1974).
4. Transcript of a conversation between Jean Whyte and Geoffrey Alley, 1981. MON 1059: 2000/68/5.
5. Andrew Osborn to Jean Whyte, December 23rd, 1958. SU: M 465.
6. Jean Whyte to Andrew Osborn, January 28th, 1959. SU: M 465.
7. Jean Whyte to Andrew Osborn, February 8th, 1959. SU: M 465.
8. Jean Whyte to Andrew Osborn, January 2nd, 1959. SU: M 465.
9. Harrison Bryan. *No Gray Profession*, 1994, 50.
10. Neil A. Radford. 'Obituaries. Jean Primrose Whyte AM', [2003].
11. Andrew Osborn to Jean Whyte, December 29th, 1958. SU: M 465.
12. 'Gets high post'. *Advertiser* [SA], February 6th, 1959, 20.
13. Andrew Osborn to Jean Whyte, January 28th, 1959. SU: M 465. Jean, in an undated curriculum vitae, possibly prepared as she was leaving the University of Sydney, outlined the responsibilities of her position as Reader Services Librarian:

    'Administration of the department responsible for circulation & reference services, and the shelving and maintenance of the collections.

    'Participation in the detailed planning of the new Fisher Library, under Dr. A.D. Osborn, librarian.

    'Building of the Undergraduate Library.

    'Selection of reference works & bibliographies.

    'Checking the collection for the Tauber Report on Australian Library Resources.

    'Checking the existing bookstock for rare books and segregating these.

    'Helping the Librarian to prepare two reports on the collections.' (Jean Whyte. 'Curriculum vitae', [1972?]. NLA: MS 9616).
14. Brideson, H.C. [Reference for Jean Whyte]. May 8th, 1956. NLA: MS 9616.
15. Jean Whyte to Andrew Osborn, February 18th, 1959. SU: M 465.
16. Jean Whyte to Andrew Osborn, January 28th, 1959. SU: M 465.

17. Harrison Bryan. 'An Australian Library in the AM'. *Journal of the Royal Australian Historical Society* 55 (3) 1969, 205–227.
18. [Jean Whyte?]. 'The Fisher Library, University of Sydney'. *ALJ* 8 (2) 1959, 62–64.
19. Harrison Bryan. 'Scholars, teachers, students and librarians'. *Arts* 2 (3) 1963, 174.
20. Jean Whyte. 'Direct service to readers', 1977, 284.
21. Imogen Garner. 'A tribute to our past leaders', 2004.
22. Jean Whyte. 'Direct service to readers', 1977, 284.
23. Harrison Bryan. *No Gray Profession*, 1994, 49.
24. David Waters. 'The education explosion'. *ALJ* 14 (3) 1965, 126–129.
25. Jean Whyte. 'Direct service to readers', 1977, 284.
26. Andrew Osborn. 'The Library Keeper's Business'. *Arts* 1 (3) 1959, 176.
27. Jean Whyte. 'Direct service to readers', 1977, 286–289.
28. Margaret Lundie. 'What Jean Whyte meant to the Sydney University Library'. *FIB [Fisher Library Officers' Association Information Bulletin]* 8 (2) 1971, 1.
29. 'You nearly saw me walk out of the place last week' (Andrew Osborn to Jean Whyte, February 10th, 1959. SU: M 465).
30. Harrison Bryan. *No Gray Profession*, 1994, 50. 'It was difficult not to sound sweetly reasonable after Andrew!' (Ibid, 48).
31. Ibid, 45. I wonder whether Harrison Bryan received similar letters when he succeeded George Chandler at the NLA?
32. Harrison Bryan. 'The new Fisher library at the University of Sydney', *ALJ* 12 (2) 1963, 67–70.
    I think that the building looks out of place: its severe outline clashes with the grandeur and grace of surrounding Sydney-sandstone nineteenth-century university buildings and gardens, which are among Australia's best examples of Gothic revival architecture. Jean did not agree with my opinion, as she wrote that the new building 'has been much imitated but seldom surpassed for its combination of functional efficiency and aesthetic appeal' (Jean Whyte and Neil A. Radford. 'Obituaries'. *The Australian*, May 7th, 1997, 14).
33. Jean Whyte. 'Retirement Reminiscences', 1988. NLA: MS 9616.
34. University of Sydney. Library Advisory Committee. 'Minutes', June 8th, 1970 and July 13th, 1970. SU Archives; Owen Slight. 'Sydney University library moves its research collections'. *ALJ* 16 (6) 1967, 240–244; Neil A. Radford. Personal communication, January 17th, 2005; Neil Radford. Person communication, June 29th, 2009.
35. Jean Whyte. 'Copyright Law in Australia', *Vestes* 8 (1) 1965, 3–9. Harrison Bryan said of the new photocopiers: 'they were breeding like rabbits in Fisher' (Harrison Bryan. *No Gray Profession*, 1994, 61).
36. Margaret Lundie. 'University of Sydney library since the War'. *ALJ* 20 (6) 1971, 8.
37. Harrison Bryan. 'Scholars, teachers, students and librarians'. *Arts* 2 (3) 1963, 182.
38. Harrison Bryan. 'University of Sydney Library. Library Automation Programme'. *Report to Library Advisory Committee*, 1972. SU Archives.
39. Jean Whyte. 'Direct service to readers', 1977, 285.
40. Jean Whyte. 'And now the videotape'. *ALJ* 22 (10) 1973, 400.
41. Transcript of a conversation between Jean Whyte and Geoffrey Alley, 1981. MON 1059: 2000/68/5.
42. Jean Whyte. 'The librarian's task, 1962: an editorial'. *ALJ* 11 (2) 1962, 55–60.

43   Harrison Bryan. *Annual Report of the Librarian*, 1971, 8. SU Archives.

44   University of Sydney. Library Committee. 'Minutes of Annual Meeting', November 18th, 1968. SU Archives.

45   Harrison Bryan. *Annual Report of the Librarian*, 1972, [1]. SU Archives.

46   When Harrison Bryan was appointed the Vice Chancellor told him 'to deal only with him on the vital matters of staff and money and "not to let the Library Committee have anything to do with them"' (Harrison Bryan. *No Gray Profession*, 1994, 47).

47   'teaching staff … are not limited as to time or number of books … The Fisher Library is designed principally, of course, to meet the needs of the University with its teaching staff of about 700, as well as its 10,000 students' ([Jean Whyte?]. 'The Fisher Library, University of Sydney'. *ALJ* 8 (2) 1959, 62–64).

48   Harrison Bryan. 'An Australian Library in the AM'. *Journal of the Royal Australian Historical Society* 55 (3) 1969, 212.

49   Interview: Wallace Kirsop, 2008.

50   Margaret Lundie. 'University of Sydney library since the War'. *ALJ* 20 (6) 1971, 5.

51   [Jean Whyte?]. 'The Fisher Library, University of Sydney'. *ALJ* 8 (2) 1959, 62–64; Neil A. Radford. 'Student borrowing from a University library'. *ALJ* 15 (4) 1966, 154–160.

52   John Cummings. 'A birthday ode for Miss Whyte, in ottava rima'. NLA: MS 9616.

53   Margaret Lundie. 'University of Sydney library since the War'. *ALJ* 20 (6) 1971, 8; Harrison Bryan. 'The Fisher "sit-ins" of April 1967'. *Vestes* 11 (1) 1968, 153–159.

Harrison Bryan appears to have later changed his mind about this protest, as he spoke of students 'spoiling for a fight – any fight so long as it was with authority – and we had a series of sit-ins in Fisher. Fortunately, the University Administration managed to divert the activists' wrath onto itself after the first sit-in and thereafter the sitters were merely using the Library as their battleground but not actually fighting us' (Harrison Bryan. 'Jean Primrose Whyte'. *ALJ* 38 (1) 1989, 11).

54   University of Sydney. Library Advisory Committee. 'Minutes', February 14th, 1972. SU Archives. Jean was Acting Librarian in early 1972 for a period of about six weeks.

55   Interview: Denis Richardson, 2006.

56   The latter figures included branch library holdings added to the main catalogue (Margaret Lundie. 'University of Sydney library since the War'. *ALJ* 20 (6) 1971, 7).

57   R.L. Cope. 'The Library Keeper's business'. *AARL* 33 (2) 2002.

58   University of Sydney. Library Advisory Committee. 'Minutes', February 16th, 1970. SU Archives; Interview: Harrison Bryan, 2005. I thought that 4,000 items was a misprint, that to have catalogued so many books in addition to his other work seemed unlikely, but he assured me that the number was correct; the work was done on Saturdays and early mornings.

59   University of Sydney. Library. *Report on the collections, 1959–1960*. Sydney: 1961.

60   Andrew Osborn to Jean Whyte, August 22nd, 1993. SU: M 465.

61   The Public Library of New South Wales was later renamed the State Library of New South Wales.

62   Harrison Bryan. 'Scholars, teachers, students and librarians'. *Arts* 2 (3) 1963, 174.

63   University of Sydney. Library Advisory Committee. 'Minutes', November 16th, 1964. SU Archives.

64   University of Sydney. Library Advisory Committee. 'Minutes', November 15th, 1965. SU Archives.

65   Harrison Bryan. *Annual Report of the Librarian*, 1966, 1. SU Archives.

66　University of Sydney. Library Advisory Committee. 'Minutes', June 8th, November 17th, 1969. SU Archives.

67　University of Sydney. Library. 'Australian University Libraries – Reader Services Unit output – Main Library only 1971', 1972. SU Archives.

Perhaps the overloaded system was responsible for a serious security problem in the new building: bundles of books were lowered out of windows after dark. This problem was resolved (?) by closing unsupervised rooms earlier (University of Sydney. Library Advisory Committee. 'Minutes', September 14th, 1970. SU Archives).

68

	Michigan	Sydney
Students	c.30,000	c.16,000
Library attendance	1,771,695	1,774,572
Holdings	107,817	59,000
Book use in library	649,128	c.2,100,000 (excludes stack use)
Home circulation	237,059	214,224
Hours open/week	105	82

Table 3.1 (Harrison Bryan. *Annual Report of the Librarian*, 1965, 1–2. SU Archives).

69　Margaret Lundie. 'University of Sydney library since the War'. *ALJ* 20 (6) 1971, 8; University of Sydney. Library Advisory Committee. 'Minutes', November 21st, 1966 and March 8th, 1971. SU Archives.

70　Harrison Bryan. 'Obituary' [Beatrice Pilcher Wines]. *ALJ* 21 (10) 1972, 451–452.

71　Harrison Bryan noted that the University took pride in its Library, but the pride was 'by no means completely well-based' (Harrison Bryan. 'Some comments and an occasional rejoinder', 1988, 228).

72　'a cumbersome title about which we had better do something' (Andrew Osborn to Jean Whyte, December 23rd, 1958. SU: M 465). Harrison Bryan commented that Osborn had moved Miss Wines to the position 'in a moment of miscalculation ... He had assumed, quite incorrectly, that she would take early retirement' (Harrison Bryan. *No Gray Profession*, 1994, 48).

73　Harrison Bryan. *No Gray Profession*, 1994, 48.

74　While this description of her relationship with Jean is not flattering to Miss Wines, Harrison Bryan wrote in Wines' obituary 'her enthusiasm, her overflowing good spirits, her cheerful dedication to the service of the reader all ensured that even those who were exasperated at the time by the Library's deficiencies, yet remember it later with admiration and affection' (Harrison Bryan. 'Obituary' [Beatrice Pilcher Wines]. *ALJ* 21 (10) 1972, 451–452).

75　Jean Whyte. 'Curriculum vitae', [1964?]. NLA: MS 9616.

76　Library Association of Australia. 'Library Association of Australia 1961 Conference Programme, August 21st-August 25th'. *ALJ* 10 (2) 1961, 110–113.

77　Inter-library Loan Committee. 'Inter-library Loan Committee'. *ALJ* (4) 1960, 211.

78　Jean Whyte. 'Who uses a University Library, why and to what effect?'. 1972, 527–537.

79　Harrison Bryan. 'Jean Primrose Whyte'. *ALJ* 38 (1) 1989, 11.

80　Jean Whyte. 'Curriculum vitae', [1964?]. NLA: MS 9616.

81　Harrison Bryan. *Librarian's Information Bulletin* 1 (10) 1963.

82　'The Availability of Scientific Information in Australia: working paper presented to the Conference of Directors of Scientific Information Centres in the Asian-Pacific Region, June 10–14, 1963, Hong Kong'. NLA: MS 9616.

83. Harrison Bryan. *Librarian's Information Bulletin* 1 (3) 1963.
84. Transcript of a conversation between Jean Whyte and Geoffrey Alley, 1981. MON 1059: 2000/68/5.
85. Jean Whyte. 'Some Reminiscences of Geoffrey Alley', 1995, 3. J. McEldowney Personal Collection, Dunedin, New Zealand.
86. Ibid.
87. Transcript of a conversation between Jean Whyte and Geoffrey Alley, 1981. MON 1059: 2000/68/5.
88. W.J. McEldowney. *Geoffrey Alley, Librarian,* 2006, 406.
89. Jean Whyte. 'Some Reminiscences of Geoffrey Alley', 1995, 3. J. McEldowney Personal Collection, Dunedin, New Zealand.
90. Transcript of a conversation between Jean Whyte and Geoffrey Alley, 1981. MON 1059: 2000/68/5.
91. Jean Whyte. 'Some Reminiscences of Geoffrey Alley', 1995, 2. J. McEldowney Personal Collection, Dunedin, New Zealand.
92. Geoffrey Alley to Jean Whyte, February 11th, 1969. J. McEldowney Personal Collection, Dunedin, New Zealand.
93. Interview: Joan Barry, 2005.
94. Jean Whyte. [Notes for a speech prepared for a celebration of the conferring of the award of Order of Australia on Harrison Bryan], [1984]. NLA: MS 9616.
95. Interview: Joan Barry, 2005.
96. Jean Whyte to Andrew Osborn, January 17th, 1959. SU: M 465.
97. Geoffrey Alley to Jean Whyte, April 16th, 1969. J. McEldowney Personal Collection, Dunedin, New Zealand.
98. Harrison Bryan. 'Jean Primrose Whyte'. *ALJ* 38 (1) 1989, 12.
99. 'H.C.L. Anderson Award. Citation for Jean Primrose Whyte, BA, MA, FLAA', [1987]. NLA: MS 9616.
100. University of Sydney. 'Minutes of a regular meeting of the Senate of the University of Sydney, August 8th, 1972'. Resolution 72/252. SU Archives.

CHAPTER 4

○ INTERLUDE: THE *AUSTRALIAN LIBRARY JOURNAL*

She was ALJ[1]

Jean told the story of her editorship of *ALJ* in this article, published in 1972:[2]

Jean Whyte

IN JANUARY 1959 I wrote my first editorial in my first issue of the *Australian Library Journal* : twenty-five editorials and seventy-three issues later I wrote my last. I had edited the *Journal* from volume 8 to volume 19 and in that time it had grown from a quarterly to a bi-monthly and finally to an eleven issues per year publication. Of the 4,517 pages that had been published by the end of 1970 I was responsible for 3,354.

When I became editor in 1959 I had never edited anything. I had only the vaguest idea of what a galley-proof was, and I even thought that pasting-up an issue would be interesting. Those who persuaded me to take the job said that it would be easy and would give me good experience in such things as proof reading! It certainly provided plenty of experience.

What were the major difficulties that I encountered during my stint as editor? The somewhat unoriginal answer is 'How to get copy good enough to publish'. As the years went by I found that increasingly I could decide what to publish, but for at least half of those twelve years there really was no choice. I published what I had.

One of the regular features of the *Australian Library Journal* in 1959 was the Examiners' Reports on the LAA examinations. They took up a great deal of space, and solved the problem of copy for one of the four issues each year. In the early days of the Association, when most of the *Journal's* readers were probably students and when professional librarianship in Australia was at a fairly unsophisticated level, the comments of examiners of the kind that stated over and over again—'The general standard was not high'; 'Candidates do too little work'; 'The role of the State Library was not well understood'— may have helped to improve the standard of librarianship, but by 1960 they would hardly improve the image of Australian librarianship in the eyes of an international audience and they had become tedious for all but the candidates concerned. In 1961 the reports ceased to be published in the *Journal*.

One of my continuing problems was the fact that some groups of librarians seldom submitted articles while others were quite prolific. In some states writing for the *Journal* was almost unheard of, and librarians in universities contributed more actively than any other group. In such circumstances what does an editor do? Should I have published anything submitted on, say, school libraries because it was all there was? Should I have rejected otherwise acceptable copy from university librarians just because it was from university librarians? I was criticized for publishing too many articles from university librarians, too many articles from South Australia, too many articles on automation, and even for publishing too many obituaries. The critics ignored the one most important fact that if you do not publish what you have, you do not publish anything. In fact, I rejected about twenty per cent of the articles submitted and returned another ten per cent for alterations.

When the *Journal* increased its frequency from a quarterly to a bi-monthly and then to a monthly (minus one issue) I heard that some readers thought that in fact the articles had become shorter and less scholarly on both occasions. Looking back now, I do not think that there was any substance in the charge. In fact, the average length of the articles that I published remained remarkably consistent at between five and six pages, increasing slightly in the last four years. It was easier to produce special issues once there were eleven issues per year but there were few of these, only some regular ones on government publications, one on law librarianship and one on orientalist librarianship. Throughout my editorship I produced special Conference issues of the *Journal*.

I have not counted the names of the contributors but I have little hope that the number of members who wrote for the *Australian Library Journal* represented a higher percentage of the membership than when Harrison Bryan was editor. In fact, the present editor's policy is probably the only way of ensuring contributions from a larger group. During my editorship I think that the people who contributed the most material to

234

THE AUSTRALIAN LIBRARY JOURNAL JULY 1972

the *Australian Library Journal* were Janet Hine (for contributions and index) Harrison Bryan, an ex-editor (Caveat Editor Laurentius Fulvus), Russell Cope, D. H. Borchardt and G. A. J. Farmer. This is, I should add, a quantitative judgement.

From 1959 to 1965 the *Australian Library Journal* retained the format that had been established from its beginning. Occasionally someone at a Council Meeting would talk about the possibility of altering the design but it was considered too expensive and difficult. When in 1965 I was given a chance to re-design the Journal I was delighted. From 1966 to 1969 the *Australian Library Journal* reflected my idea of the appropriate presentation for a professional journal. In achieving this I had a great deal of help from Mr D. R. Hall. Of course we had to be careful of costs, we had to be economical of space and paper, and every now and again there were mistakes in layout that shouted at me from the printed page — too late to be corrected. In designing the 1966 *Journal* we set out to produce a publication which would be a professional journal and would convey the fact that it was concerned with books and print. Its effects were to depend on the layout, on the spacing of letters and the harmonious arrangement of type. At that time in Sydney there was little choice in typefaces and we were determined that the total *Journal* must be printed in one face : but we were fortunate in being able to find a printer who had Bembo which was my first preference.

The story of the re-designing of the *Journal* is too long to recount in detail. Perhaps some idea of the difference between today and those more amateur days can be conveyed by the fact that the lettering for the cover of the *Australian Library Journal* from 1966 to 1969 was worked out by the Editor over one weekend in eighteen hours of work on the Piscator Press in the Library of the University of Sydney.

Misprints — the fear of missing them! Misprints — the shame of them! They go with every editor, and they are the things that librarians notice and comment upon most frequently. It is my opinion that the editor of the *Australian Library Journal* could issue a Stop Press copy warning that all the materials in our libraries were about to dinistegrate or that the reading of books was about to be prohibited on pian of death and that the only response would be from members pointing out that he had misspelt *disintegrate* and *pain*.

My own copies of the *Journal* have the misprints that I discovered noted and there were certainly some that may have sent some editors into the harbour or to the tranquilizer bottles. A heading for *Recent Referent Books*, the 'September, 1968' running head reading 'October, 1968', the omission of an author's name and even 'Quarterly' misspelt on a cover : certainly the *Journal* was under-edited and I did not then believe that it could be otherwise. There was not enough time to read all the proofs more than once. It took about thirty-two hours of editorial time to produce each issue of the *Journal*.

Today the editorial policy of the *Australian Library Journal* is published in the *Handbook* of the Library Association of Australia. This policy was first adopted by the Council of the Association in 1968. Certainly it may be said that the Association's *Journal* has no other objectives than those of the Association, but editors have a habit of thinking about these objects and their translation into cold or hot print in the pages of the *Journal*.

The first editor's policy was expressed on the first printed page of volume 1, number 1, under the title 'Over to Us', and Harrison Bryan has quoted some of his words. In 1954 Harrison Bryan, the second editor, meditated on his duties:

To go no further, the Journal must reflect the constitution and objects of the Association whose organ it is. On the one hand, it must concern itself with the professional competence of librarians in this country. To this end, clearly, it should offer space for professional articles of high standard. . . .
Being a working librarian, my natural bias is towards more articles of a professional nature, any present unbalance, I think, tends to react against them. I think too, that there is scope for a type of material that so far has not figured prominently in our columns and which must appeal to all classes of our membership. I refer to reports from particular libraries, and especially of course the larger ones, of notable

developments, including, particularly, valuable acquisitions...[1]

In 1959 I began my period of editorship with an editorial expressing the objects of the *Journal* as I saw them. My definition of objects is not very different from that of Harrison Bryan and the only new note is expressed in the final paragraph:

> Finally this Australian Library Journal belongs to the librarians of Australia. It is their record of ideas and achievements and it is the medium through which Australia's place in international librarianship must be judged....[2]

Looking back over the twelve years as editor of the *Australian Library Journal* I see my own professional preoccupations in the editorials that I wrote. The subjects that they covered included the need for pre-publication cataloguing, the need to compile bibliographies, the value of LAA Conferences and of the *Australian Library Journal* itself: but the subjects most frequently dealt with were education for librarianship, the nation's library resources and the importance of supplying library materials on all subjects to all the people.

The only issue of the *Journal* that ever brought real comment from its readers was that of June 1964. In publishing it I had decided that I had to do what I could to arouse members of the Library Association of Australia to take a stand against censorship. In August of that year the *Statement on Freedom to Read* became Association policy.

It is, I suppose, some indication of my conservatism that I would not now repudiate the views that I expressed in those editorials. I still believe:

> There are a hundred articles that could be written for this Journal. The members of the Library Association of Australia have enlisted in the struggle against ignorance but not as soldiers to be commanded and led, rather as explorers to discover new routes through the desert, or as scientists to find better ways of combating the disease.[3]

Harrison Bryan has mentioned the difficulty of publishing regular features in the *Journal*. I, too, wanted to establish the 'Australian Library Scene' and the 'Diary of forthcoming meetings', but with little success. I regard the regular features that I did publish as among the most successful articles to appear. Janet Hine's witty and perceptive reviews of Australian reference books, Russell Cope's reports on government publications, Laurie Brown's looks at the 'Public Library Scene' and Geoffrey Farmer's 'Notes on Australian book design' were all features that people read. Margaret Lundie was a book review editor who was so successful that I had to ration the amount of space that the reviews could have.

I remember reading the first *Australian Library Journal*. I remember the excitement with which we greeted it and how pleased we were at this evidence of growth of the profession. Years later I looked critically at its production and was appalled by the mixture of types. Most of the text was in Benedictine, some of the headings in Garamond, sans-serif, bold and italics were used almost at random. But it was our Journal and the words were more important than the clothes they wore. (In this computer-ridden age many may wonder that I would even notice such minor details as type faces!)

Since then there have been many changes, many experiments that failed, some that succeeded. If it is to serve the profession well the *Journal* should change in design and in content. I am a spasmodic believer in the notion that one good custom may corrupt the world.

They were busy years. There was never any question about what to do with my weekends. There were many crises, many urgent and after-hours meetings with the printer, and, fortunately for my sanity, there were always professional colleagues ready to help. Every time that I cut up the galleys for pasting I thought of resigning, every time that the latest issue arrived on my desk I decided that it was a job worth doing.

One of the depressing reflections is that the reality fell so far short of the vision: the performance was so much less than the ideal. But thinking and saying is always so much easier than doing.

[1] 'Banana benders all'. *Australian Library Journal* 3(2) : 41, April 1954.

[2] Whyte, J. 'Editorial'. *Australian Library Journal* 8(1) : 2, January 1959.

[3] Whyte, J. 'Editorial'. *Australian Library Journal* 9(3) : 164, October 1960.

ENDNOTES

[1] Interview: Harrison Bryan, 2005.

[2] Jean Whyte. 'Twenty-one years of the *Australian Library Journal*: Jean Whyte'. *ALJ* 21 (6) 1972, 234–236. Courtesy of the Australian Library and Information Association.

CHAPTER 5

○ MISS JEAN WHYTE, BA (HONS) (ADELAIDE), AM (CHICAGO), FLAA, 2ND DIVISION APS
JEAN'S SHORT STAY AT THE NATIONAL LIBRARY OF AUSTRALIA

far and away the best librarian in Australia[1]

Jean Whyte's life would fit neatly into periods each between thirteen and nineteen years if it were not for her two-year stint at the NLA. The reason for this anomaly, said Jean, was that there was an 'unfortunate change in librarians'[2] ... Alan Fleming, Director General of the NLA, was succeeded by George Chandler.

Fleming, a friend of Jean's, was not a librarian, so there was an uproar when he was appointed, but Jean defended him. Fleming, a senior public servant, became popular with the staff at the NLA. He had been head of the Joint Intelligence Organization and brought to the position a wide knowledge of the public service and a range of useful contacts. When he heard of Jean's application for the NLA position he was so amazed by his good fortune that he checked with Harrison Bryan to find out whether the application was genuine.[3] Like Osborn before him, Fleming was keen to have Jean work with him and anxious to make the rough places plain, to the extent that he ensured a welcome for Baggins: 'I am nevertheless wondering whether you'd like a furlined basket or a plush lined filing cabinet drawer for Baggins (& directions as to whether he should be filed under CAT or PERSON)'.[4]

Baggins and Miss Jean Whyte arrived at the NLA in September 1972. Jean's new position, Branch Director, one level below that of the Director General, was classed in the Second Division of the Commonwealth Public Service, in which there were 850 men and one woman (there were no women in the first division). Jean said that 'not being familiar with the Commonwealth public service ... the second division classification had not meant a darn thing to her until she read the PSB [Public Service Board] report and realized how small the division was'.[5]

The NLA, set up in 1901, had been housed first in Melbourne (where it was known as the Commonwealth Parliamentary Library) taking over the Victorian Parliamentary Library building, before moving to Canberra in 1927 (Andrew Osborn, who then worked in the Library, had assisted with the move). The Library occupied various locations around Canberra until, in 1968, it was moved into its current building on the shores of Lake Burley Griffin. Jean described the new building in her *ALJ* article 'The National Library' shortly after it opened.[6]

By the time Jean arrived the Library held more than 1,250,000 volumes (fewer than the University of Sydney), subscribed to 54,000 serial titles and held many special collections. The collection was increasing rapidly and new technology was extending the way materials and services were made available locally, nationally and internationally – this was the time of the 'information explosion', 'the days of the STISEC Report, the Tell Seminar, the amendment of the National Library Act which enlarged the Library's ambit ... a central role for the Library ... the time of ALAIN, the projected Australian Library Assisted Information Network, the first vision of effective coordination of the national bibliographic and information service resource'.[7] It was a time of acronyms: 'the language of a world increasingly organized in formal groups for exchange of ideas and co-operative action; a world of fast travel and communications; a world continually expanding its powers of handling information through computers'.[8]

The Library had recently been reorganized into three branches; Jean became Director of one of these, the Information, Reference and Research Branch, which had 120 staff and was itself divided into Reference, Australiana and the special collections, the last of which Jean especially enjoyed[9] – the National Film Collection, the National Photographic Collection and the newly formed National Collection of Sound Recordings.[10] The Branch also arranged the restoration and permanent display of Captain Cook's journal and the purchase of expensive materials such as *Parrots of the World*, which cost $50,000 for the full set, more than the cost of the average Australian suburban house at the time.[11] Jean enjoyed developing the National Collection, which involved requesting and receiving donations, much of it from public figures in Australia such as authors, politicians and academics, and she was especially interested in acquiring manuscripts and personal papers.[12] Jean, again, led a department involved in rapid, ground-breaking change.

Although there was excitement in the challenge of the NLA's work, in comparison with the University of Sydney there was an 'astonishing quiet'[13] – contrast the problem of thousands of overdue loans in Sydney with Jean's attempt at the NLA to retrieve emu eggs and a painting which had been loaned to Dame Zara Holt in 1966 to 'decorate' the Prime Minister's Lodge for the Queen Mother's visit.[14] Jean enjoyed working in the NLA[15] and had the 'best job in the place',[16] but she found the first twelve months difficult (but not as difficult as in Sydney).[17] And, said Harrison Bryan, 'It was just the time for librarians with vision and enthusiasm to be in Canberra, an atmosphere in which Jean thrived'.[18]

Not only the Library but also Canberra itself was a world away from Sydney. Overcoming early loneliness,[19] she claimed to enjoy living in Canberra (and it appears that Baggins did too – 'Glad Baggins feels he can be a Canberra cat' wrote Alan Fleming).[20] Her enjoyment of Canberra is surprising (I am not sure whether Baggins shared her enjoyment: he suffered from hay-fever and conjunctivitis in Canberra),[21] given the Canberra of the 1970s: Canberra can be very cold (especially in contrast to the Outback); most people left work at 4.51 p.m. (but Jean was used to working long hours after other staff had left), there was little social life and few restaurants, and there were no harbour views (she said that the Canberra hills made up for this loss).[22] She planned to stay in Canberra and was quite comfortable financially, enjoying her work and her life. She bought a 'guvvy' house (built for government employees) and enjoyed her garden, planting roses, which became a continuing interest.

Then into her Garden of Eden came the snake. Dr. George Chandler became Director General of the NLA in 1974, following Alan Fleming's early retirement. Chandler was British and came to Australia with excellent qualifications, experience in large British public libraries and an international standing in librarianship, along with the expertise to develop automation at the NLA and automated resource sharing in Australia.

And his own plans. There appear to be two strands, perhaps three, to Jean's problems with Chandler: his plans for the NLA, his management style, and perhaps his British library education. Chandler wanted to reorganize the Library on the subject department basis he knew from British public libraries, with plans for 'a whole lot of National Libraries. E.g. National Music Library, National Film Library, National Humanities Library, etc.',[23] which did not include ALAIN/ALBIS and overrode all that the Library has been working towards: 'he thinks he can just superimpose it [his own plans] & his answer to criticism is that we will be promoted!'[24] Chandler's management style was not consultative (in contrast to that of Fleming, who was always ready to listen to librarians),[25] which compounded the problems caused by his lack of knowledge of Australia, Australian systems and the public service (possibly an important factor in Chandler's being appointed, as Fleming's public-service background had helped him maintain the independence of the NLA). Chandler's plans were not supported by senior staff, and he 'appeared not to find it easy to understand completely the Australian scene, far less adjust to it'.[26]

Jean reacted quickly (to avoid an experience similar to that of working with Brideson at the PLSA?):

April 1st, 1974: Chandler arrived;
July: Jean questioned whether she was wasting her time at the NLA;[27]
October: Jean discussed a position with Monash University;
December: Jean accepted the Monash position, and by
January 1975 she had left.

Although this sequence was rapid, Jean knew of Chandler's appointment before he began work – there is an intriguing letter to Jean from Geoffrey Alley dated February 23rd, 1974 in which Alley in New Zealand – in reply to a letter from Jean which I have not seen – wrote that Chandler was an 'English import ... usual crippling limitations'.[28] Jean would have known quite a bit about Chandler before he arrived: she knew people who knew him, he had a worldwide reputation, and, while Jean was editor of *ALJ*, she had published a review of a book by Chandler (it was damned with faint praise).[29] And Chandler's 1971 publication *Libraries in the East* had received an even less favourable review by NLA staff member Dulcie Penfold, who wrote 'one cannot help wondering "East of where?"'.[30]

Although Jean later said that, had it not been for Chandler, she would have remained at the NLA[31] (I presume she meant until her retirement), there were other factors which influenced her decision, including the decline of the Whitlam (Labor) Government, which had given so much support to the development of the NLA. And the Monash offer may have been too good to refuse. Also, there was little possibility of furthering her career at the NLA, both because the most senior appointment would not be vacant again for some years and because the appointment of a woman still seemed impossible. Also the Garden of Eden had not been without its problems: although Osborn had encouraged her to apply for the position of Director General following Fleming's retirement – 'I feel that you are far and away the best librarian in Australia and would like to get things going to propose your candidacy. I feel that it is an opportune time, especially with Whitlam's expression of equality for men and women'[32] – Jean did not apply, 'because ... I do not want to have anything to do with the politicking, intrigue and the gossip that is certain to break out here in the next few months'.[33] The stress at this time led Jean to visit a doctor, who recommended that she take a month's leave because she was 'showing signs of nervous exhaustion' and had been under 'considerable strain'.[34]

The stress may also have been caused by her usual heavy workload: in addition to her work Jean continued her involvement in the LAA, attending conferences, giving papers, mentoring, accrediting library schools, writing about librarianship, etc. She also wrote *A report on the administration of public libraries in South Australia.*[35] At the time her friend and past colleague, Ray Olding, was State Librarian of South Australia. Olding said that there was an attempt by elements within the Premier's Department to move the Libraries Department into the Premier's Department instead of allowing the State Library to be a government department with the State Librarian being the Permanent Head of Department reporting directly to the Minister for Education. Olding and the then Minister for Education, Hugh Hudson, opposed the move, and Hudson asked Jean to write a report on this and other library matters. Nobody was surprised when Jean agreed with Olding and Hudson that the Library should remain independent (although this independence was to last only a short time).

Jean's brief stint at the NLA could be called unfinished business. There had been the early 'excitement of the Fleming years at the NLA when we worked so hard to realize our dream of a nation-wide information service',[36] dreams which looked possible because the Library had the support of the Whitlam Government. Looking back while she was still at the Library, she thought that she had been 'of some use',[37] and perhaps been the most successful in Films and Music, which was not where she expected it.[38] But there were too many problems: 'Fido is really winning on so many fronts'.[39] As Jean wrote to Alan Fleming, 'Of course I feel a bit of a weasel already – & I really like & believe in the NLA – always have. But I just cannot stand the present set-up. You would have a fit …'[40]

ENDNOTES

1. Andrew Osborn to Jean Whyte, May 15th, 1973. SU: M 465.
2. Transcript of a conversation between Jean Whyte and Geoffrey Alley, 1981. MON 1059: 2000/68/5.
3. Harrison Bryan. 'Jean Primrose Whyte'. *ALJ* 38 (1) 1989, 11.
4. Alan Fleming to Jean Whyte, March 24th, 1972. NLA: MS 9616.
5. 'Doubling the number'. *Canberra Times,* September 28th, 1972.
6. Jean Whyte. 'The National Library'. *ALJ* 17 (8) 1968, 257–258.
7. Harrison Bryan. 'Jean Primrose Whyte'. *ALJ* 38 (1) 1989, 12.
8. Janice Kenny. *National Library of Australia*, 1984, 15. When I was a librarianship student, I was given a list of steps for developing projects, the first step (before any planning whatsoever) was to choose an acronym.
9. Jean Whyte. 'Retirement Reminiscences', 1988. NLA: MS 9616.
10. Also referred to as the National Sound Archive.
11. William T. Cooper. 158 watercolour paintings reproduced in Joseph M. Forshaw. *Parrots of the world,* 1973.
12. Interview: Graeme Powell, 2008. The National Archives of Australia collected only public records of government.
13. Harrison Bryan. 'Jean Primrose Whyte'. *ALJ* 38 (1) 1989, 11.
14. Jean Whyte to D. Eddowes, December 12th, 1972. NLA: MS 9616. Materials were for loan only in special circumstances.
15. Jean Whyte to Karen Foley, November 14th, 1972. NLA: MS 9616.
16. Jean Whyte to Alan Fleming, October 21st, 1973. NLA: MS 9862.
17. Ibid.

18. Harrison Bryan. 'Jean Primrose Whyte'. *ALJ* 38 (1) 1989, 12.
19. Jean Whyte to Alan Fleming, September 3rd, 1974. NLA: MS 9862.
20. Alan Fleming to Jean Whyte, September 23rd, 1972. NLA: MS 9616.
21. Jean Whyte to Alan Fleming, October 15th, 1974. NLA: MS 9862.
22. Jean Whyte to Malvina Overy, August 14th, 1973. NLA: MS 9616.
23. Jean Whyte to Alan Fleming, September 3rd, 1974. NLA: MS 9862.
24. Ibid.
25. Interview: Graeme Powell, 2008.
26. 'Chandler, George (1915–[1992])'. In Harrison Bryan, ed., *ALIAS*, 1988–1991, Vol. 1, 144–145.
27. Jean Whyte to G.R. Manton, July 24th, 1974. NLA: MS 9616.
28. Geoffrey Alley to Jean Whyte, February 23rd, 1974. J. McEldowney Personal Collection, Dunedin, New Zealand.
29. Spencer Routh. Review of *How to find out, a guide to sources of information for all, arranged by the Dewey Decimal Classification* by G. Chandler. *ALJ* 13 (2) 1964, 85.
30. Dulcie Penfold. Review of *Libraries in the East* by G. Chandler. *ALJ* 21 (3) 1972, 128–129.
31. Transcript of a conversation between Jean Whyte and Geoffrey Alley, 1981. MON 1059: 2000/68/5.
32. Andrew Osborn to Jean Whyte, May 15th, 1973. SU: M 465.
33. Jean Whyte to Andrew Osborn, June 15th, 1973. SU: M 465.
34. Brian Andrea. [Medical certificate], October 4th, 1973. NLA: MS 9616.
35. Jean Whyte. A report on the administration of public libraries in South Australia. NLA: MS 9616.
36. Jean Whyte. 'Retirement Reminiscences', 1988. NLA: MS 9616.
37. Jean Whyte to Alan Fleming, October 21st, 1973. NLA: MS 9862.
38. Jean Whyte to Alan Fleming, September 3rd, 1974. NLA: MS 9862.
39. Ibid. Jean (and others) privately referred to Chandler as 'Fido'.
40. Jean Whyte to Alan Fleming, October 15th, 1974. NLA: MS 9862.

Figure 7: George Chandler, Alan Fleming, Kenneth Myer, Harrison Bryan and Harold White

Figure 8: Hector Monro

Figure 9: Dame Roma Mitchell

Figure 10: Andrew Osborn

CHAPTER 6

PROFESSOR JEAN WHYTE, AM, BA (HONS) (ADELAIDE), AM (CHICAGO), FLAA
JEAN BECOMES THE FOUNDATION PROFESSOR OF THE GRADUATE SCHOOL OF LIBRARIANSHIP, MONASH UNIVERSITY

> one of the dominant figures in Australian librarianship in the second half of the 20th century[1]

The story of Professor Jean Whyte at Monash University is not the history of the Graduate School of Librarianship (GSL), although part of the GSL's story will be told here, as it is bound up with Jean's story.[2]

Planning for a post-graduate school of librarianship in Victoria began in the 1960s: Axel Lodewycks, the Melbourne University Librarian, claimed to have been the first person (in 1958) to propose that a graduate school of librarianship be set up at a Victorian university,[3] and, with others, he continued to campaign for a school. Monash had begun discussing the founding of a library school by 1964 but had had to wait while the University of Melbourne debated – and eventually decided against – a similar proposal.[4] In 1967 the Monash Faculty Board made a tentative proposal to the Australian Universities Commission (AUC) for a library school.[5] But Monash, in an about-turn, decided not to proceed, on the grounds that the Royal Melbourne Institute of Technology (RMIT) course was adequate for Victoria's needs; then, on the advice of the La Trobe University Librarian, Dietrich Borchardt, it returned to its earlier proposal.[6] This proposal passed through all levels of Monash administration, was supported by the LAA,[7] and received funding approval from the AUC in 1972.[8] Monash's Dean of the Faculty of Arts, Professor Guy Manton, who became the chief advocate for a library school, travelled overseas in 1973 to look at library schools, in order to help set up the GSL. Jean thanked him for his assistance, saying that the GSL 'would not exist if you had not believed that it should do so'.[9]

Why was Monash the place in which to set up a library school? Monash had been established in 1958 – named in honour of the Australian soldier Sir John Monash (with whom Jean shared a birthday) – set up to cater for the rapidly growing number of students wanting tertiary education. A number of factors made Monash an appropriate place for a library school, including that it was still new and more amenable to fresh ideas and to directions which would differentiate it from the older University of Melbourne; librarianship fitted in with Monash's technological direction, with the bibliographic work in the English, French, and German departments, and with the new Department of Information Science.[10] Other reasons included the need for more graduates than could be produced by RMIT and for a more academic level of study, especially as 'with the tremendous growth in the amount of information to be dealt with and the diversification in the methods of storing and imparting it, the librarian of the future will need to be familiar with and control a far wider range of activity than in the past'.[11] Perhaps, too, Manton and a number of other academics who were married to librarians supported the proposal because they thought of librarianship as a genteel occupation for the wives of academics.

The proposal of the first Monash Librarian, Ernest Clark, that the University establish a school of librarianship was accepted by the University,[12] and the quality of the Library contributed to the proposal: Monash was proud of its Library, which was well supported by the Professorial Board, had a big budget, and held the materials needed by its staff and students,[13] pointing to Monash's decision-makers understanding the importance of libraries in education and therefore understanding the importance of graduate education for librarianship (the Library's quality was important to Jean in her role in accrediting library schools). Perhaps these factors contributed to the old question of whether librarianship should be taught at a university not being raised.

Monash set up a Council Committee with eleven members – including one librarian, Brian Southwell, Clark's successor as Monash Librarian – presided over by the Pro-Vice-Chancellor, Professor W.A.G. Scott, to appoint a Professor of Librarianship and Director of the Graduate School of Librarianship.[14] The position was advertised world-wide in 1974, and there were nine applicants, three of them from overseas, all senior in the library profession. Jean did not apply but lent her support to another applicant.[15] The Committee, wisely, consulted three librarians (Margery Ramsay, Laurie Brown and Denis Richardson) for comments on a shortlist of four and for suggestions of others who might be suitable for the position, an indication that the Committee was not happy with the shortlist. The three librarians unanimously rejected the entire shortlist.[16] Two of the librarians recommended that Jean Whyte be approached, as they thought that she was better than anyone on the shortlist.[17] The Committee followed their advice.

Manton flew to Canberra to urge Jean to apply. She turned him down, giving three reasons: that she had gone to Canberra 'to help realize a vision of national services' and was 'not ready to give up yet'; that she had lent her support to another candidate; and 'I wouldn't be my first choice'. She was tempted, she wanted the School to do well, but no, she would not apply.[18]

Her suitor persisted. He wrote to Jean: 'Your name has been suggested in several quarters, and I have been asked by the committee to write to you. We would like to know in the first place whether you will allow yourself to be considered'.[19] Jean 'thought for a week & said yes'.[20]

Jean's reply to Manton's invitation is glorious:

> Dear Professor Manton,
>
> Your letter of September 25th has caused me some perturbation and many hours of thought. I really cannot see why 'several quarters' should suggest my name as a person who should be considered for the Chair of Librarianship.
>
> But they have, and I know that I must say yes – if only so that the Committee really has a chance to be sure that they do not want me.
>
> I shall send you a formal application as soon as possible but for the present I have taken up your suggestion and have asked three people whether they will allow me to give their names as referees. As I have told you before I am well known in the profession in Australia and I think you should ask anyone you please what they think of me. My referees are, of course, all people who will probably give you favourable reports, but I have chosen them carefully because I want the Committee to be as well informed as possible about me. I think it is true to say that the three people listed below know me and my abilities and failings very well. I cannot think of any among the living who know me better. They are [Harrison Bryan, Librarian, University of Sydney, and future Director

General of the NLA, Geoffrey Alley, former National Librarian of New Zealand, and Alan Fleming, former Director General of the NLA]

...

You also asked me when I could be released from my present position, if the Committee should decide to offer me the Chair. The Australian Public Service has no requirements of notice to leave, but I think that I should probably give two months notice. I would also wish to take some leave, possibly with the idea of talking to some of my colleagues in the United States who are Deans of library schools. Naturally there would have to be discussions about what leave I would carry over from this position, but I expect that my long service entitlements would carry over. If not I have about five months of this leave owing at present.

Yours sincerely,

Jean P. Whyte[21]

Monash flew Jean to Melbourne for a weekend of interviews and discussions. They paid for her economy return airfare on TAA Flight 473 ($52.60) and accommodation at Monash's North East Halls ($6.60) and stretched the budget to a luncheon with South Australian wines (Mildara dry sherry $1.69; Queen Adelaide Riesling $2.00; McLaren Vale Claret $4.20 – South Australian wines: they were wooing rather than interviewing her – luncheon for eleven people: $40.89).[22] The Committee voted unanimously that Jean be offered the position.[23] She accepted the offer. Her salary was to be $19,614 per annum, a little higher than that advertised, plus extra amounts, such as up to $1,000 for removal expenses, which would have pleased her[24] (her salary at the NLA was $17,776).[25] Despite Jean saying that she would not accept any nonsense about medical examinations,[26] the appointment was subject to a medical examination (which would have terrified her). However, the medical report proved satisfactory.[27]

In her letter accepting the Monash appointment Jean said that she would rent out her house in Canberra to someone who would look after Baggins (who was, by now, at least eighteen years old) while she travelled overseas before taking up her appointment.[28] 'I feel Baggins will adjust well to higher learning & absence of irritating Canberra hay-fever dust', wrote Alan Fleming.[29] Jean moved from Canberra to Melbourne in January 1975, to a house in Mount Waverley close to Monash belonging to her friends Audrey and Douglas Muecke. A few months later she bought her own home in Mount Waverley, moving the rest of her possessions there from Canberra, including about 2,000 books – 'I hate possessions – they trap you (but on the other hand I like my books!)' she wrote.[30]

Why did Jean at last agree to Manton's proposal to be interviewed, knowing that if she did so she would almost certainly be offered the position? She said that she liked teaching and knew that she could teach, that she liked universities and that the position would give her an opportunity to write more about libraries, that it was a new school, without left-over staff, and that Monash had courses in computing, education, sociology and bibliography. The School would have a masters program and students could learn about new technology,[31] and she was especially impressed by the amount of cooperation within Monash.[32] Most importantly, the School was to be at a university and the course at post-graduate level, implementing Jean's view of librarianship as a graduate profession and allowing her to put into practice her theories of education for librarianship. She said that she did not want to be influenced by her antipathy towards Chandler but that she would not have considered Monash if Fleming or Bryan had been Director General.[33]

Jean had a year in which to set up the GSL. She waited until after Auntie's ninetieth birthday celebrations in March 1975[34] before travelling overseas for five months, visiting library schools and associations in Continental Europe (the Netherlands, Germany, Austria, Yugoslavia, Denmark, Sweden and Finland), Great Britain (where she bought books at Hay-on-Wye for the Monash University Library – memories of Andrew Osborn), New Zealand, and the United States of America (where she attended the Annual Conference of the American Library Association in San Francisco and caught up with friends from her previous visits).[35] She also began interviewing prospective staff overseas, which prompted Manton to arrange for Monash to contribute $500 to her expenses, as she would be acting on behalf of Monash before her official appointment.[36]

Jean took up the position of Professor of Librarianship and Director of the GSL officially in July 1975. The GSL was given a space on the Fourth Floor South of the Menzies Building (the 'Ming Wing') at Monash (Clayton), but this space was inadequate, as space was at a premium because building the necessary extensions had been postponed. The GSL was assigned the academic dress of 'jet black piping around the Monash Master of Arts cowl' and colours to be 'jet black, old rose and turquoise blue'.[37]

A university department, a master's degree, academic dress: education for librarianship had changed since Jean's entry into the profession in 1942: her first librarianship qualification, the Qualifying Certificate in Librarianship, had been replaced by Registration, which by 1975 was being phased out – Jean wrote of the changes in 'Control and diversity: a short history of course recognition in Australia'.[38] By the time that the GSL was set up there were eleven librarianship courses in Australia at seven institutions,[39] which, Jean wrote, were close to sufficient for the basic professional level, whereas more advanced courses were needed. One such course, the first (Australian) Master of Librarianship, had been set up at the University of New South Wales in 1964, under the leadership of Professor Wilma Radford.[40] But Jean saw the need in Australia for further courses, believing that Australia lagged behind other countries in advanced education for librarians: 'The U.S. has had advanced courses for librarians for 40 years … It's possible to gain a Doctorate of Philosophy in the subject there … I also believe Australian universities should offer more advanced courses – the more schools and the more specialists the better'.[41] In 'The Accreditation of Courses in Librarianship' (1974) she had written that 'librarianship today is a much more complicated discipline than it was when I studied for the first Preliminary examination ever offered in Australia. There is more to read and learn than there was when I studied at the University of Chicago ten years later. Professional education for librarianship in Australia is today much more concerned with the basic philosophy and purposes of libraries, much more concerned about the problems – social, administrative, technical – that librarians must try to solve, than about the details of cataloguing and reference books'.[42]

Jean presented a concise statement of her theory of education for librarianship in her 1984 article 'Librarians and scholars':

> Librarianship is an academic discipline but at present it occupies a basement in the house of intellect. It will climb upstairs when it can present a more firmly based tradition of scholarship, more certain and significant research findings, a less didactic approach to its subject matters so that students in library schools participate in academic questioning and argument rather than concentrating on learning a body of facts that will, inevitably, be out of date; and a more pervading sense of urgency and purpose.[43]

In this article Jean developed the theme she had first written about in 1956, the need for graduate education in librarianship.[44] This time she did not argue that librarianship should be studied at a university; instead she wrote that one of the reasons the question of whether librarianship should be taught at a university arose was that librarianship was too new as an academic discipline to have established traditions of scholarship. She gave many reasons for this lack of scholarship, mostly blaming library schools which emphasized teaching rather than research, had poor academic standards, were isolated from other parts of the university, lacked finance and were under pressure to produce professionals for the workforce; to these she added 'the domination of the practitioners in every branch of librarianship, including education for librarianship'.[45]

Jean's set out her plans for the GSL in *Preliminary notes on the School of Librarianship at Monash University*: the preamble was self-effacing, noting that she had had little involvement in library education during the previous fifteen years, although she had been interested in the subject and involved in the Board of Examination, and, in an interesting contrast to her views in 'Librarians and Scholars', she wrote that her views on education for librarianship had been determined by staffing needs in the libraries, which led her to the opinion that the combined wisdom of the staff was more important than the ideas of 'the Director'[46] (with her involvement with the Board of Education, teaching and examining, and her writings on education for librarianship, little recent involvement may be an exaggeration).[47]

Under the heading 'Objectives' Jean said that she saw the GSL's 'first responsibility' to be a Masters program in librarianship (which became the Master of Librarianship course), to offer 'librarians of superior academic qualifications the opportunity of advanced studies in their profession so that they are equipped to fill senior positions in libraries and library schools'.[48] This program, for experienced librarians, would be designed to make students aware of – and find solutions to – Australian librarianship problems, to introduce students to research skills, and to allow them to specialize in an area of librarianship. She also planned a Diploma course to teach librarianship to graduates who did not have library experience but who wanted to take up 'junior professional positions in libraries' (this became the Master of Arts course, not the Diploma course). She thought that students could visit 'working libraries as laboratories' (she did not say so, but this was in contrast to the SLIS library), that their librarians could visit the GSL, and that the interaction could benefit both.

The GSL courses were to emphasize professionalism and the future of Australian librarianship. Libraries were seen as 'service institutions', and the courses would deal with 'problems of service to the library's users'. The philosophy was of librarianship as an entity (SLIS methodology) rather than being broken into many different parts: 'computing studies' as part of the traditional courses (i.e. not separated by process), materials not separated by form, as 'the informational content of all library materials is more important than their physical form', library environments rather than courses on types of libraries, and administration through the Department of Business Studies, as 'the administrative problems of libraries are generally not unique'.[49] Jean said: 'I don't really believe in teaching librarianship in little bits called "acquisition, cataloguing, readers' services, readers advising, and so on". I think that you teach librarianship as one thing and you talk about the building of the collection and the use of it and the organisation of it all as one central problem'.[50]

The GSL would conduct research into Australian librarianship, acknowledging that research interests would include the interests of the staff and of other Monash departments, such as historical bibliography, publishing, Australiana, and services to the disadvantaged, Aborigines and students. And courses for librarians in special subject libraries, similar to those which were available in some American schools, were a possibility. Students would be introduced to the work done by technicians and also learn traditional librarianship skills such as reference and cataloguing.

Jean's planned teaching methodology, which took into account Monash guidelines, included discussions, seminars and lectures, while assessment would be through seminars, written work and examinations, with students learning to work together on projects (SLIS methodology).[51] Each course would be the responsibility of one member of staff but include the participation of other staff. Initially there would be few staff, so it was important that they have a range of abilities, with the possibility of extra staff being brought in to cover subjects such as 'Archives, Historical bibliography, Information Science, automation and mechanized systems; [and] School librarianship'. A specialist in 'Information science and library automation' should be appointed, and the possibility of a visiting 'American teacher' could open the GSL to other teachers of librarianship.[52]

These *Preliminary notes on the School of Librarianship at Monash University* were written in 1975, and by March 1976 *ALJ* had published 'In the mainstream: the Graduate School of Librarianship at Monash University', in which Jean set out her plans as the GSL opened:[53]

> As a school within Monash University, and a part of the Faculty of Arts, the Master's Degree must be comparable in admission requirements, course content, amount of work and time required with any other degrees such as the MA degree. My first suggestion was that we would offer an MA, but this seemed to carry with it a greater restriction in admission regulations and time requirements. The MA degree, for example, requires a preliminary year of work for those who are not Honours graduates. The Master of Librarianship degree has arrived at a compromise in having a degree in two Parts. Part 1 is our version of preliminary work. It is designed to test whether those who enrolled can write a research paper complete with an adequate bibliography (if they cannot, there would seem to be little hope that they will ever finish a Thesis). It is also designed to bring students up-to-date with the literature of librarianship and give them a critical attitude to it. This first course on the *Literature of Library and Information Science* can also serve as model for the study of any

other subject field. Once admitted to Part II of the course, the student has a number of choices ...

The School is offering an advanced degree. We hope that those who undertake it will be among the potential leaders of the profession. We assume that through academic and professional studies and through experience, they will be reasonably competent librarians already.

We want to make them more than this. We want them to address themselves to the problems of the profession ... to worry about the future of library and information services ... to develop a critical attitude towards the profession but one that is constructively critical ...

SPECIAL SUBJECTS

... *Historical Studies in Australian Librarianship*. Perhaps I should make it clear that I think that Australian librarians, and their colleagues in other lands, are engaged in one profession. The word *Australian* appears in the title of this course because the history of Australian librarianship has not yet been written, and our students and staff may contribute to that writing, and because we want to understand our own environment ...

We want our students to worry about the problems of the profession – and the course in *The Future of Library and Information Services* is a key course in the school ... should address itself each year to the current challenges and worries of the profession. The other compulsory course is *Literature of Librarianship and Information Science B* ... a research methodology course ...

[two courses for students who wish to specialize in an area of librarianship]:

The first is in the area of historical bibliography and textual criticism. Our course on *Bibliography and Textual Scholarship* will be especially useful for those who want to work in rare book and special collections, but it is also an area of importance to those who work anywhere in scholarly and research libraries. It can even illuminate decisions about the use of microforms and the purchase of art reproductions ...

Education for Library and Information Services ... to offer those who are or could be involved in the teaching of the subject a chance to study the problems and to think about the directions in which it could go ...

Special Topic is ... in a subject not otherwise covered in the syllabus. It also allows us to offer courses which we may well have developed by next March or April but which were not ready for the Handbook.

The areas that we hope to cover more adequately are library administration and the implications of computer, microform and telecommunications technology for library and information services. We have already committed ourselves to offering a course on *Library and Information Services for Migrants* in 1977.

About 30–35 per cent of the work for the Master of Librarianship degree is taken up with a Minor Thesis and this has influenced our courses. They are all, I hope, subjects which offer scope for thesis topics and investigation. I think that this is important because the definition of a thesis topic and its investigation are often the most difficult part of a student's work. I hope that students will be sufficiently stimulated by the unanswered questions and the problems raised in the courses to want to investigate them …

Our courses will include the considerations of machine information services and automatic and electronic data processing methods whenever they are appropriate …

I see the Graduate School of Librarianship at Monash University as in the mainstream of education for librarianship. Its specific objectives have been stated as being –

(1) To study the problems of library and information services and to contribute towards the solution of those problems through research;

(2) To specialize in a specific area of librarianship and information services and thus to fit themselves for senior positions as specialists in that area;

(3) To undertake studies which will fit them for a career in education for librarianship;

(4) To undertake courses which combine studies in librarianship and related fields such as management, computer science, sociology and education.

Its general objective is of course that of the Library Association of Australia: to promote, establish and improve libraries and library services and (most obviously) to improve the standard of librarianship and the status of the library profession.[54]

Three lecturers were to be appointed to the GSL. The positions were advertised internationally, but the choice was left to Jean – Elizabeth Morrison said that she was not formally interviewed for the position; instead she had a chat with Jean (whom she had known professionally for some years) and was then taken to meet Manton, who appeared to have given Jean a 'free hand in choosing staff'.[55] The staff, besides Jean, were lecturers Brian McMullin, Radha Nadarajah (Rasmussen) and Elizabeth Morrison, and the secretary was Valda Twaddle[56] (succeeded by Irene Bouette and then Mary Lou Maroney). During the first year Richard Stayner, a specialist in economics, joined the staff (Jean's study of economics at the University of Adelaide led her to believe that librarians should study economics and management). Elizabeth Morrison thought that the original staff were a 'judicious and cleverly balanced mix',[57] Harrison Bryan that Jean had attracted colleagues who shared 'her dedication to teaching and research',[58] and Neil Radford that 'Jean's clarity of vision, infectious enthusiasm and passionate commitment to the scholarly enterprise enabled her to attract first rate academic staff and students'.[59] The staff were augmented by a number of visiting lecturers, including staff from other departments and a number of overseas academics. As the GSL and the number of courses grew, so did the number of staff.

The GSL lecturers travelled widely in 1975, visiting libraries and library schools, taking part in activities beneficial to the future GSL, gaining ideas for setting up their own areas of teaching, and designing their courses with a minimum of oversight, with Jean showing trust, confidence and support. The first courses were inspired, planned by having an initial theme and a catchy acronym (such as LOLIS – Literature of Librarianship and Information Science, FOLIS – Future of Librarianship and Information Science, and BATS – Bibliographical and Textual Studies) and then developed by a staff member.[60] According to Elizabeth Morrison, Jean 'did not allow us [the staff] to take life easy. She, at the same time, made conditions as easy as possible for us. I suspect she not only went into the university political fray with guns blazing but also sheltered us from the flak'.[61] Jean expected staff to be available when she wanted them, such as at weekends,[62] would ring to see whether people were still at work when she herself was not there, and continued her own long working hours.

Initially a Master of Librarianship degree and a Diploma in Librarianship (which focused on technology and management and also was for experienced librarians) were offered, and additionally, in 1980, the Master of Arts, a two-year full-time basic professional degree, for graduates only, while the Diploma was phased out. There were 40 applicants for the first Master of Librarianship course; all were interviewed and twenty-five offered places, five more than the GSL's quota. Of the twenty-five, twenty-two began the course in the first year of teaching, 1976; by the end of the year fifteen remained, the most common reason for withdrawal being that 'despite an explicit statement in the Handbook and despite warning at the interview, some students simply did not accept the fact that part-time study for the degree required 12–15 hours of work each week'.[63]

The Master of Librarianship students, as Jean expected, were experienced librarians holding middle-to-senior-level library positions,[64] and with a variety of academic and professional qualifications, who wanted the opportunity to undertake further study and research.[65] Diploma students held less senior positions, many returning to work or moving to larger libraries. The Masters of Arts students were mainly new graduates, without library experience: 'as they were fresh from demanding academic study but, usually, with no experience of the practical side of librarianship, one often had to dampen academic debate with consideration of practicalities. This was in contrast to the approach in M Lib and Diploma seminars, where often one had to work hard at keeping discussion focussed on concepts and theory'.[66]

The subjects taught at the GSL, not surprisingly, reflected many of Jean's interests, such as library services to migrants and education for librarianship and information science. She wrote that 'Perhaps foolishly I have put myself down to teach a course in Education for Librarianship and the more I think about it, the less I know about it, which is I suppose strange because most of my professional writing has been in this field. I only decided to teach it because it has been completely neglected in Australia and I think the results are only too obvious in the library schools'.[67] Other subjects Jean taught in the early years included Historical Studies in Australian Librarianship, The Future of Library and Information Services, and, with other staff, Information Needs and Services in a Specific Subject Field.

Cooperation in many areas was important to Jean: in the University, the Faculty, the library profession and between students. Cooperation within Monash was important, as Jean thought that the GSL had to be part of the University and contribute to its work, in contrast to SLIS, which, Jean said, 'was in the university but not of it … I do not remember any academics outside SLIS visiting us or vice versa'.[68] Students were given the opportunity to study in other disciplines, and there were exchanges of lecturers, such as with Computer Science; and Jean gratefully received assistance from staff from other parts of Monash early in the GSL's life. The GSL 'was perceived as an integral part of the university and a valuable contributor to its work'.[69]

Cooperation within the Faculty was also important. The GSL was set up by, and became part of, the Faculty of Arts, an important decision in line with Jean's view of education for librarianship, and in contrast to many of the library schools in Australia, which were in colleges that had a vocational orientation. Preparation for the inclusion of the GSL in the Arts Faculty included a paper by Margery Ramsay entitled Librarianship as a field for academic study.[70]

Jean's idea of cooperation with the library profession was one of leadership of the profession, rather than being advised by it: she wrote that 'the teaching of librarianship, like the teaching of any other profession, should not be a "state of the art" survey, but rather should aim to lead professional thinking'[71] (she largely ignored an Advisory Committee). Her teaching methodology was based on her understanding of the principles of library education rather than the more applied approach of librarians. Jean wrote that 'the influence of advisory committees anxious that the product should match specific jobs … work[s] against the development of scholarship and research'.[72]

Examples of cooperation in the first year included three research seminars held in co-operation with the Departments of English and French; research seminars and public lectures and the visits of twenty-four librarians.[73] Monash staff and other librarians were invited to the seminars, which were followed by lunch so that students could meet the librarians and form links with the profession. The students enjoyed the seminars, and the visiting librarians were impressed by the high quality of the lectures, their relevance to librarianship, and the social interaction.[74] Jean was always ready with a pertinent comment or question.

Cooperation was also in the form of social interaction between students: projects to work on together, opportunities for students to socialize, with a common room for students, seminars, discussions, library visits, an annual tour to visit Canberra libraries, time to meet other professionals, an annual party at Jean's home in Mount Waverley, and, later, an Alumni Association. Students were encouraged to travel overseas, with the first study tour, to Denmark, led by Radha Rasmussen, taking place in 1978.[75] Students travelled to the United Kingdom on GSL/Blackwell's study tours, beginning with students Sandra Penny and Brian Hubber in 1982.

Did Jean have carte blanche in how she set up the GSL? It seems so, within the Monash limits. Harrison Bryan wrote that 'a prescient university gave her her head and got a prestige School of Librarianship in return',[76] Neil Radford that 'Jean had pretty much a free hand',[77] and Ross Harvey 'carte blanche with setting up the department'.[78] Perhaps Jean would agree: she said that one of the reasons that she had been attracted to Monash was because it was a new school, perhaps meaning that she thought that she would be able to set it up in the way that she wanted.[79] And it appears that she did, although there were limits imposed by finances and Monash rules. The ideas, themes, and the emphases on scholarship and research were Jean's. In another way,

Jean had carte blanche: she set up the school according to guidelines which she herself had helped to formulate through her work on the Board of Examination (and its successors), where she was, at the time of her appointment to Monash, Chair of the Board and Convenor of the Accreditation Sub-Committee.

The GSL appears to have been based on Jean's wisdom collected over her lifetime of librarianship, of educating librarians and of being a member of the Board of Education, with an emphasis on her experience of library schools in North America: the Graduate Library School in Chicago, 'the best library school in the English speaking world',[80] and SLIS (selectively). There was also the negative influence of the British model of librarianship, which had been the basis for education for librarianship in Australia (and for George Chandler).[81] Although Brian McMullin wrote that there was no formal plan to emulate the GLS, but to develop courses as the staff saw fit, Boyd Rayward wrote that the GSL 'might be called the GLS of the Southern Hemisphere, a school critically focused in all its work like its counterpart, on scholarly investigation'[82] (because this link was so strong many people wrongly assumed that Jean gave the GSL its name based on the GLS).[83] Similarly, Neil Radford thought that the GSL was

> modelled in many ways on her alma mater, the Graduate Library School at Chicago ... [the GSL was to be] a genuinely academic school of librarianship where study and teaching would be carried out alongside research, where education would be valued over mere training, and where the principles and philosophies underlying practice would be emphasised ... [Jean believed] that research was the way to develop good students into critical thinkers, and to move the profession forward intellectually.[84]

Finance became a concern. Jean wrote that the GSL 'was established almost too late' because of lack of finance.[85] Two former members of the GSL staff have written of the poor timing, both linked to finance: Ross Harvey, who called the GSL 'one of the brave experiments in Australian library education', referred to the proliferation of courses in librarianship in the 1980s leading to the GSL then being unable to 'attract sufficient students with acceptable academic entry qualifications',[86] and to concerns that there might be an over-supply of librarians.[87] And Elizabeth Morrison wrote that the timing was poor because of funding cutbacks following the greatest expansion of tertiary education in Australian history: 'in the course of 1975, the Whitlam Labor Government decided that there would be no growth for universities and colleges in 1976 ... Triennial funding would be halted and there would be heavy cuts to the funding of research bodies ... with modifications triennia were reinstated in 1977, but growth was not'.[88] By 1975 Monash was Australia's fifth largest university, with more than 13,000 students, but now there was little prospect for continuing growth, as there was a declining birth-rate matching the economic pressures. The new Vice-Chancellor, Ray Martin, wanted growth to be replaced by excellence in scholarship.[89] Under Jean's direction this was assured.[90]

Some help came from a $12,000 grant from the Myer Foundation, spread over two years,[91] which was to assist in the Diploma course, but the financial problems continued throughout Jean's time at Monash. The GSL was affected by the increased student-to-staff ratios and by the loss of coursework scholarships, initially allocated nationally, but diverted by Monash to research students. And the GSL's first Annual Report noted that about $12,000 spread over three years was needed to provide librarianship resources in the Monash University Library.[92] Inevitably, in the competition for the limited funds, the question of whether librarianship should be taught at a university was raised, but there was no great enthusiasm for closing down an established department, though this was a recurring theme, especially when Jean retired.[93] Cuts to funding caused problems for the GSL, and throughout Monash, as departments competed for funding: Monash 'is beginning to show signs of indulging in internal bickering. The pressures caused by government cuts in funding are certainly considerable, and having to make appointments and plans afresh each year really invites nervous breakdowns'.[94]

This 'internal bickering', years after Manton and Matheson retired, led to the Arts Faculty being unhappy about having the GSL among its members. In dealing with this dilemma Jean was politically astute: she called in a consultant archivist, Frank Upward. Her interest in archives had begun with her association with George Pitt, and teaching archives had been considered as the next step in the GSL's early days, but it had not proceeded because of lack of funds. Upward's recommendations led to funding for a post-graduate course in archives and records management: Upward was appointed as the lecturer, beginning teaching archives in 1988, shortly before Jean's retirement, and the GSL survived.[95] Perhaps Harrison Bryan was referring to these events when he described Jean as having 'very real success as an academic in the world of academic administration and policy making'.[96]

Jean's other activities at Monash included her membership of the Bookshop Board, the Professorial Board and the Monash University Council (she was elected to represent the professors and served on the Board from August 1983 to March 1985. She was also a member of the Art Advisory Committee and its Chair in 1982, giving her an important role in the future of the Monash art collection, which, although it was originally planned 'to decorate and enliven the walls',[97] by this time had grown to a large and valuable collection, and the vulnerable University walls were no place for such valuable works (dead walls and graffiti were preferred). While Monash recognized the increasing value of the collection, the Committee received only a small allowance each year, a pittance.[98] Discussions proceeded on the need for a University gallery, now the Monash University Museum of Art, which was eventually opened on March 12th, 1987. Jean was also a member of the Vera Moore Fund Committee from 1977 to 1981. This Fund had been set up in 1976 to provide 'such support for the creative and performing arts as may enhance the teaching of those departments in the Faculty [of Arts] which are concerned with the understanding and criticism of those arts'. The Committee funded events organized by the Faculty, such as piano recitals, film-making, concerts, play readings, seminars, art and photography exhibitions.[99]

Another of Jean's Monash activities was involvement with the Monash University Library. Cooperation with the Library had always been important, and many GSL students were able to find work at the Library. Jean, along with other GSL staff, was involved with the Friends of the Monash University Library, and one of her chief interests, hand-printing, took place in the Library basement, where the Ancora Press was set up.

Jean made a number of overseas trips during her time at Monash, which incorporated conferences, study leave, holidays and, importantly, keeping up with overseas friends and maintaining contacts. There is a change from the Jean who found Australia chafing when she returned from her overseas study to the Jean who years later set up her own department along the lines of the ones she had studied and worked in overseas, giving librarians access to post-graduate qualifications in Australia instead of their needing to travel overseas; she now wanted not to return overseas but to encourage others to visit and lecture in her department. She also continued her travel in Australia, much of it for the LAA. She continued to attend the Board of Examination meetings in Sydney and went to Canberra for her work on the Commonwealth Committee on Overseas Professional Qualifications (COPQ)[100] and the Council of the NLA.

When Jean reached the compulsory retirement age of 65 in 1988 she did not go willingly (she reminded people that 65 was not the compulsory retirement age in South Australia).[101] Retirement plans? 'I don't plan. I finish the work in hand and look for the next job'.[102] But the accolades were grand. There were a retirement party, honours and a seminar, 'Librarianship in Australia: a seminar to honour Jean P. Whyte Foundation Professor and Chairman of the Graduate School of Librarianship', sponsored by the newly formed GSL Alumni Association. A booklet was published from the seminar.[103] Looking at the names of the participants in the seminar – many of whom were GSL graduates – we could echo Harrison Bryan's comments when he looked back on the Metcalf Seminar, saying that the participants looked like a *Who was who* of Australian librarianship.[104] The keynote address was given by Bryan, now the former Director General of the NLA (Jean was later to edit, with Neil Radford, a festschrift in honour of Bryan).[105]

According to Monash University Council's Minute of Appreciation, 'Jean Whyte has launched a department of librarianship which in its short existence has established itself as the leading research body in the country';[106] and Neil Radford wrote that 'It is no exaggeration to say that the GSL at Monash, under Jean Whyte, was one of the leading schools of librarianship in Australia, fully equal to the best in the world'.[107]

Elizabeth Morrison saw Jean as a 'a powerful administrator and planner: pragmatic, with a broad understanding of librarianship and education'.[108] She was both authoritarian and democratic, consulting widely.[109] This consultation was important: it was a characteristic lacked by Brideson, Osborn and Chandler.

And not only the hierarchy: students over the years have expressed a great deal of appreciation for Jean's work. So many spoke of her care for them and support, including financial assistance.[110] The students were impressed by her organizational abilities,[111] intellectual prowess and approachability.[112] The overall impression of the GSL given by most students, was that it felt 'organized' early in its life and that they had enjoyed, appreciated and benefited from the experience. The GSL was compared favourably with other library schools of the time, and some students had, like me, wanted to study at the GSL because it was said to be the best library school in Australia. The only student unrest at the GSL during Jean's time took place while she was on leave, prompting the thought that while the cat was away … During Jean's time at the GSL graduates were to include 34 Masters of Arts, 43 Masters of Librarianship, 38 Diplomas of Librarianship and 2 Doctors of Philosophy.[113] And some wonderful work was done by the students, especially in the field of the history of the book.[114]

As Jean left Monash and the library profession, a poem about her, published anonymously, appeared in *ALJ*. It was purportedly found at Jean's send-off:

JPW – A PANEGYRIC

Jean! You're leaving us! We're more or less miffed;
Of time, your learning stands the test. Shift
Not your friendship from us; it's your great gift.
That's why we're here – a living festschrift!

So: here's a vote for Jean P. Whyte.
Scholar, professor, leading light.
Founding Chair of the School at Clayton;
A nod from her's an ultimatum!

Cheerful. Tolerant. Democratic.
And with a well-stocked mental attic;
A mind alert, to every tactic,
In Monash politics took the hat-trick.

Tall, austere, in manner, regal,
Fierce, high-flown, professional eagle.
Broadminded, tolerant of anything legal,
But of charlatans, a moral beagle!

Most widely read, bibliographic grazer;
In debate and discourse a forensic razor.
Bluff, bluster, bombast, never faze her;
Yet could charm the pants off
Malcolm ******

A fluent, and a powerful teacher,
Of library history, she's the preacher.
None can follow: none over-reach her;
On our horizon a major feature.

Her hospitality! A Clayton morning, damp and foggy;
One tottered in; with flu and soggy –
Feeling much like a distempered doggy
Jean's whisky made one feel less groggy.

O Jean, O Jean, editorial Nero!
Of syntax, grammar, you're my hero!
Compared with you: we're less than zero;
Can't see you leave without a tear-oh!

What shall we do now that you're going?
Along a different row you're hoeing.
Whilst we're low flyers, to- and fro-ing,
You've been a bibliographic Boeing.

So! Here's a toast, Jean Primrose Whyte!
Of our profession, leading light!
We hope that you won't fall from sight;
We know that you're still full of fight!

One phase of your career has ended;
Professional standards long defended.
To you our deepest thanks extended.
To put it in one word: you're
SPLENDID!'[115]

ENDNOTES

1. Brian McMullin. 'Yadlamalka girl shaped Australian librarianship'. *The Age*, April 18th–19th, 2003, 19.
2. A brief history of the GSL may be found in Appendix 4; a comprehensive history is yet to be written.
3. See Appendix 3. See also K.A. Lodewycks. 'A proposed university school of librarianship'. *ALJ* 17 (1) 1968, 32–33 and [K.A. Lodewycks]. 'University of Melbourne. Proposed Post-graduate School of Librarianship. Specimen Scheme', 1962. MON 1059: 2000/68. 93.
4. Interview: Wallace Kirsop, 2008.
5. R. Selby Smith to K.A. Lodewycks, June 20th, 1967. MON 1059: 2000/68. 93.
6. Victorian Universities Committee. 'Item 46.2'. *Victorian Universities Committee. AUC Fifth report – collaboration between universities*, April 1972. MON 1059. 2000/68. 93.
7. Harrison Bryan to J. M. Swan, May 24th, 1971. MON 47: 1986/56. 95. Also, Jean wrote privately, as a member of the Board of Examination, to Margery Ramsay, Chairman of the Board, commenting on a Conference discussion of various courses: 'I said openly that we welcomed the setting up of schools at Monash and Adelaide' (Jean Whyte to Margery Ramsay, September 17th, 1973. NLA: MS 9616).
8. G.R. Manton. 'Preliminary Proposals for a Graduate School of Librarianship', [1972]. MON 1059: 2000/68. 93.
9. Jean Whyte to G.R. Manton, [1977?]. MON 1059: 2000/68. 13.
10. Monash University. Faculty Board. 'Minutes'. January, 1970. MON 1059: 2000/68. 93.
11. G.R. Manton. 'Preliminary Proposals for a Graduate School of Librarianship', [1972]. MON 1059: 2000/68. 93.
12. Interview: John Legge, 2008.
13. Ibid.
14. Monash University. Council Committee for an appointment to a Chair of Librarianship. 'Minutes. Meeting No. 1', [early 1974?]. MON 1059: EA/195/1.

15. Following her appointment, Jean wrote an apology to the applicant she had supported, saying that she had not planned to apply for the position herself and had agreed to accept the position only because circumstances had changed.

16. A comment on one candidate was: 'I believe that his appointment to Monash would be a disaster not only for the university but for Australian library education at large' (MON 1059: EA/195/1).

17. One of the librarians consulted, Margery Ramsay, then Principal Librarian at the State Library of Victoria, wrote that Jean Whyte 'had very good academic records in her bachelor's and master's degree work, and she has an unusually wide knowledge of librarianship. She is one of the most able librarians in Australia, with numerous overseas contacts, and she would undoubtedly establish the school on a broad basis ... she is interested in research, but as a practising librarian has not been able to undertake very much' (Margery Ramsay. [Untitled note], [1974]. MON 1059: EA/195/1).

    In hindsight the NLA had been a good career move: although Jean had an outstanding reputation, without the NLA her experience was limited to two libraries. Monash, in choosing to appoint her, would have been impressed by her appointment as second in charge at the NLA and a member of the Second Division of the Commonwealth Public Service.

18. Jean Whyte to Alan Fleming, September 3rd, 1974. NLA: MS 9862.

19. G.R. Manton to Jean Whyte, September 25th, 1974. MON 1059: EA/195/1.

20. Jean Whyte to Alan Fleming, October 15th, 1974. NLA: MS 9862.

21. Jean Whyte to G.R. Manton, October 10th, 1974. MON: SLO 72330.

    Geoffrey Alley warned Jean that 'If (when) you are offered the job A Fleming's, Harry B's and my letters should be retrieved somehow so that you can have an idea of what you will need to live up to!' (Geoffrey Alley to Jean Whyte, October 18th, 1974. J. McEldowney Personal Collection, Dunedin, New Zealand).

22. Monash University. [Internal debit /credit note], 1974. MON: SLO 72330.

23. Monash University. 'Minutes of Council'. Item 4.1.1. December 9th, 1974. MON EA/195/1.

24. J.D. Butchart to Jean Whyte, December 11th, 1974. MON: SLO 72330.

25. Jean Whyte. 'Curriculum vitae', 1974. NLA: MS 9616.

26. Jean Whyte to Alan Fleming, October 15th, 1974. NLA: MS 9862.

27. W.F. Northam. [Memo]. December 12th, 1974. MON: SLO 72330.

28. Jean Whyte to J.D. Butchart, December 17th, 1974. MON: SLO 72330.

29. Alan Fleming to Jean Whyte, November 15th, 1974. NLA: MS 9616.

30. Andrew Osborn to Jean Whyte, January 14th, 1959. SU: M 465.

31. Jean Whyte to Alan Fleming, October 15th, 1974. NLA: MS 9862.

32. Jean Whyte to Alan Fleming, September 3rd, 1974. NLA: MS 9862.

33. Jean Whyte to Alan Fleming, October 15th, 1974. NLA: MS 9862. Harrison Bryan was an unsuccessful candidate for the position of Director General when Alan Fleming retired but later was to succeed Chandler.

34. Jean Whyte to Lester Asheim, January 3rd, 1975. NLA: MS 9616.

35. Monash University. Graduate School of Librarianship. *Annual Report*. 1975, 4.

36. G.R. Manton to I.B. Tate, [1975]. MON: SLO 72330. Jean undertook this work for Monash during her accumulated recreation leave from the NLA.

37. Monash University. Graduate School of Librarianship. *Annual Report*. 1975, 3.

38. Jean Whyte. 'Control and diversity', 1985, 5–25.

39. The Australian schools which existed when the GSL was set up were at the University of NSW, the NSW Department of Technical Education, RMIT, the South Australian Institute of Technology, the Canberra College of Advanced Education and the Western Australian Institute of Technology. The Tasmanian College of Advanced Education was seeking accreditation, and the Sydney Technical College course was closing (Jean Whyte. 'The Accreditation of Courses in Librarianship', 1974, 593–608).

40. Wilma Radford. 'The School of Librarianship, University of New South Wales'. *ALJ* 19 (11) 1970, 417–419.

    At the end of 1973 Wilma Radford retired from her position as Professor at the School of Librarianship, University of New South Wales. The position was advertised, but Jean did not apply: 'I have all the snobbiness of a Sydney "man" when I think of [the University of NSW]' (Jean Whyte to Alan Fleming, September 3rd, 1974. NLA: MS 9862).

41. Barbara Hooks. 'Advanced librarian course from Monash'. *The Age*, January 10th, 1975, 12.

42. Jean Whyte. 'The Accreditation of Courses in Librarianship', 1974, 603.

43. Jean Whyte. 'Librarians and scholars', 1984, 261.

44. Jean Whyte. 'In-service training or library schools'. *ALJ* 5 (1) 1956, 1–5.

45. Jean Whyte. 'Librarians and scholars', 1984, 243–262.

46. Jean Whyte. *Preliminary notes on the School of Librarianship at Monash University*, [1975]. NLA: MS 9616.

47. Notice, too, the title of Jean's 1981 paper 'Random remarks from a long-time librarian, short-time teacher of librarians'.

48. Jean Whyte. *Preliminary notes on the School of Librarianship at Monash University*, [1975]. NLA: MS 9616.

49. Ibid.

50. Transcript of a conversation between Jean Whyte and Geoffrey Alley, 1981. MON 1059: 2000/68/5.

51. Ibid.

52. Jean Whyte. *Preliminary notes on the School of Librarianship at Monash University*, [1975]. NLA: MS 9616.

53. In a note to the editor of *ALJ* Jean wrote 'this is my first statement on the School and is designed to acknowledge the work of earlier library educators' (Jean Whyte to C. Datar, January 14th, 1976. MON 1059: 2000/68. 47).

54. Jean Whyte. 'In the mainstream'. *ALJ* 25 (2) 1976, 51–58.

55. Interview: Elizabeth Morrison, 2008.

56. The descriptions of academic staff

    The Staff

    Professor Jean P. Whyte, B.A. Hons (Adel.) A.M. (Chic.) F.L.A.A. took up her position on 10 July. Her professional interests are National, State and research library services; user studies; education for librarianship; history of librarianship; library administration.

    Dr. Brian J. McMullin, M.A. (N.Z.) M.L.S. (West Ont.) Ph.D. (Leeds) was appointed as a Lecturer and arrived at the School on 28 September. His interests are historical and analytical bibliography; printing practices especially in the seventeenth and eighteenth centuries; problems in the transmission of texts; the building of library collections.

Ms. Elizabeth Morrison, B.A. (Melb.) A.L.A.A. was appointed as a Lecturer and takes up her duties in February 1976, her interests being microform, computer and telecommunication in the library, bibliographic control and library planning; management techniques in librarianship.

Ms. Radha Nadarajah, LL.B. (Sing.) M.Lib. (Wales) A.L.A. will take up the position as a Lecturer in March 1976. Her interests are public librarianship, especially services to the disadvantaged; the influence of the mass media; the economics of library provision and services; education for librarianship; library development in South-East Asia. (Monash University. Graduate School of Librarianship. *Annual Report.* 1975, [1]).

57 Elizabeth Morrison. 'The Graduate School of Librarianship at Monash University: the beginning'. *Education for Librarianship: Australia* 6 (2–3) 1989, 6.

58 Harrison Bryan. 'Jean Primrose Whyte'. *ALJ* 38 (1) 1989, 14.

59 Neil A. Radford. 'Obituaries. Jean Primrose Whyte AM', [2003].

60 Interview: Elizabeth Morrison, 2008.

61 Elizabeth Morrison. 'The Graduate School of Librarianship at Monash University: the beginning'. *Education for Librarianship: Australia* 6 (2–3) 1989, 6.

62 Interview: Rachel Salmond, 2005.

63 Monash University. Graduate School of Librarianship. *Annual Report.* 1976, [1].

64 Elizabeth Morrison. 'The Graduate School of Librarianship at Monash University: the beginning'. *Education for Librarianship: Australia* 6 (2–3) 1989, 8.

65 Barbara Hooks. 'Advanced librarian course from Monash'. *The Age,* January 10th, 1975, 12.

66 Elizabeth Morrison. 'The Graduate School of Librarianship at Monash University: the beginning'. *Education for Librarianship: Australia* 6 (2–3) 1989, 8.

67 Jean Whyte to Lester Asheim, September 12th, 1975. MON 1059: 2000/68. 6.

68 Jean Whyte. 'Some Reminiscences of Geoffrey Alley', 1995, 2. J. McEldowney Personal Collection, Dunedin, New Zealand.

69 Neil A. Radford. 'Obituaries. Jean Primrose Whyte AM', [2003].

70 Margery Ramsay. 'Librarianship as a field for academic study', [1972?]. MON 1059: 2000/68. 93.

71 Monash University. Graduate School of Librarianship. *Annual Report.* 1976, 6.

72 Jean Whyte. 'Librarians and scholars', 1984, 257–258.

73 Research Seminars: John Spring 'Joseph Bennet, Restoration Printer' and Dr. Wallace Kirsop 'Early Editions of Corneille's Le Cid'; Professor David Bradley 'Textual Problems and Playhouse Copy' and Dr. Brian McMullin 'A consideration of some editorial orthodoxies'; Dr Angus Martin 'Specialized Retrospective Checklists: the example of eighteenth-century'; Professor Perry Morrison 'Sociological and Psychological Survey Methods applied to librarianship'; Dr Edward Kazlauskas 'Instructional Technology, University of Southern California'; Professor Perry Morrison 'Case Study Methods'; Dr. Robert Rosenthal 'The future of Rare Book and Special Collections'; Harrison Bryan 'The Future of Research Libraries'; Barrett Reid 'Future of Public Libraries'.

Public lectures: Phillip Bryant 'Library Research: The Bath University Projects'; Dr. Edward Kazlauskas 'Library Automation in California'; Dr. Robert Rosenthal 'Dealing in the Past; the acquisition of books and manuscripts for research collections'; Professor C. West Churchman 'The Library as an Inquiring System' (Monash University. Graduate School of Librarianship. *Annual Report.* 1976, [1]–2).

74 Elizabeth Morrison. 'The Graduate School of Librarianship at Monash University: the beginning'. *Education for Librarianship: Australia* 6 (2–3) 1989, 7.

75 *Librarianship in Australia*, 1988, 27.
76 Harrison Bryan. 'Jean Primrose Whyte'. *ALJ* 38 (1) 1989, 5.
77 Neil A. Radford. 'Obituaries. Jean Primrose Whyte AM', [2003].
78 Interview: Ross Harvey, 2005.
79 'Late start, but Jean Whyte has the last word'. *Monash Reporter*, 9–88, 1988.
80 Ibid.
81 Interview: Ross Harvey, 2005.
82 W. Boyd Rayward. 'The future of library education in Australia – and its past'. *ALJ* 38 (2) 1989, 115–123.
83 Graduate school of librarianship was used (in files held at Monash University) as a descriptive term – that Victoria needed a graduate school of librarianship – as early as 1970; by 1974 it had changed from description to title.
84 Neil A. Radford. 'Obituaries. Jean Primrose Whyte AM', [2003].
85 Jean Whyte to G.R. Manton, [1977?]. MON 1059: 2000/68. 13.
86 Ross Harvey. 'Losing the quality battle in Australian education for librarianship', [2004].
87 See, for example, Neil A. Radford. 'Education for librarianship and the manpower problem'. *ALJ* 26 (8) 1978, 197–202.
88 Elizabeth Morrison. 'The Graduate School of Librarianship at Monash University: the beginning'. *Education for Librarianship: Australia* 6 (2–3) 1989, 5.
89 Ibid.
90 'I have said many times that the value of the Graduate School of Librarianship can only be judged by the quality of its graduates and unfortunately as part-timers they will be slow in coming' (Jean Whyte to G.R. Manton, [1977?]. MON 1059: 2000/68. 13).
91 Monash University. Graduate School of Librarianship, [1974?]. MON 1059: 2000/68. 47. Ken Myer chaired the Council of the NLA when Jean was a Council member.
92 Monash University. Graduate School of Librarianship. *Annual Report*. 1975.
93 Interview: Brian McMullin, 2008.
94 Jean Whyte to Geoffrey Alley, October 16, 1981. MON 1059: 2000/68. 5.
95 Interview: Frank Upward, 2008.
96 Harrison Bryan. 'Jean Primrose Whyte'. *ALJ* 38 (1) 1989, 14.
97 Monash University Council. 'Minute of Appreciation. Professor J.P. Whyte', 1989. NLA: MS 9616.
98 Interview: Grecian and Ross Day, 2008.
99 Vera Moore Fund Committee. MON 1059: 2000/68. 1.
100 Monash University. Graduate School of Librarianship. *Annual Report*. 1976, 5.
101 Interview: Rachel Salmond, 2005.
102 'Late start, but Jean Whyte has the last word'. *Monash Reporter*, 9–88, 1988.
103 *Librarianship in Australia*, 1988.
104 Harrison Bryan. 'The Metcalf seminar – 25 years on'. *ALJ* 33 (1) 1984, 32.
105 Jean Whyte and Neil A. Radford, eds. *An enthusiasm for libraries*, 1988.
106 Monash University Council. 'Minute of Appreciation. Professor J.P. Whyte', 1989. NLA: MS 9616.
107 Neil A. Radford. 'Obituaries. Jean Primrose Whyte AM', [2003].

[108] Elizabeth Morrison. 'The Graduate School of Librarianship at Monash University: the beginning'. *Education for Librarianship: Australia* 6 (2–3) 1989, 6.
[109] Interview: Elizabeth Morrison, 2008.
[110] Interview: Steven Kafkarisos. 2005.
[111] Interview: Sara Miranda, 2008.
[112] Interview: Steven Kafkarisos. 2005.
[113] A list of GSL graduates during Jean's term may be found in *Librarianship in Australia*, 1988, 57–58.
[114] Interview: Elizabeth Morrison, 2008.
[115] [Hector Monro?]. 'JPW – A panegyric'. *ALJ* 38 (2) 1989, 191. 'Cheerful'?

CHAPTER 7

○ EMERITUS PROFESSOR JEAN WHYTE, AM, BA (HONS) (ADELAIDE), AM (CHICAGO), HON DLITT (MONASH), FLAA

What a richly rewarding life you have made out of librarianship![1]

1. THEMES FROM JEAN'S WORK

There are themes which run through much of Jean's work and life which I have not written about earlier, many because they extend over more than one chapter of her life. I have divided these themes into work and life and will begin with those about her work, although many people would echo Joan Brewer when she said of Jean 'libraries were her whole life'.[2] More than that, as George Pitt said, 'What a richly rewarding life you have made out of librarianship! We both remember the rather placid, unenterprising, drifting career it seemed to offer. Not now!'[3] Jean's life was rewarding, her career had not been placid, unenterprising or drifting, and later in life it led to various honours.

Jean had been awarded a Fellowship of the LAA in 1963; she said that she was a Fellow 'by birthright more than merit' because all foundation members were automatically created Fellow.[4] She received the H.C.L. Anderson Award, appropriately, at the LAA's 50th anniversary in 1987. Jean's citation – two A4 pages – begins:

> The H.C.L. Anderson Award may be conferred on a professional member of the Association 'who has rendered outstanding service to librarianship or to the library profession in Australia or to the Library Association of Australia or to the theory and practice of librarianship'. Professor Jean Whyte satisfies eminently every single one of these criteria.[5]

Another honour was Member of the Order of Australia (AM), awarded in 1988 'for services to education, particularly in the field of librarianship'.[6] It was, her friend Agnes Gregory wrote, 'some sort of recognition for all the blood, sweat and tears you've put in on behalf of the profession. When we talk about the giants there used to be in the old days, we sometimes forget that there are a few of them still extant'.[7]

Importantly to Jean, on her retirement she was awarded the title of Professor Emeritus as 'a formal recognition of the high esteem by which you will always be remembered at Monash'[8] ('Professor Emeritus' was conferred; it was not a rite of passage on the retirement of a Monash professor). Later, Monash awarded her an Honorary Doctor of Letters (Hon DLitt). Jean said, in her acceptance, 'I realize that this invitation is indeed an honour and I accept it in the belief that, in so doing, librarianship is also honoured'.[9] The award was presented at a graduation ceremony, where Jean was described as a 'distinguished Australian librarian';[10] she gave the Graduation Address, which was another version of 'A word from Callimachus'.[11]

Jean wrote 'A word from Callimachus' in 1957 and tinkered with it for the rest of her life. It is remarkable for its breadth of scholarship, whimsicality and longevity – 43 years from its first publication to its last. It portrays library history in poetry, imitating the language and poetic form of various periods. It is a history of librarianship, named in honour of the Greek scholar and poet Callimachus of Cyrene, Librarian of Alexandria, who created the first national author bibliography.[12] Jean refers to Callimachus as one of the first librarians whose name is known. She casts him in a supernatural role as a living witness to the history of libraries – 'he has lived as long as the world has had libraries, and he lives today. I saw him last night in the stacks'.[13] Its final form *The Poems of Callimachus*, was hand-set and printed by the Ancora Press at Monash in 2000, thus combining Jean's interests in poetry, library history and hand-printing.[14]

Hand-printing had become a hobby during Jean's time at the University of Sydney (although she was already interested in typography). Andrew Osborn bought two printing presses for what became the Fisher (later Piscator) Press, set up by Harrison Bryan,[15] which Jean used for printing and teaching at the University of Sydney. Her interest continued at Monash, where she founded the Ancora Press in 1976. Jean and her friend Margery Ramsay arranged for the State Library of Victoria to transfer to Monash on indefinite loan an Albion Press,[16] on which the first Ancora imprint was produced, a keepsake for the Friends of the Monash University Library. Professor Arthur Brown, Chair of the English Department at Monash, bought a Columbian Press (now at the entrance to the Matheson Library at Monash Clayton); Jean thought that while the Columbian was a magnificent press, looking 'resplendent in black and gold and red', the Albion was probably more reliable.[17] Like the Piscator at the University of Sydney, the Ancora Press was used for teaching, including bibliography and textual studies in the GSL and other Monash departments.

The hand-press operation was named the Bibliographical Laboratory[18] until Jean suggested that the name be changed to 'Ancora', which was derived from the Monash motto 'Ancora imparo' (I am still learning); the anchor was a common device among early printers, and, appropriately, Ancora was housed in the Library basement. When Prince Charles visited Monash a security cordon cut the students and staff off from the press, but Jean used her authority to insist that she be allowed into the building, saying: 'I'm a professor. Let me through'.[19] The press is now housed at Monash Caulfield Campus and continues to produce hand-set booklets and to act as an informal teaching press, while also being central to the artists' book program in the Faculty of Art and Design.

Hand-printing was one of Jean's many interests which were a way of preserving the past; other aspects included conservation, archives, rare books and library history. Jean taught classes on conservation such as the 'Production, publication, history and care of books' in Sydney and introduced a subject on the conservation of library materials at Monash, taught by Ross Harvey – forward thinking for the time, as conservation of library materials was not a subject popular with librarians.[20] Also at Monash Jean had introduced a post-graduate degree in archives and records management. Her interest in archives began under the early influences of George Pitt and Andrew Osborn, who wrote that 'the oldest function of the librarian is conservation'.[21] And her interest in rare books (perhaps begun at the PLSA when so many books were discarded) was in evidence at the University of Sydney, the NLA, the Friends groups she belonged to, and in her donations to purchase rare books.

Jean's interest in Australian library history began when she started to teach librarianship.[22] At Monash she taught Historical Studies in Australian Librarianship, which included biography in Australian librarianship – the people were more interesting to Jean than were the institutions (I agree): 'our libraries have been made as much by people as by systems and legislation. Those individuals were librarians and benefactors. Often they were fiercely committed and unreasonable'.[23] In the following extract from *Uniting a Profession* note that Jean placed 'who' before 'how': 'the chronology – the 'when?' – is not difficult, but when we start to ask the more interesting questions of 'why?' and 'who?' and 'how?' the answers are not so readily found. Those which are readily found are not always convincing'.[24] She wrote many articles on library history, possibly more than on any other subject, as her later articles began with a historical overview; she also provided Monash support to establish and continue the Library History Forums.

The first Library History Forum, held at Monash in 1984, was the idea of GSL staff member Elizabeth Morrison, who, with Michael Talbot, the GSL's first PhD. graduate, edited that Forum's papers: *Books, libraries and readers in Colonial Australia*.[25] At subsequent forums, when Jean was sometimes acknowledged as their initiator, she would stand and say 'I just want to make a correction, Elizabeth Morrison started it'.[26] But Morrison acknowledges that it is what Jean wanted, it was just that Jean did not think of it first.[27] Jean supported and was involved in organizing some of the subsequent conferences; she was the chief organizer of the 1989 conference, the papers from which she edited with Frank Upward.[28] The forums continue in various locations around Australia; the 9th was held in Melbourne in June 2009.

The forums were another way of preserving the past, as was Jean's interest in writing the history of Australian libraries: she worked on writing the history as long as she was able. At first she planned two books on the subject, the first to be a collection of articles by various authors which she would edit, the second her own larger work on the history of the Associations, both of which she wanted to publish in time for the LAA's 50th anniversary in 1987.[29] But it was not to be. The history of the Institute was published as *Uniting A Profession*, completed after Jean's death by David Jones,[30] who wrote that she

> was fascinated by the origins of professional library associations in Australia and intrigued by the actions and motives of the people who created them. As a library educator, she was curious about the genesis of the Institute's system of library training and examinations. As a participant, she was interested in the workings of Branches and Committees, their achievements and their failures. As a frequent delegate, she hoped to provide an assessment of the significance of the Institute's conferences. Perhaps most of all, as a keen observer of people in action, Jean found the study of the leading figures in the Institute and their relationships with each other – the core of any association – especially absorbing. The fact that she had met or corresponded with many of the foundation members gave an added dimension to any historical study which she would undertake. Little wonder, then, that she was stimulated to delve into the diverse and scattered records of the Institute and, indeed, found it hard to stop delving and to start writing ...

> Jean worked her way methodically through AIL documents in a number of libraries and archives, making copies of the most relevant items or sitting in a reading room or at a borrowed desk in the Association's old Ultimo building whispering notes into a tape recorder for later transcription ... her research

was a lengthy process – she was for most of this period running a demanding department at Monash University and had, of course, many other calls on her time ... She mastered one computer and word processing programme and then another, carefully backing up copies of her drafts, gradually becoming aware that she might run out of time and that someone might have to take over the project from her.

No-one could be as well equipped as Jean – a contemporary observer and a rigorous scholar – to tackle the history of the Institute ... Jean saw this history as in part repaying a debt which she believed she owed to the profession. I see completion of this work rather as a part repayment of the much larger debt which I, in common with other library and information professionals in Australia, owe to Jean Whyte.[31]

Jean's involvement with the Associations – the Institute and the LAA – had begun when she started work at the PLSA, and it continued throughout her working life and into her retirement. She was consultant to the LAA 50th-anniversary celebrations in 1987,[32] having been involved in the entire length of the LAA's life. I have tried to track Jean's involvement with the LAA, which has been a daunting task, as it was multifarious, and I think that Jean became selective when she recorded her committee memberships. She began her Institute committee work in 1946 and continued attending Institute and LAA committees, meetings and conferences throughout her career, as well as encouraging others to attend. She was an examiner for most of her career, and John Lowe, who was an examiner with her in New South Wales, said that Jean suggested asking students to discuss a quotation; John asked her which one, and she replied that one could be made up, that she had made up dozens in her time.[33]

Examining was part of the involvement in Jean's long association with the Board of Examination, from 1955 to 1968, and from 1971 to 1977,[34] being Deputy Chair 1960–1962 and Chair 1962–1963[35] (succeeding Wilma Radford). During this time the Board was known variously as the Board of Education, the Board of Examiners, the Board of Examination and the Board of Examination, Certification and Registration of Librarians. The Board dealt with Registration examinations, qualifications for membership of the Association, recognition of qualifications of overseas applicants, new qualifications and courses, course accreditation, etc.

While in the Chair Jean played a leading role in the decision that future members of the LAA would have to be university graduates. This was a stormy period for the LAA, as members argued about whether 'graduate' required a post-graduate degree or whether an undergraduate one (in librarianship) would suffice. The argument caused 'deep division' within the profession until 1968, when an undergraduate degree in librarianship was accepted as fulfilling the requirements for membership.[36] Jean's view was that librarians should be graduates with a bachelor's degree (in another field) as well as qualifications in librarianship.[37]

Also while Jean was Chair a new syllabus was introduced for Registration, but possibly the Board's most important action during her membership was the move from examining students to accrediting courses offered by library schools, as education for librarianship was moving from in-house library training to stand-alone library schools, as Jean advocated. This process began with the LAA's decision in 1961 to recognize the Diploma of the University of New South Wales

Postgraduate School of Librarianship and led, gradually, to the end of the Association's role as an examining body and the phasing out of Registration. When Jean chaired the Board it began to consider how to respond to the increasing number of library schools. The Board took on responsibility for the accreditation of courses (setting up the Accreditation Sub-Committee in 1971, with Jean as the first convenor).[38] The Board looked at the types of courses which could be accredited and how to assist tertiary education institutions in setting up such courses, and it was continually involved with advising, negotiating and discussing these courses with the institutions.[39] With Jean's involvement it is no surprise that accreditation was on the American Library Association pattern, and she was responsible for the first 'Statement on recognition of courses in librarianship'.[40] In an interesting twist of fate Jean was a Board member when the possibility of setting up a library school at Monash was discussed. She wrote: 'I said openly that we welcomed the setting up of schools at Monash and Adelaide Universities'.[41] The GSL was set up in accord with guidelines which she had helped prepare, and it was this same Board which accredited and reaccredited its courses.

Membership of the Board required a considerable amount of travel and work: 'I think it is the sort of committee that requires constant attendance and that is worrying enough even for those of us who are constantly involved in the game'.[42] And it had a large mandate, with, in 1962, 919 candidates sitting for the examination in 46 centres, including seven located overseas.[43]

Why was the Board so important to Jean? In her first published article on librarianship she wrote that 'the greatest single factor contributing towards the realization of [the Institute's objectives] … is the appointment of a Board of Examination and Certification'[44] – the objectives of the Institute being 'to unite persons engaged in library work, and to improve the standard of librarianship and the status of the library profession in Australia'.[45] Although this was written so early in Jean's career, her opinion did not change. She also wanted the best people on the Board – as early as 1959 she wrote: 'I can probably fix (or rather suggest) the SA and Tasmanian votes. The Board is the important body & we want the best people'.[46]

Another LAA involvement was attending their conferences, seeing them as an important function of the Association in seeking to improve standards of librarianship.[47] The first conference Jean attended was the 1946 Institute Conference in Hobart, and she continued to attend Association conferences throughout her career, giving lectures and seminars at many; she was also known to be good at questioning other speakers (this was a trait often commented on, from the Metcalf Seminar to the Library History Forums). She chaired the Adelaide 1957 conference committee[48] and edited the proceedings of the 16th Conference.[49] The last time Jean spoke at an LAA conference she said: 'I do not think that I shall appear again upon a conference platform – but don't expect complete silence. After all I am a life member'.[50]

Jean's LAA involvement gave her a national profile: as she wrote to Guy Manton, she was 'well known in the profession in Australia', so he could ask anyone he pleased what they thought of her.[51] She was well known through her editorship of *ALJ*, her membership of many committees and her attendance at conferences, and also because of her work at the NLA. She was also a member of the Council of the NLA from 1981 to 1987,[52] appointed to represent librarians,[53] the first woman to be a member, and the first librarian, 'the only voice of librarianship on that body ever, apart from successive Directors General'.[54] Ken Myer was the Council Chair, Harrison Bryan the Director General (following the retirement of George Chandler in 1980). Bryan had proposed that Jean become a Council member, perhaps in the hope of influencing the Council towards his views.[55] She visited Canberra frequently for Council meetings but saved money by staying with friends and returning the fee she received as a Council member to the NLA to purchase materials.[56] Another NLA Committee of which Jean became a member was the Advisory Committee in the Humanities. Here she represented the LAA from 1976 until 1982.[57]

Jean was also a member of the COPQ Expert Panel on Librarianship from 1971, when it was founded, until it was disbanded in 1979. COPQ was set up by the Minister for Immigration to assess the qualifications held by people educated in other countries who wished to work in Australia. Jean assisted here not only with her ability to assess the qualifications of librarians but also by visiting library schools when she travelled overseas.[58] Jean said that her association with COPQ had 'shown that our Australia-wide system has much to commend it, and is a state towards which other professions aspire'.[59] Jean combined her experience of teaching, examining, Board membership and COPQ membership in her article 'Control and diversity: a short history of course recognition in Australia', as well as editing *Librarianship in Australia* for COPQ.[60]

Jean was involved with many other associations and societies, including international interests, begun at school with her support for the World Federal Union; also in her South Australian years she was a member of the Australian Institute of International Affairs and the United Nations Association, and in Canberra she was a member of the Australia-China Society.[61] She was also a member of a number of international and overseas librarianship associations, giving her a broader perspective for Australian librarianship, such as the Canadian Library Association,[62] the American Library Association and its Divisions of Library Education, and Resources and Technical Services,[63] and the Beta Phi Mu Honour Society in Librarianship.[64]

Other groups Jean was a member of at different times included the English Association,[65] the Fellowship of Australian Writers, the Fulbrighters Association,[66] the Book Collectors Society,[67] the Australian Institute of International Affairs, the UN Association,[68] the Bibliographical Society of Australia and New Zealand,[69] and the Association of College and Research Libraries.[70] She was keen on supporting libraries she was associated with by joining Friends of the Library organizations, becoming a member of the Friends of the Public Library of South Australia,[71] of the Sydney University Library (which she helped to establish),[72] and of the Monash University Library, continuing her active association with the Monash Friends after her retirement.

The variety of librarianship issues Jean was interested in covered (almost) the whole spectrum of librarianship, as can be seen by her large and varied published output, especially the variety of books she reviewed. I will look, briefly, at a few of these interests, chosen because they are not mentioned elsewhere in this biography or because of their importance to her.

The first is her interest in library buildings, perhaps an interest arising from the poor state of the PLSA buildings (she spent years in temporary accommodation) and continuing with new buildings: the 'new' Fisher, and the four-year-old NLA. Jean was appointed to the Library Council of Victoria and the Council of the NLA in the same week in 1981, staying on both until 1987. Membership of the former led to membership of the State Library of Victoria Building Advisory Committee when controversial plans for redeveloping the State Library were being considered. Jean resigned from the Committee, disappointed by the state government's 'recycling a monument to nineteenth century librarianship'.[73]

Reader education was another long-term interest, an underlying theme of her report 'Who uses a University Library, why and to what effect'.[74] The report was the result of the largest survey of borrowers and loans ever in Australia, carried out at the University of Sydney, and the value lay in Jean's description of the survey's purpose. It was later re-published in a collection of what the LAA considered the most important statements made in their own publications.[75]

A further long-term interest was the provision of information in languages other than English, begun with the Adelaide Lending Service; she recalled at her retirement 'all the displaced persons as we called them in those days, coming in to borrow from our small but hard won collection of books in foreign languages'.[76] At Monash there was an emphasis on services in languages other than English.

A theme, rather than a deliberate interest, was Jean's pattern of involvement in new and groundbreaking work: her involvement with setting up the Adelaide Lending Service and being appointed to a position there reserved for men, and perhaps her work with the provision of material in languages other than English; being one of the earliest librarians to study overseas; her editorship of *ALJ*; at the Fisher the development of services to undergraduates, 'almost unbelievably in advance of any previous achievement in this country';[77] the pioneering work in technology and, at the NLA, using technology to extend the ways material was provided nationally; her ranking in the public service; and setting up the GSL.

The area of librarianship Jean was longest associated with was teaching. Her ability to teach was a family trait: Alexander Macully, the teacher of elocution and the art of reading; Kitty, who was 'second to none in her methods of teaching and instilling confidence in her pupils';[78] and Billie, who was known for her teaching ability. Harrison Bryan was to refer to Jean as 'a born teacher and teaching, in my view, is what she has done best'.[79] In her retirement speech notes she wrote: 'Images that I recall with so much satisfaction ... the first day that I stood in front of a class and lectured (on classification) – 1948 and, after the first 15 minutes of nerves, knew that this was something I liked doing'.[80] Teaching librarianship was to be the path which Jean would follow for the rest of her career, although teaching was part-time until her last position, and from the beginning her students were wanted by libraries.

Jean's life is the story of education for librarianship in Australia in the 20th century. Did I say why education for librarianship was important to Jean? She said it clearly herself in 1949:

> Our most pressing need is more education for librarianship, but let us not lose sight of the reasons for this education. We want better librarians to organize better libraries because we believe in books for their help in the ordinary business of living and working, and for the happiness and wisdom that is in them, and because we know that the proper functioning of a Democratic state depends upon the education of the people.[81]

Yet another long-term interest was also an unhappy association, that of dealing with technology (as it was for many people in the sixties and seventies, when the technology was new and more difficult to use). At the Fisher and at the NLA Jean had to deal with enormous changes in library automation. She recognized the value of automation, took a leading role in implementing its use in libraries, made sure that it was taught from the beginning at the GSL, but found it difficult to deal with on a personal level.[82] She said: 'I think the computer is in libraries to stay and it's important and I think we take it over rather than it takes us over'.[83]

One more long-term interest was censorship, both within and outside librarianship. Censorship is a perennial topic: as I first wrote this chapter there was public debate on an exhibition in Melbourne of photographs of naked children, and as I edited it I was asked to sign a petition against Internet censorship. An early memory of Jean's was of

> a Member of the Board of Governors of the Public Library of South Australia telling me that the nine volume set of the Memoirs of Casanova should not be on the open shelves of the library – it was immoral. He finished by asking, 'Reach me down volume seven please Miss Whyte, I've just returned volume six'. He was a small man.[84]

Most librarians were against censorship and in favour of freedom to read, so Jean's opposition to censorship, perhaps influenced by George Pitt,[85] is not surprising, but it was held with surprising fierceness. She first publicly opposed censorship at an Institute meeting in 1946: '23rd July. Misses Whyte, Gledhill and Laughton discussed with some vigour "Censorship and the Library"'.[86] At that meeting 'Miss Whyte condemned censorship for adult readers'.[87] Her attitude would later have been compounded by her U.S. experience and by her editorship of *ALJ* during the time of public discussion of censorship, in particular in libraries, by the banning of books (such as *Lady Chatterley's Lover*), and by bizarre behaviour (this was the time of Sir Arthur Rylah's 'teenage daughter').[88] For example:

> The 'Bizarre' Mayor
>
> Barry Humphries' Book 'Bizarre' is now back in the Moorabbin (Victoria) Library.
>
> Earlier in the year the mayor of Moorabbin, Cr. R. Butler, directed the Town Clerk to have 'a certain book' withdrawn from the Library. At the time Cr. Butler said that he had not read all the book, but had seen some of the cartoons and plates and professed not to understand the cartoons.
>
> The Mayor in a press interview gave three reasons for his action. He regards it as positive action in regard to the increasing number of sex maniacs and maintenance claims. Secondly, he feels that there must be some form of censorship in all things. 'You are not entitled to take opium, or liquor above a certain strength. The same applies to literature.' Thirdly, three copies at $10.00 each! 'I think the money could have been better spent.'
>
> During the period of the books withdrawal, the Moorabbin Public Librarian continued to take reservations for it …[89]

Jean's simplest expression of her opposition to censorship, and the reasons behind it, is to be found in her Presidential Message of 1949:

> We do not serve the majority alone but all men whatever their needs, whatever their political, religious or social ideas. The test of Democracy after all is not whether the majority rule, but whether the minority is free. Service to the few can be only too easily overlooked because it does not improve our statistics and because their influence for the cause of libraries is negligible.
>
> As librarians, we can have no political, religious or other bias, but we are not therefore neutral. We believe in the freedom of the written word and must oppose censorship and restriction as strongly as the American Library Association is opposing it ...[90]

The high point of Jean's opposition to censorship was to come in the LAA campaign 'to persuade the librarians of Australia to take a stand against censorship'.[91] The campaign began with a Presidential address by Jean's friend W.G.K. Duncan, then Professor of History and Political Science at the University of Adelaide. Duncan argued that a librarian's 'vocation is to promote and foster the free flow of information and ideas throughout his community',[92] a statement which Jean published in *ALJ* and later referred to as 'the most significant statement of professional attitudes to censorship that has appeared in the Journal'.[93] But to Jean it 'seemed to those librarians who agreed with the 1961 president that their professional association would never take a firm stand'.[94]

Jean continued her campaign: the June 1964 issue of *ALJ* highlighted the censorship controversy. It included a ten-page article by John Bray, Q.C. (a long-time friend of Jean and Chief Justice of South Australia), which was 'an excellent statement of the folly of censorship'.[95] Frederick May outlined other follies in 'The concupiscence of the oppressor: some notes on the absurdity of the book censorship'.[96] May was 'the brilliant, if controversial'[97] Professor of Italian at the University of Sydney and a close friend of Jean. His article included examples of material which had been censored in Australia; Wilma Radford called the article 'an anthology of erotica, a scholarly study of some erotic passages in various literatures, and what its subtitle stated it to be: some notes on the absurdity of the book censorship'.[98]

The *ALJ* issue provoked a storm, as Jean had hoped: the next issue contained five pages of correspondence discussing censorship: 'For the first time in the life of the *Australian Library Journal* its readers have been sufficiently stirred by its contents to write a number of letters to the Editor ... [the Editor] welcomes articles of a highly controversial nature from members of the Association because only by fearless debate and informed consideration can the members of the Library Association of Australia decide on their professional attitudes and further the objects of the Association'.[99] Most correspondents favoured May's opinions and congratulated *ALJ* for publishing them. For example:

> Dear Madam
>
> I felt quite proud that the 'profession' has gone ahead to the extent that May's article could be printed in its *Journal*. It seems to me that this is worth a hundred pompous letters to the press against censorship or waffly resolutions at meetings. Instead we are seriously and emphatically considering censorship.

> Whether it was prudent to publish the article I don't know, but your reader response will have shown that. I'm sure it was right to publish it.
>
> For my part, thanks,
>
> Jack Ward
>
> Royal Melbourne Institute of Technology, Melbourne.[100]

And Pitt's (personal) letter to congratulate Jean: 'You have fired a fierce and well-aimed broadside into the prudish absurdities of literary censorship … you have made library history in Australia, setting up another mile-post on the road to literary freedom here'.[101]

The *ALJ* issue was praised outside librarianship, but Jean's effort was not just to secure material for the correspondence pages: it was to stir the LAA to action to endorse a statement on censorship – as Jean demanded in her editorial of the issue, 'it is time that the Library Association of Australia announced publically and unequivocally where it stands on the issue of censorship and the freedom to read', which could be 'invoked whenever a librarian was faced with attempts to suppress and censor the books in his library'.[102] The LAA was moved to endorse the 'Statement of Principles on Freedom to Read' in 1964,[103] which 'helped libraries to adopt a position concerning censorship in general and to resist attempts to censor particular books during the next decade'[104] – for example:

> Censorship in Sandringham
>
> The Sandringham [Victoria] Council decided to remove Edna O'Brien's *Girls in their Married Bliss* from its shelves and rebuked the Librarian, Mr. [Lee] Ellis, for not selecting the right type of book. Mr. Ellis in his reply cited the L.A.A.'s Statement on Freedom to Read.
>
> A committee of 'interested citizens' was formed to wage a campaign against the Council's decision … The campaign has not, so far, succeeded in reversing the Council's decision, but it should deter similar decisions in the future.[105]

Jean wrote of one of the battles in her poem 'Namoi Regional Library bans "The Thin Red Line"', which ends:

> Our women hear, but must not read these words men only say,
> To keep our wives and children pure we've thrown the book away.
> No matter what the critics say we councilors know best
> How to preserve the morals of the women of the West.[106]

Jean wrote a lot about censorship, including 'Trends abroad: Australia' for *Library Trends*, an international journal.[107] She began writing this as a joint paper on intellectual freedom in Australia and New Zealand with Geoffrey Alley, retired National Librarian of New Zealand. Their ideas differed, and so they wrote separate articles on their own countries, with Jean's being characterized as 'impressionistic and fairly gloomy', with observations such as 'to try to state whether intellectual freedom exists in Australia today, and if so to what extent, is a task which increases in difficulty as the evidence is gathered'.[108] As well as writing, Jean chaired the LAA's Freedom to Read Committee,[109] spoke about censorship, asked her friends to speak about it at meetings,[110] and was a member of committees on censorship in libraries[111] and of the LAA working party on the LAA 'Statement on Free Library Service to All'.[112] Her opposition to censorship carried through to all material, including seeing as a censor a librarianship student who did not want to stock books which trivialized women.[113]

Jean was involved in another censorship row which erupted in the 1970s. A group named Library Workers Against Uranium Mining was formed. The problem, as this group saw it, was that available information on uranium, including information from the government (which planned to restrict information on uranium being made available to the public), was not impartial; therefore materials against uranium mining should be made available in libraries. In her 1977 *ALJ* article 'Head not heart: why I am against Library Workers Against Uranium Mining' Jean wrote again of the importance of freedom of information, that 'the library must never try either to suppress or to promote any of the evidence or any of the argument. It can only promote the seeking of information, debate, discussion and understanding'.[114] She was, she explained, against the existence of a library group which promoted only one side of an argument, whether for or against uranium. Helen Modra, in her thesis 'The short march: social responsibility in Australian librarianship 1970–1983', described Jean's attitude as 'the classic liberal arguments in support of intellectual freedom, in which active promotion of issues was not seen as commensurate with professional obligations. [Whyte] has certainly earned her reputation in the profession as a staunch supporter of intellectual freedom during the sixties in particular, and was understandably cautious about any sort of activity that might appear to be incompatible with intellectual freedom principles'. Jean commented that she was 'not against considering social issues but [she was] against a party line'.[115] Both sides wanted information to be available, but Jean's chief concern was with the name of the group, which implied that they represented one side only. That Jean upheld the idea that both sides of an argument should be represented in libraries is seen in her 1966 *ALJ* editorial 'Are we failing our public?',[116] where she wrote about the need to ensure both sides of the debate over the Vietnam War were available in libraries, deploring the lack of materials opposing the War, to the extent of advising readers where material on peace could be found and acquired. Perhaps her attitude could be summarised in 'A word from Callimachus', where she wrote: 'Librarians defend the right of man to read what 'ere he will'.[117]

To return, now, to Jean's other professional interests. She was also interested in library administration, becoming early on in her career a Councillor for professional officers in the South Australian Public Service Association[118] and later a member of the Royal Institute of Public Administration Regional Group (in Canberra).[119] These memberships may have politicized her to think about her own rights and prepared her for the administrative role at Monash, where she showed her ability in administration and leadership. And, by holding the senior position at Monash, at last she did not need to defend the views of a senior librarian whom she did not agree with, and, instead of Andrew Osborn's mixture of impractical, infuriating and brilliant ideas, Jean's administration of the GSL was characterized by ideas which were practical and usable.

I think that we could say that a world perspective could be called an interest. Jean travelled for work and pleasure, taught in Canada, and gave her paper at the Conference of Directors of Scientific Information Centres in the Asian-Pacific Region in Hong Kong in 1963. She was among the earliest Australian librarians to gain overseas qualifications and kept up friendships with those she had met in the United States through visits there, having some visit Australia, to the benefit of students at Monash. She wrote about Australia for various overseas journals and reviewed books on librarianship in other countries. And she wrote of librarianship from a world perspective, with the lack of resources in Australia being a constant theme. Her style of librarianship had an overseas influence, a North American slant, perhaps begun with Pitt, dominated by Chicago (GLS) and Canada (SLIS), and increased by her association with Osborn (and reinforced by her antipathy for the British George Chandler) – she wrote to Osborn of professional loneliness in Australia, and the attraction of returning to the United States.[120]

And could we call 'working hours' an interest? Certainly Jean's work was characterized by her long working hours. She usually worked 50–60 hours per week,[121] preferring her long working days to begin late, complaining that Harrison Bryan 'was considered efficient for arriving at 7.30 am [at Sydney University] whereas I was inefficient because I was still around at 7.30 pm'.[122] She worked through public holidays and was irritated by 'the Australian habit of stopping work a week before Christmas and sleeping thru office hours in order to be fit for yet another party'[123] – this written shortly after she went to the Metcalf Seminar in place of Hedley Brideson, who, Jean claimed, did not want to interrupt his summer holidays, thereby giving an unexpected boost to her career.[124] George Pitt commented: 'Do you never weary of having so many things to do at once? I suppose not. It has been your mode of living for as long as I can remember'.[125] She also expected that others would work longer hours than required, so she would call meetings after working hours and ring to check that staff were still at work.

The last interest (and talent) I will look at is the selection and mentoring of talented librarians. As Neil Radford wrote:

> For four decades she encouraged countless younger people – staff members and, later, students – to perform better than they thought they could, to set their sights higher and achieve more, to believe in themselves and their own abilities, and to become active in the profession.[126]

Jean mentored in many ways, including encouraging people to study overseas, as she had done so early in her career. She enjoyed combining work with social events which furthered both library activities and networks. Her students spoke of her support in continuing their studies or undertaking new areas:

> students could remain in awe of her, but those who were prepared to meet her standards were likely to become life-long friends in whose careers she continued to take a practical interest. She recognised dormant talent in both students and colleagues and encouraged them to higher things, to strive to attain the ideals she herself espoused.[127]

Recruitment became part of Jean's work at the PLSA, and she had 'a great eye for talent'.[128] Some people thought that her most important contribution to librarianship was 'recruiter,' 'facilitator,' and 'catalyst,' a person who has over the years and continues constantly, indeed relentlessly, to put people in touch with each other and with enriching opportunities in wide ranging aspects of the profession.[129]

There were to be many selected during her career. One example will suffice: one of the first people Jean 'mentored' was Ray Olding, who was to become State Librarian of South Australia. When Jean became Staff Training Officer she persuaded Hedley Brideson to centralise the Library's cataloguing services, and she chose Olding, who was part of the Ranganathan Study Group, to head the new section, which, he said, surprised him. Olding, who says that he owes his start to Jean, wrote that

> the S.A. Branch of the LAA had a casual vacancy for a General Councillor on the LAA's General Council. For some reason I was elected, aged a callow 27 if you please. I do not now remember, but am perfectly sure, that Jean fixed this … [giving me] the opportunity of meeting and mixing with the top rank of Australian librarians on both professional and social levels, through which I received life-long benefits … I was appointed Conference Secretary for the 1957 LAA Conference in Adelaide. I became an Examiner in the cataloguing and classification papers of the Registration Examination, and later a member and then Chair of the Board of Examiners.
>
> A further means of reputation exposure directly attributable to Jean, was a series of *ALJ* articles, and many book reviews during Jean's tenure as Editor … the study group on Ranganathan's Colon Classification that Jean and George Buick started back around 1950 and which first stimulated my interest in cataloguing and thus shaped the rest of my career … In 1967–68 I took leave without pay from the State Library and taught cataloguing at the Library School of the University of Minnesota at Minneapolis. Whilst there I was offered, and appointed to, a professorship at the University of California, Los Angeles, specifically and explicitly as a replacement for Seymour Lubetzky … had it not been for those study discussions on Ranganathan …[130]

Frank Upward also spoke of Jean recruiting by challenging people,[131] as she did when she asked him to consult, then to design a course and finally to teach it. And Rachel Salmond wrote of Jean respecting 'those she employed for what they had to offer'.[132] Being good with recruitment meant that the staff Jean chose were of a high standard, and many of the staff became her friends. Although her chief role in selection was within the library profession, her ability in the area of selection was recognized by Monash, and she became a member of numerous selection committees, which left another mark on the history of Monash.

The other side of this ability with people was that Jean had favourites and idols. The favourites were those people she encouraged, but it was not always clear why she chose them, nor why some others were not her favourites. Some reasons were obvious: she appears to have encouraged more males than females, although career-oriented women, preferably without children, were acceptable, and being a South Australian was an advantage. Her favourites were usually young men.

She also had idols, always male, the earliest of whom (professionally) was George Pitt, with whom she retained a friendship until his death, whereas, although she and Andrew Osborn remained friends, she soon found that he had feet of clay. She was loyal, holding people in esteem even when they made mistakes,[133] most obviously Osborn, when so many others criticized him. She was better at choosing her favourites than she was in choosing her idols.

With this ability to select people I found it odd that she wrote: 'You know – I'm not looking forward to meeting new people at all – I never do'.[134] Another anomaly was that Monash may have been the only time Jean herself was interviewed for a position. There may have been an informal interview for the PLSA position (she said that she knocked on the door); she was not interviewed for the University of Sydney position; and it is unlikely that she would have been interviewed for the NLA position, given Fleming writing: 'I was delighted to find that you had offered to throw in your lot with us here in trying to turn this place into what it ought to be & can be'.[135] Jean may have been interviewed for positions she unsuccessfully applied for: I found a number of curricula vitae prepared over a long period (evidence that Jean had wanted to leave the PLSA and the University of Sydney many years before she was able to do so). She wrote to Osborn after writing her application for the Sydney position: 'I just hope that I never have to apply for another job – its embarrassing and boring'.[136]

As there were few areas of librarianship which did not interest or involve Jean at some point in her career, they are worth mentioning, even if that interest or involvement was one of criticism. Early in her career Jean was a member of the children's libraries section,[137] but she did not think that organizations lending toys, tools, etc., should be called 'libraries', a term which she thought should be restricted to those lending books (and their substitutes). This view was marked by a satirical article in *ALJ*, 'New service for Wombat Beach'[138] (perhaps tied in with retrieving emu eggs from the Prime Minister's Lodge?).[139]

The other area of librarianship Jean shied away from was cataloguing: 'I am not of the right sex to understand cataloguing'.[140] She appeared to have enjoyed cataloguing with Pitt, catalogued the Mines Library, had an early interest in Ranganathan's Colon Classification,[141] taught cataloguing (that first lecture), wrote about it and was an examiner in the subject, but disliked it so much that Harrison Bryan was to refer to her 'well-known lack of personal attraction to cataloguing'.[142]

I cannot let the story of Jean Whyte's career end without reference to the changing role of women in Jean's lifetime and how this change affected her career, starting with a 'glass ceiling' at the beginning of her career, when her desire to study at university was met by her parents' belief that girls should not go to university. Jean said they could not afford to send her to university,[143] but the Whyte family appear to have been comfortably off, with wealthy relatives; Jean and Billie had both been to an expensive boarding school; and Prim was still working. This was in 1942, and many young women were discouraged from attending university, being encouraged instead to enter 'suitable' occupations such as teaching and nursing (working at Yadlamalka for Jean). But the university was more enlightened and allowed girls to enrol. So Jean was able to study, despite her parents' wishes, but she had to earn her living to support herself.

Women might be allowed to work, but they were paid less than men, and Jean encountered this at the beginning of her career, when she was employed in her first job at the lower salary of clerk (the position held by women) rather than at that of library assistant (held by men). Her first move was to the Reference Department, which was staffed by males, 'most of whom did not welcome a female, so my first jobs were putting away everything that readers had used – books, pamphlets, newspapers and maps'.[144]

Jean soon found that women in many lower-paid positions did the same work as men employed in higher-paid positions, and perhaps she acknowledged this situation when she described herself as 'Second-in-charge' at the Adelaide Lending Service from 1946, which is correct in that she was in the third-highest position and there was no-one in the second-highest – the top two positions were reserved for men.[145] It was the enlightened George Pitt who recommended that Jean be appointed to the position of second-in-charge. Then came 'one time when being a woman' was to Jean's advantage in her career:[146] winning an American Association of University Women Fellowship, awarded 'to help women of outstanding ability who may be expected to do constructive work on returning to their own country';[147] Jean wrote that 'I shall do my best to see that librarianship in Australia benefits as much as possible from my visit to the United States'.[148] But discrimination came again when she was unsuccessful in her application for the position of Flinders University Librarian, supposedly because she was a woman.[149]

Jean had entered librarianship when the majority of librarians were women but when few held senior positions in big libraries. Despite this, Jean's career had flourished at the PLSA, when the senior positions in other libraries were not hers. Other opportunities were there: teaching librarianship, President of the South Australian Branch of the Library Association of Australia and editorship of *ALJ*.

When Jean moved to the University of Sydney there was little likelihood of promotion to the position of University of Sydney Librarian due to the 'glass ceiling' for women – even if there were women elsewhere reaching the position of University Librarian,[150] no woman had (or has yet) held the position of University of Sydney Librarian. Again, when Jean went to a high-level appointment at the NLA it seemed unlikely that a woman would be appointed to the position of Director General (it has since happened, but long after Jean had left). In the Minute of Appreciation for Jean Whyte I read: 'Guy Manton was able to persuade Jean to take up the chair [of librarianship at Monash]; in other circumstances she might well have become National Librarian'.[151] I wondered what other circumstances were being referred to. If a woman could have been considered for the position? If Jean had remained at the NLA until Chandler's retirement? Perhaps the other circumstances would come with developments in women's liberation.

Jean's appointment at the NLA lifted her to the Second Division of the Commonwealth Public Service, where there was one other woman among 850 men,[152] and no women were yet at the top level. When Jean was interviewed by the *Canberra Times* following her appointment to the NLA she said that she had been unaware of the paucity of women at the top of the ladder: 'there was a preference for men in the higher echelons of her profession, she admitted, "But it's encouraged by women being so silly. They don't apply for a job and then go round saying it was earmarked for one of the boys"'.[153] Despite saying this, there had been times when Jean had been encouraged to apply for positions which she did not in the event apply for, such as that of National Librarian (by Osborn),[154] Macquarie University (by Alley), Professor of Librarianship at UNSW (by Alley)[155] and the Monash position (by Manton).

Jean worked her way up the public-service ladder, spending seventeen years in various positions at the Public Library of South Australia before she was appointed to the number three position at the University of Sydney and then to the number two position, before accepting the number two position at the NLA, but never applying for the position of National Librarian. Perhaps we could contrast this with the career of Harrison Bryan. Bryan, unlike Jean, did not go directly from school into librarianship but first gained his arts degree and completed war service. His first position after completing full-time librarianship education – which was at a level not achieved by Jean until she had had many years of experience – was as Assistant to the Librarian at the University of Queensland Library, at a time when there was no Librarian and the Acting University Librarian was in poor health, so Bryan was doing the work of the University Librarian in his first appointment and was appointed University Librarian in little more than a year.[156]

Jean's appointment to Monash followed the Committee's rejection of an all-male short-list (and long-list), showing that there were few women at her level. She became one of few women then at Monash (and in Australia) to hold the title 'professor' and the second woman to be a Professor of Librarianship in Australia. She became very conscious of being one of the few women professors and was honoured by and proud of the title.[157]

When Jean went to Monash it was time for her to be in a top position, after so many second-in-charge positions, always second to men, some of whom she disagreed with: Brideson (she 'considered that everything that she accomplished was against what he wanted, and loathed defending his views – which she did not agree with – to the staff'); Andrew Osborn (he 'generated ideas. Many of them were impractical, some were infuriating, but a few were brilliant. He did not know which were which');[158] and George Chandler (with whom Jean clashed immediately).

And, in line with many of that time, Jean was aware of the power of words, perhaps more so because of her interest in poetry. An example is from Monash: although she was not the first woman to be appointed a professor at Monash (at the time of her appointment she was one of five),[159] several newspapers reported: 'Woman takes new chair at Monash'.[160] Jean's reply to one newspaper was:

> Thank you for announcing my new position in your paper ... May I suggest that all journalists resolve to mark International Women's Year by banning such irrelevant headings as 'New chair goes to woman'.
>
> There is nothing remarkable in the fact that Monash University has appointed a woman to a professorship.[161]

2. THEMES FROM JEAN'S LIFE

Now to turn to Jean's interests which were not her work, beginning with her strong friendships, importantly with animals. She loved animals, lived with them all of her life and, depending on one's opinion, was devoted to or ruled by them. In Jean's personal papers are many references to her animal friends at Yadlamalka (and photographs, such as one of Jean riding a camel), and, when she was working at the PLSA, sending food to London for a dog Pitt had met (soon after the end of the War).[162] Baggins the cat lived with Jean in Adelaide, Sydney, Canberra and Melbourne; he was a feature at all the libraries Jean worked in, and she had a habit of forgetting that she had left his meat in the refrigerator at work. She was understandably upset by the death of her long-time companion after their move to Monash. Baggins was succeeded by other cats, and by Fergus and Tansie, miniature schnauzers, and finally by the silky terrier, Quingle. Jean took her dogs to work with her, they slept under her desk at Monash, and she enjoyed walking them in Valley Reserve. She was also known for imitating animal noises – George Pitt wrote (in 1968): 'when I first saw you (usually flying and baa-ing down the lane by the old C.L.S. building)'.[163]

Jean had lifelong friends, some dating from childhood and school, others from each of the libraries she worked in, from Monash, and from her Chicago days. Long-standing friends included Geoffrey Alley, John Bray, Harrison Bryan, Mavis Crawford, Margaret Lundie, Brian and Lisbeth McMullin, Elizabeth Morrison, Ray Olding, George Pitt, Neil Radford, Margery Ramsay, Radha and Henning Rasmussen, Boyd Rayward – and the list could go on and on. There was an interweaving of the personal and the professional: Jean's colleagues and her staff were her friends and continued so into her retirement. I have chosen to write about three friends, Roma Mitchell, Andrew Osborn and Hector Monro.

Roma Mitchell, later Dame Roma, was often referred to as 'Roma the First', as she was the first woman to receive a number of honours, such as Queen's Counsel, Justice of the Supreme Court of South Australia, state governor, Deputy Chancellor of a university, and later Chancellor, etc. I am unsure how the Whyte and Mitchell families met, but as Adelaide had a population of about 250,000 in the early twentieth century there were many opportunities for the children of two wealthy families to meet (as the eligible Kitty Macully had met the eligible Prim Whyte). Perhaps Jean and Roma's fathers had been friends: Prim Whyte and Roma's father, Harold Mitchell, were similar in age, both had been educated at St Peter's, both were eligible bachelors, both had spent some time in South Australia's north and both served in World War I, though Harold did not return.

Roma saw Kitty die: 'When someone asked young Roma Mitchell how the shark had taken Mrs Whyte – surely a strange question to address to a twelve year old – she thought for a moment, then gave a wonderfully literal and unemotional reply: "By the femur bone"'.[164] Jean was three when her mother died, Roma four when her father died; they were to be lifelong friends, and Roma was often referred to as 'like a sister' to Jean and Billie. Roma wrote references for Jean, while Jean wrote the entry for Roma in the *Oxford Companion to Australian History*.[165] Jean became a visitor to Government House, and she stayed at Roma's home during Roma's last illness, answering letters on her behalf.[166] Jean was devastated by Roma's death, and it may have precipitated Jean's slide into dementia.[167]

The second important friendship was with Andrew Osborn. Although Jean said that Andrew's major influence on her was to change the direction of her career[168] it was far more than that. It was due to Andrew's offer of a job for Jean at the University of Sydney that she was, at last, able to leave the PLSA and to make her first move interstate; it was also through his influence that she did not return to the United States in the 1950s. Andrew encouraged her to continue editing *ALJ* in 1963 (she did); to do a PhD. (she never did); to teach at the University of Western Ontario (she did, but for a shorter time than stipulated in his invitation); and to apply for the position of National Librarian (she did not). She was influenced by his book-buying and proposed – but never took – a year away from the Library to buy books.[169] Under his influence she also wrote of the scarcity of resources in Australian libraries in 'The librarian's task, 1962: an editorial', seeing the increase in the total resources as one of the librarian's chief tasks at that time.[170] Her interest in printing began with Andrew, but his greatest influence on her (both positive and negative) was in the way she set up the GSL.

It is hard to tell when Jean became disillusioned by Andrew – perhaps when she had to deal with his impracticalities in Sydney – but she did not criticize him to her friends at the time. She said later that 'he was innovative ... whether the innovations would always be sensible is another matter'.[171] Perhaps we could call him a fallible role model: she learned from his talents and his mistakes. She wrote (although unfortunately without saying when she reached this conclusion) 'that life with Andrew was not easy and that he was a very contrary person who certainly did not practise what he preached'.[172]

Although Andrew was to have such a big influence on Jean's career there was little influence on her personal life, as their early relationship soon lost its intensity. This evolved from Jean's infatuation with him to his wanting Jean's friendship, although his was a more restrained and less emotional admiration. When his wife died he married one of Jean's close friends at the University of Sydney, Margaret Lundie, who had been Associate Editor of *ALJ* when Jean was Editor. Jean, with a later University of Sydney Librarian, Neil Radford, was to write Andrew's obituary.[173]

A later friendship was with Hector Monro. Hector and his wife Joyce were New Zealanders, both librarians before Hector's career in philosophy, which led him to Australia to take up the position of senior lecturer at the University of Sydney and later to become the foundation Professor of Philosophy at Monash: 'within five years he had built up one of the best departments of Philosophy in Australia'.[174] Hector was

> a renowned moral philosophy and ethics scholar both in Australia and overseas, and the author of four books and numerous papers in philosophical journals ... Dr Aubrey Townsend says Professor Monro was an unusual academic. 'His interests were broad – ranging over philosophy, literature and history – and his publications commonly combined these interests in ways that made his books appealing to an audience wider than usual for an academic writer ... He wrote about ethics, humour, literary figures and the environment. And he is the only philosopher I know of who was able to publish poetry in an academic philosophy journal'.[175]

More than an unusual academic, Hector wrote a book on humour while he was in gaol in New Zealand (as a conscientious objector during World War II)! Jean became friends with Joyce and Hector, and the friendship with Hector developed after Joyce's death in 1980.

Jean and Hector shared many interests, including censorship, crosswords, dogs, librarianship, printing, poetry, rare books, travel, walking, wine and the theatre (they had season tickets to the Melbourne Theatre Company – they would leave their car at the railway station and catch a train to Melbourne, and perhaps that was where they were going when I saw them last). They kept up their friendships at Monash after retirement through frequent attendance at the Banquo Club, a monthly lunch gathering of retired academics. Hector donated his non-philosophical books and a substantial bequest from his will set up the Hector Monro Fund for the purchase of significant seventeenth- and eighteenth-century works for the Library.[176]

Jean and Hector set up house together when Hector was becoming frail. Jean was rather awkward in telling her friends of the arrangement, and visitors to the house were shown over it and were able to note the separate bedrooms.[177] Hector's family was pleased that Jean was able to help him stay at home[178] – but not for long, as he was unsteady on his feet and would fall, whereupon Jean would need the help of one of her friends to help lift him. Hector went into a nursing home, but, when the time came, Jean was not able to move into the same home, as it did not have the facilities for dementia patients. Hector died in 2001.

Various people have asked about or commented on Jean's relationships with other men. There were many admirers, but few relationships: when younger she wore her heart on her sleeve and seemed emotionally immature, having crushes on various men, but there was no-one significant until her friendship with Hector late in life.

To turn now from friends to other interests, beginning with poetry: she read poetry, 'had a remarkable memory bank of English verse',[179] wrote poetry and doggerel and reviewed books of poetry. Childhood isolation gave her time to read the books at home, which included much poetry because of the interests of Macully, Kitty and Prim. Jean said that she 'was stuffed with the English poets', and 'brought up on bush ballads'.[180] She said that her degree was in poetry rather than in literature;[181] her interest was encouraged at university by Charles Rischbieth Jury, Professor of English at Adelaide University and author of a number of books of poetry, who invited Jean and a dozen or so other people, such as John Bray, to his home to read poetry; many were to become her long-term friends. This group, known as 'The Poetry', began their monthly meetings in 1947; the remaining members still meet monthly. Douglas Muecke, who has attended meetings of the group since its inception, and is still a member, recalls Jean, who continued to attend meetings when she visited Adelaide, reading, among others, Banjo Paterson.[182] I suspect too that there was another Jury influence – Jury was always trying to find homes for the kittens from his cat, Claribel, so I wonder whether Claribel was the mother of Baggins.

Jean kept many poems written in Yadlamalka days, but it is not clear who actually wrote them – whether it was Jean, Billie or Prim. Her poetry has been described as somewhat derivative and competent;[183] she wrote for the school magazine, for library occasions and for *ALJ*, as well as more serious poetry for university magazines such as *Phoenix* and *Poetry Monash*, and doggerel for special occasions. An example of the latter is a farewell poem to Elaine de Cure and Pam Wollaston (from PLSA), typical both of the poems she wrote for special occasions and of her thoughts on staff turnover:

'QUALIFICATIONS NECESSARY FOR JOINING THE STAFF OF THE PUBLIC LIBRARY OF S.A.'

Young ladies must be pigeon-toed,
Cross-eyed and toothless too,
Their shoulders drooped as with a load,
Their stockings always blue.

They should not dress in anything
Brighter than black or brown,
And when a book they're forced to bring
They must bring too, a frown.

They must not laugh, or even smile
Or speak with one another
<u>On no account will we employ
A lass who has a brother.</u>

With sorrow we draw up these rules
Experience dictates
Because past choices we have found
Too good at getting dates.

For we must bid a fond farewell
To our dear Wooly sheep
But since she is so glad to go
We must forbear to weep.

We do not blame you, Pam that you
Desert us for another,
But we regret we e'er employed
A lass who had a brother.

The A.L.S. is quiet without
Their Elaine Margaret Mary,
But laughter will return no doubt
With Mrs. Gerald Carey.

Elaine and Pam we wish you joy
We're glad to set you free –
Because you see, you do not fit
Our new staff policy.

And while we are assembled here
Note – this advice to mothers –
We won't employ your Daughter Dear,
Unless she has no brothers![184]

Jean's Outback childhood was the origin of her interest in literature: her reading and learning of the classics of English and Australian literature, her 'fierce attachment to things Australian, not least to its literature'.[185] She was to say in later life that she had 'an old passion for Australian literature – perhaps I am sick of that old passion (but not desolate)'.[186] She said that she probably would have stayed in literature had she studied full-time, 'almost certainly and there I would be stuck',[187] and that she had probably been able to contribute more to libraries than she would have to English literature.[188] Her two unfinished theses were in English literature,[189] and she co-authored two reports on Australian literature in Australian libraries.[190] It seemed to some that she had read everything.[191]

Art, especially contemporary art, also played a part in Jean's life. At Monash she was a member of the Vera Moore Fund Committee and the Art Advisory Committee, and the walls of her homes were covered with paintings and prints, with an emphasis on contemporary Australian works: 'What spaces weren't taken up with bookshelves were taken up with art', said her friends Grecian and Ross Day.[192]

Holidays and travel were important interests. Later holidays, the highpoint of Jean's year,[193] were at Carrickalinga, a coastal resort 78 kilometres south of Adelaide on the Fleurieu Peninsula, where she, Billie and Roma had a kit home built, with a room added later for Hector. She travelled a lot during her career and in retirement, seeing much of Australia, frequently visiting North America and Europe, and also South America, taking in the Galapagos Islands, Thailand, Nepal and East Africa, doing much of this travelling with Hector.[194] She visited the Alleys in New Zealand several times, she enjoyed walking, and Harrison Bryan told of Jean visiting his family when they were camping at the Warrambungles – she provided 'iron rations': a bottle of whisky and a camembert.[195]

The whisky is not surprising. Jean enjoyed alcohol, especially South Australian, such as wine from McLaren Vale and the Fleurieu Peninsula,[196] Coopers Ale, champagne,[197] and Grange Hermitage. She was a social drinker, saying that she drank a glass of sherry or two glasses of beer a day, but the only effect was to make her more serious and gloomy than ever.[198] Just before she left Adelaide she hosted a party for about 35 people and 'remembered to order enough drink for twice as many, but forgot all about food'.[199] There was sherry in her office, and she would take staff out for a drink, including the army of shelving staff at Fisher.[200] She became knowledgeable about wine, possibly under the tutelage of Professor Jury,[201] and had an admirable collection of wine – and a few of the good bottles from her cellar were consumed after her funeral.[202]

The last major interest to note is Jean's continued worries about her health. Pitt wrote to her: 'I am very happy to find you beginning to doubt whether you will die young'.[203] There were rumours of a misplaced heart, but this is no more than a rumour. She had a cardiac murmur,[204] had had a broken arm (probably accounting for her claim that she could write with either hand, although her writing with her right (usual) hand was difficult enough to read), and there were various operations over the years. There was a scar on her lungs, known to be present in 1959;[205] perhaps this is why she gave up smoking. She had some anxiety symptoms, sometimes mild panic attacks, often associated with driving,[206] and the leave that she took from the NLA in late 1974 would now be called 'stress leave'. Some thought that she was a hypochondriac, others that she exaggerated her symptoms. On the other hand, she sought help when others might have soldiered on, which may have helped maintain her independence.[207] Her real concern should have been dementia.

Now to some things which I have grouped as interesting non-interests. First, driving. Jean rode horses and camels at Yadlamalka, but driving a car in the city was a lot different. Before gaining her licence she organized lifts. Ray Olding said that she felt 'like a sack of potatoes' on the back of his motorbike in Adelaide,[208] and she travelled more comfortably in the Mercedes in Sydney. She obtained her licence (Fisher apparently went through trauma when she was learning to drive) and bought her first car when she lived in Sydney. She was not comfortable while driving and was easily flustered.[209]

Another non-interest was sport (after leaving school, where she had been active in tennis and hockey), despite the sporting interests and abilities of both parents. Yet another was religion: Prim was a Congregationalist, Kitty the daughter of an Anglican priest, and though Jean was baptised an Anglican, and went to an Anglican school, she described her beliefs as 'Religion: once fiercely Anglo-Catholic (caused by school). Now: nil'.[210] Although she quoted the Bible, the quotes were derived not from a religious bent, but from her knowledge of the classics. So, for example, 'Whenever two or three Australian librarians are gathered together',[211] 'Libraries exist so that men may live more abundantly',[212] and, in her poetry, 'Must I give / To Caesar all that unto him belongs?'.[213]

Jean had little involvement in politics, describing herself as 'theoretically slightly left of center'.[214] Neil Radford said that 'politically she sided more with the common man and the goals of the labour movement than with conservative ideology'.[215] Her main involvement appears to have been dealing with the effects of government economic decisions on the libraries in which she was working, as well as hosting parties on election nights.[216] Jean's lack of involvement in politics and religion and her opposition to censorship may be summed up in her own words: 'the professional belief that the library has no politics, no religion, no moralities to push'.[217]

From interests to characteristics, what David Jones called Jean's 'formidable intellect'.[218] As I found this area so difficult to write about I asked David to comment; he wrote:

> Her achievement with [the history of the Institute] was really remarkable, as she retained an enviable objectivity in writing about events in which she often played a part and on issues on which she more often than not had firm views. She managed to bring alive most of the characters who played a significant part in the development of the library profession, with sidelights which informed but never trivialised, and with a respect for their motives, an appreciation of individuals as products of their times – in other words, a real historian's flair. She could grapple with issues of great complexity and throw light on them in easily comprehended sentences and often with humour and verve. She was comprehensive in her approach, but did not overwhelm with facts and occurrences. And above all she breathed life into an organisation by showing how it was all too human – with the same vices and virtues of the species. It was all the more remarkable that although she had been working on the history on and off for twenty years, she was still writing of it with enthusiasm and commitment – right up to the time when she realised that her mind was fading and that she would need to try and leave some pointers for someone to follow in her footsteps. She had a masterly view of the big picture, could see linkages and influences across geographical divides and chronological gaps, could absorb a mass of detail whilst blazing a trail through a forest of documentation, and

was able and willing to share her discoveries, ideas, opinions and conclusions with interested audiences. I actually think it is a sign of a remarkable intellect to be able to leave an unfinished work in such a way that a colleague can complete it.[219]

Referees found many good things to say about Jean; one which encapsulates many of her characteristics was written by Roma Mitchell:

> I have known Miss Jean P. Whyte all her life. Her character is one of integrity: to any problem she applies an honest, fearless and enquiring mind. Her enthusiasm for and interest in librarianship appear to be limitless. She is an interesting and fluent speaker. Furthermore she combines with academic learning a wide interest in people and current affairs which renders her admirably fitted for her contacts with the general public and, I believe, with the members of a library staff.[220]

Jean had a good sense of humour, she was polite, sociable, loyal to her friends, had few weak points, met deadlines, and didn't like 'small talk'.[221] But many found her 'formidable': this was my experience, not surprisingly, as she was by that time close to the end of her career, a professor, and I was a new student. Many people told me their own stories of a memorable first meeting, such as Brian McMullin, who met Jean at SLIS, in the Rare Book Collection. She barged into the room saying 'Have you got Watt?' (i.e. Robert Watt's *Bibliotheca Britannica*, which he was using, that had been acquired for teaching purposes).[222] And Neil Radford (nephew of Professor Wilma Radford) wrote that, when they were introduced on Jean's first day at the University of Sydney, Jean said 'Humph! Radford! You have a famous name to live up to!'; Radford said that he was seventeen years old and she was bigger than he. 'Yes Miss Whyte', he quaked.[223]

Many students saw her as aloof, imposing, sometimes abrasive, impatient with pretension, but also inspiring, doing much to help the individual student, including providing financial and emotional support. Although she kept a distance between herself and students, if a student became a member of staff, the relationship could change to a friendship.[224] Part of this aloofness was due to her height. To describe herself to Andrew Osborn she wrote: 'I've got gingery hair, a grumpy expression & am above average height'[225] (she was about 178 centimetres tall according to her passports, about the same height as Prim). Her school photographs show Jean almost a head taller than her peers, gangly and awkward, a giraffe among the gazelles. But later her height was an advantage, as it added to her imposing nature. She dressed well, was well groomed, and her hair was always well done. I think that she looked rather like her grandfather, Alexander Macully.

I sometimes wonder whether Jean was most like Macully, who was said to be 'A most lovable man, and such a mixture of contradictions! Believed all things, hoped all things; to him nothing was impossible but what was impracticable'.[226] Macully died before Jean was born – they were similar in looks, educated at private schools, where they distinguished themselves in English literature, loved poetry, were careful with their appearance, well-loved by many people, moved interstate a number of times because of work and suffered from dementia – and, although he was a minister of religion, Macully does not appear to have been 'religious'. Both were good public speakers, Macully known for his 'remarkable power as a reader and reciter',[227] while Jean presented her lectures with 'elegance and power'[228] and with impressive 'Churchillian cadences'.[229] It was a pity that she missed hearing her grandfather read poetry at his 'An evening with the poets' at the South Australian Institutes – I think that she would have enjoyed the experience.[230]

Macully was probably the only university graduate before Jean in her family, they both became teachers, and they both gained and enjoyed the title 'professor' (his was a courtesy title). Macully continued his career in a form of literature; Jean thought that she was lucky not to have been stuck there. They both enhanced their backgrounds – Macully's claim to Irish birth and Jean's claim to being head prefect. Macully went through bankruptcy and bounced back, and perhaps the family story led to Jean's worries about her finances.

Jean always worried about her superannuation, from the time of her work at the PLSA. Although she was always a government employee she worked for different governments, and superannuation was not able to be transferred (nor other benefits, such as holiday leave), although she and Andrew Osborn tried, unsuccessfully, to transfer her superannuation from the PLSA to the University of Sydney. By the time she left Monash there was sufficient superannuation for her retirement, and she had no dependants. She had benefited from a lifetime's work and saving, and also from inheritances from family members.

In her will Jean left large amounts to Monash's school of librarianship (by then absorbed into the Faculty of Information Technology), to the Monash University Library, to the Art Gallery of South Australia, the R.S.P.C.A., Ryder Cheshire, and the Winston Churchill Memorial Trust, where Roma had been Deputy Chair of the South Australian committee which awarded fellowships and President of the Trust (all the other committee members were men).[231] The Churchill fellowship donated by Jean has been used to provide fellowships for the study of an aspect of library and information services by a South Australian; a fellowship sponsored by Roma was for excellence in the performing arts. Jean's bequests to Monash will be used to support research and publication, including an annual lecture, and to add to the Library's research collections in areas of Jean's interest, including literature, librarianship and philosophy (many of her poetry books were left to the Library).[232] Jean asked that her friends be invited to take books from her own collection after her death, which prompted Elizabeth Morrison to comment that she had not fully appreciated 'the length and breadth of Jean's learning' until she saw the collection.[233]

Much of her art was valuable, and items were given to galleries after Jean's death. The William Robinson painting (known as 'The mad cow' to Jean's friends) and two of Robinson's engravings went to the Art Gallery of South Australia, and another painting to the Monash Museum of Art. Other paintings, jewellery, and various possessions of Jean were chosen by her friends after Jean's death. If I had had the opportunity I would have chosen the binary clock, a fascinating machine on Jean's mantelpiece – I have not been able to find out who has it.

In her final years Jean became more and more dependent on her friends – she would ring at any time to get the help that she thought she needed. She had been known for her organising skills, 'her astonishing ability to organise her friends, not, I hasten to say only in her own interests'.[234] Manipulative? But she was also generous, giving much to those who helped her during those last years.

Jean forgot many of the practical skills she had learned at Yadlamalka. She had enjoyed cooking and entertaining, with good wines and conversation, but she seems to have forgotten how to cook and increasingly relied on bought food. She needed more and more help as she grew older, and her friends from this period laughed when I told them that in her younger days she claimed to be 'reasonably good with an axe, a saw, nails & pieces of wire'.[235] She had never been a keen housekeeper, and there were problems in moving house a number of times (all within Mount Waverley), from her home in Rob Roy Street, then to Bruce Street, to be closer to the park where she walked the dogs and to have more room for her vast collection of books, then to Valley Road with Hector.

Jean had few relatives in later life. Auntie died in 1978, having retained close contact with both Jean and Billie. Jean wrote that 'I'm one of those lucky people who have a really good step-mother – but then she is my mother's sister'.[236] There were no relatives on Kitty's side, as none of her siblings had had children, and few on Prim's side, despite his being from a large family. Prim retired to Adelaide and died in 1958, in Parkside Mental Hospital, Eastwood, a few weeks after being admitted with 'senile dementia'.[237] Billie outlived Jean, but had dementia years before Jean succumbed to it. Perhaps they both inherited dementia, as their grandfather, Alexander Macully and their father both had dementia. Perhaps Jean's health concerns were based on her knowledge of the presence of dementia in her own family. Rachel Salmond said that she took meals for Jean on most Thursdays from July to October 2000, when Jean was 'mostly coherent' and seemed 'mentally prepared' for what proved to be her extraordinarily rapid decline in November-December 2000. They 'talked about ALIA things and other library-type things, which a year or so earlier she would have still discussed in terms of what was ahead, as if they were all over as far as she was concerned'.[238]

It is difficult to know when Jean began deteriorating mentally: it is said that intelligent people may be better able to hide their decline. She became forgetful and certain oddnesses in her behaviour were noticed,[239] while her driving became more erratic, her practical skills lost. She was devastated by Roma's death in March, 2000, and the slide downhill quickened. Jean's last public appearance was at the launch of the 2000 edition of *The poems of Callimachus*, on October 19th, 2000. She was admitted to hospital the following day. From there she moved to a series of three nursing homes. As dementia developed she talked nonsense, often in rhythm and rhyme. According to her friend from The Poetry, Douglas Muecke, she was speaking in the rhythm of a bush ballad: 'If you asked if she remembered someone she would reply "Yes, I remember him. A tumpty tumpty tim", inventing words to continue the rhythm and provide a rhyme'.[240]

She gradually forgot people. 'That marvelous mind, razor-sharp, comprehensive, humane yet intolerant of any pretensions unwisely offered it, preceded her into oblivion', wrote John Levett.[241] Some of her friends were able to visit, some found it too difficult.

Jean died on March 18th, 2003; her funeral was held on March 24th. She was cremated.

Jean was unusually gloomy on the anniversary of her mother's death. Her lifelong friend Mavis Crawford wrote:

> This date was etched in our memories; Jean never let us forget that 18th March was the anniversary of an event that changed her life dramatically. We all treated her with extra consideration that day. How fitting, then that she herself should leave us on 18th March.[242]

As A.D. Hope wrote,

'THE UNKNOWN ANNIVERSARY'

Birthdays, holidays, days that always come round,
Christmas and Easter, Ramadan, Yom Kippur,
Wedding days, celebrations of lovers or friends,
We mark them on calendars; they are always found
In diaries, rise regular as stars, are due to recur
Year after year; they are dates on which one depends.

But there is one other day, masked by the circling year,
A strange anniversary; nobody knows what it is;
Yet it waits for each one of us, destined, certain and true,
Unknown, yet we know for a fact that it has to be there
As it brushes the cheek with a cold, unconditional kiss
And whispers, 'Be ready for me: I am ready for you.'

When we least expect it, it signals and no one knows why,
Flashes out to the zodiac as the planet turns round and round,
A day which is all your own yet you may not celebrate,
Like a private moon it already circles your sky,
Turning the same face toward you, attentive, profound,
Keeping watch like a lover each night beside your gate.

There it raises faint tides that rise and fall in your blood
It keeps but it does not observe the solar year,
For its secret clock does not run to a regular beat,
And refuses to sound the hours as a timepiece should.
Yet pressing my ear to the pillow each year I hear
The steady tramping of its remorseless feet.

Do you hear it, my love, their crunch on a rough country track
As we march on side by side? There is no trunk road to the grave—
Are we in step? Are you wondering which of the two
Will come first to the turn-off, and which one will not look back
When the other stands able only to watch and to wave
Before going on to the lonelier rendezvous?

The anniversary whose date not one of us knows
For the art to read that horoscope nobody learns.
It would be nice to celebrate in the usual way;
To be waked with a cup of tea and dew-fresh rose,
A kiss and a smiling: 'Many happy returns!'
But it will not happen. It is not, of course,
      that sort of day.[243]

Jean Whyte died on the anniversary of the death of her mother.

ENDNOTES

1. G. H. Pitt to Jean Whyte, December 30th, 1971. SLSA: PRG 1335/3-4.
2. Interview, Joan Brewer, 2008.
3. G. H. Pitt to Jean Whyte, December 30th, 1971. SLSA: PRG 1335/3-4.
4. Jean Whyte. 'Curriculum vitae', [1972?]. NLA: MS 9616.
5. 'H.C.L. Anderson Award. Citation for Jean Primrose Whyte, BA, MA, FLAA', [1987]. NLA: MS 9616.
6. 'Australia Day honours'. *Advertiser* [SA], January 26th, 1988.
7. Agnes Gregory to Jean Whyte, February 4th, 1988. NLA: MS 9616.
8. M.I. Logan to Jean Whyte, December 14th, 1988. NLA: MS 9616.
9. Jean Whyte to R. J. Pargetter, January 3rd, 1995. NLA: MS 9616.
10. [Monash University]. 'Monash University Graduation Ceremony', [1996], 5. NLA: MS 9616.
11. Jean Whyte. 'Graduation address Monash University. 1996. For Faculty of Arts Graduands 15/5/96'. NLA: MS 9616.
12. Rudolf Blum. *Kallimachos*, 1991; Barry Jones. *Barry Jones' Dictionary of World Biography*, 1994, 122.
13. Jean Whyte. 'A word from Callimachus'. *ALJ* 6 (3) 1957, 95.
14. Jean Whyte. *The Poems of Callimachus*, 2000.
15. Brian McMullin. 'Harrison Bryan, bibliographer and hand-printer', 20–34.
16. Interview: Brian McMullin, 2008.
17. Jean Whyte to Jane [Bald], September 6th, 1976. MON 1059: 2000/68. 42.
18. Interview: Brian McMullin, 2008.
19. Interview: Michael Talbot, 2005.
20. Interview: Ross Harvey, 2005.
21. Andrew Osborn to Jean Whyte, December 29th, 1958. SU: M 465.
22. Jean Whyte to Andrew Osborn, January 2nd, 1959. SU: M 465.
23. Jean Whyte. 'Waltzing with Matilda', 1988, 87.
24. Jean Whyte and David J. Jones. *Uniting a Profession*, 2007, 3.
25. Elizabeth Morrison and Michael Talbot, eds. *Books, Libraries and Readers in Colonial Australia*, 1985.
26. Interview: Elizabeth Morrison, 2008.
27. Interview: Elizabeth Morrison, 2008.
28. Frank Upward and Jean P. Whyte, eds. *Peopling a Profession*, 1991.
29. Jean Whyte to S. Acutt, October 28th, 1981. MON 1059: 2000/68. 46.
30. Jean Whyte and David J. Jones, *Uniting a Profession*, 2007.
31. Jean Whyte and David J. Jones. *Uniting a Profession*, 2007, viii–ix.
32. 'LAA 50 – National Committee'. *ALJ* 36 (4) 1987, 192.

33 Interview: John Lowe, 2005.
34 Jean Whyte. 'Personal notes', [1987?]. NLA: MS 9616.
35 [Board of Examination]. 'Board of Examination'. *ALJ* 9 (4) 1960, 184.
36 Margaret Trask. 'Judgement, energy, intellectual capacity, and vision'. *ALJ* 36 (4) 1987, 234.
37 Jean Whyte. *The Recruitment of Librarians,* [1959?], 3.
38 Harrison Bryan. *No Gray Profession*, 1994, 157.
39 Harrison Bryan. 'A decade of change'. *ALJ* 20 (1) 1971, 18.
40 Harrison Bryan. *No Gray Profession*, 1994, 155.
41 'We' refers to the collective opinion of the Board, which was also Jean's own opinion (Jean Whyte to Margery Ramsay, September 17th, 1973. NLA: MS 9616).
42 Jean Whyte to Cecily Brown. August 12th, 1976. MON 1059: 2000/68. 42.
43 Library Association of Australia. 'Annual Report for 1962'. *ALJ* 12 (2) 1963, 78–83.
44 Jean Whyte. 'Presidential message'. Australian Institute of Librarians. South Australian Branch. *Quarterly Bulletin*, 10, 1949.
45 Ibid.
46 Jean Whyte to Andrew Osborn, February 19th, 1959. SU: M 465.
47 [Jean Whyte]. 'Editorial'. *ALJ* 8 (2) 1959, 57.
48 'Branches and Sections'. *ALJ* 5 (4) 1956, 147.
49 [Jean Whyte, ed.]. *Proceedings of the 16th Biennial Conference held in Sydney, August 1971*, 1972.
50 Jean Whyte. 'Waltzing with Matilda', 1988, 88.
51 Jean Whyte to G.R. Manton, October 10th, 1974. MON: SLO 72330.
52 Jean Whyte. 'Personal notes', [1987?]. NLA: MS 9616.
53 Harrison Bryan. *No Gray Profession*, 1994, 14.
54 'H.C.L. Anderson Award. Citation for Jean Primrose Whyte, BA, MA, FLAA', [1987]. NLA: MS 9616.
55 Interview: Denis Richardson, 2006.
56 Interview: Michael Talbot, 2005.
57 S. Acutt to Jean Whyte, April 28th, 1982. MON 1059: 2000/68. 46.
58 Harrison Bryan. 'Jean Primrose Whyte'. *ALJ* 38 (1) 1989, 14.
59 Jean Whyte. 'The Accreditation of Courses in Librarianship', 1974, 604.
60 [Jean Whyte, ed.]. *Librarianship in Australia*, 1974.
61 Jean Whyte to Lindy Decker, July 25th, 1975. MON 1059: 2000/68. 37.
62 Jean Whyte. 'Curriculum vitae' [1972?]. NLA: MS 9616.
63 Jean Whyte. 'Position application and curriculum vitae', 1959. NLA: MS 9616.
64 Jean Whyte. 'Curriculum vitae', 1974. NLA: MS 9616.
65 Harrison Bryan. 'Jean Primrose Whyte'. *ALJ* 38 (1) 1989, 9.
66 Jean Whyte. 'Curriculum vitae', [1962?]. NLA: MS 9616.
67 Harrison Bryan. 'Jean Primrose Whyte'. *ALJ* 38 (1) 1989, 5.
68 Jean Whyte. 'Position application and curriculum vitae', 1959. NLA: MS 9616.
69 Jean Whyte. 'Curriculum vitae', [1972?]. NLA: MS 9616.

70 Jean Whyte. 'Position application and curriculum vitae', 1959. NLA: MS 9616.
71 Jean Whyte. 'Curriculum vitae', [1962?]. NLA: MS 9616.
72 Interview: Wallace Kirsop, 2008.
73 Jean Whyte to Ian Cathie, May 5th, 1988. NLA: MS 9616. The sorry saga of the State Library of Victoria is outlined by Axel Lodewycks in *The campaign for a new State Library of Victoria*, [1990]. Jean was one of the many librarians who were disappointed with government planning. In mid-2009 renovation of the State Library is not yet complete.
74 Jean Whyte. 'Who uses a university library, why and to what effect?', 1972, 527–537.
75 Eric J. Wainwright. *Readings in Australian librarianship II*, 1979.
76 Jean Whyte. 'Retirement Reminiscences', 1988. NLA: MS 9616.
77 University of Sydney. 'Minutes of a regular meeting of the Senate of the University of Sydney', August 8th, 1972. Resolution 72/252. SU Archives.
78 ['It is with sincere regret']. [Newspaper clipping], [1926]. SLSA: PRG 1335/1.
79 Harrison Bryan. 'Jean Primrose Whyte'. *ALJ* 38 (1) 1989, 5.
80 Jean Whyte. 'Retirement Reminiscences', 1988. NLA: MS 9616.
81 Jean Whyte. 'Presidential message'. *Australian Institute of Librarians. South Australian Branch. Quarterly Bulletin*, 10, 1949.
82 Interview: Ross Harvey, 2005.
83 Transcript of a conversation between Jean Whyte and Geoffrey Alley, 1981. MON 1059: 2000/68/5.
84 Jean Whyte. 'Waltzing with Matilda', 1988, 84–85.
85 For example, G. H. Pitt to Jean Whyte, July 30th, 1964. SLSA: PRG 1335/3-4.
86 'Secretarial notes'. *Australian Institute of Librarians. South Australian Branch. Quarterly Bulletin*, 8, 1946, 4.
87 Australian Institute of Librarians. South Australian Branch. Minute Book October 8, 1937–December 17, 1952. SLSA: SRG 109 Series 2, Vols. 1–7.
88 [Arthur Rylah]. http://adbonline.anu.edu.au/biogs/A160190b.htm.
89 'The "Bizarre" Mayor'. *ALJ* 16 (2) 1967, 75.
90 Jean Whyte. 'Presidential message'. *Australian Institute of Librarians. South Australian Branch. Quarterly Bulletin*, 10, 1949.
91 Jean Whyte. 'Trends abroad: Australia'. *Library Trends* 19 (1) 1970, 127.
92 W.G.K. Duncan. 'A librarian's first loyalty'. *ALJ* 10 (4) 1961, 163–174.
93 Jean Whyte. 'Issues in Australian librarianship', 1976, 193.
94 Jean Whyte. 'Trends abroad: Australia'. *Library Trends* 19 (1) 1970, 128.
95 Jean Whyte. 'Issues in Australian librarianship', 1976, 193.
96 Frederick May. 'The concupiscence of the oppressor'. *ALJ* 13 (2) 1964, 73–84.
97 Harrison Bryan. 'Jean Primrose Whyte'. *ALJ* 38 (1) 1989, 10.
98 Wilma Radford. [Correspondence]. *ALJ* 13 (4) 1964, 193.
99 Jean Whyte. [Introduction to] 'Correspondence'. *ALJ* 13 (3) 1964, 129; 'Correspondence'. *ALJ* 13 (3) 1964, 129–135.
100 Jack Ward. [Correspondence]. *ALJ* 13 (3) 1964, 133.
101 G. H. Pitt to Jean Whyte, July 30th, 1964. SLSA: PRG 1335/3-4.

102 Jean Whyte. 'A policy for the Library Association of Australia? An editorial'. *ALJ* 13 (2) 1964, 57.
103 'Statement of Principles on Freedom to Read'. *ALJ* 13 (3) 1964, 136.
104 Derek Fielding. 'Censorship'. In Harrison Bryan, ed., *ALIAS*, 1988–1991. Vol. 1, 142–144.
105 'Censorship in Sandringham'. *ALJ* 18 (11) 1969, 394.
106 Jean Whyte. 'Namoi Regional Library bans "The thin red line"'. *ALJ* 13 (1) 1964, 17. The Library Board of NSW and the LAA were able to stop the Library banning the book (Jean Whyte. 'Trends abroad: Australia'. *Library Trends* 19 (1) 1970, 122–130).
107 Jean Whyte. 'Trends abroad: Australia'. *Library Trends* 19 (1) 1970, 122–130.
108 W.J. McEldowney. *Geoffrey Alley, Librarian*, 2006, 412.
109 Jean Whyte to M. J. Ramsden, November 5th, 1974. NLA: MS 9616.
110 'Branches and Sections'. *ALJ* 5 (4) 1956, 147.
111 Library Association of Australia. 'Annual Report, Branches and Sections'. *ALJ* 7 (3) 1958, 92.
112 Jean Whyte to S. Acutt, October 26th, 1982. MON 1059: 2000/68. 46.
113 Jean Whyte. 'Waltzing with Matilda', 1988, 85.
114 Jean Whyte. 'Head not heart'. *ALJ* 26 (10) 18, 1977, 326–328.
115 Helen M. Modra. 'The Short March', 1986, 195–197, 208–209.
116 Jean Whyte. 'Are we failing our public?' *ALJ* 15 (1) 1966, 19.
117 Jean Whyte. 'A word from Callimachus'. *ALJ* 6 (3) 1957, 98.
118 Jean Whyte. 'Position application and curriculum vitae', 1959. NLA: MS 9616.
119 Jean Whyte to E.L. Knaus, August 2nd, 1973. NLA: MS 9616.
120 Jean Whyte to Andrew Osborn, January 2nd, 1959. SU: M 465.
121 Jean Whyte to K. Enderby, June 15th, 1973. NLA: MS 9616.
122 Jean Whyte. [Notes for a speech prepared for a celebration of the conferring of the award of Order of Australia on Harrison Bryan], [1984]. NLA: MS 9616.
123 Jean Whyte to Andrew Osborn, December 30th, 1958. SU: M 465.
124 Transcript of a conversation between Jean Whyte and Geoffrey Alley, 1981. MON 1059: 2000/68/5.
125 G. H. Pitt to Jean Whyte, May, 1971. SLSA: PRG 1335/3-4.
126 Neil A. Radford. 'Obituaries. Jean Primrose Whyte AM', [2003].
127 Brian McMullin. 'Yadlamalka girl shaped Australian librarianship'. *The Age*, April 18th–19th, 2003, 19.
128 Harrison Bryan. 'Some comments and an occasional rejoinder', 1988, 248.
129 James R. Cox to Jean Whyte, November 18th, 1988. NLA: MS 9616.
130 Ray Olding. Personal communication, August 8th, 2008.
131 Interview: Frank Upward, 2008.
132 Rachel Salmond. Personal communication, 2008.
133 Interview: Ross Harvey, 2005.
134 Jean Whyte to Andrew Osborn, February 21st, 1959. SU: M 465.
135 Alan Fleming to Jean Whyte, March 24th, 1972. NLA: MS 9616.
136 Jean Whyte to Andrew Osborn, January 3rd, 1959. SU: M 465.
137 Jean Whyte. 'Position application and curriculum vitae', 1959. NLA: MS 9616.

138 Jean Whyte. 'New service for Wombat Beach'. *ALJ* 26 (1) 18, 1977, 9.

139 Although I note lending organizations as an area of librarianship in which Jean was not involved, she might argue that it was not an area of librarianship; I include it here because it is a subject discussed by librarians.

140 Jean Whyte. Review of *Information indexing and subject cataloging, alphabetical: classified, coordinate: mechanical* by John Metcalfe. *ALJ* 6 (4) 1957, 187.

141 Jean began having the PLSA collection reclassified to the Colon Classification before she left for Sydney (the reclassification was abandoned soon after).

142 Harrison Bryan. 'Jean Primrose Whyte'. *ALJ* 38 (1) 1989, 14.

143 Jean Whyte to the Secretary, American Association of University Women, 1952. NLA: MS 9616.

144 Ibid.

145 Jean Whyte. 'Curriculum vitae', [1972?]. NLA: MS 9616.

146 'Doubling the number'. *Canberra Times,* September 28th, 1972.

147 'Valuable grant for study in U.S.'. *Advertiser* [SA], March 18th, 1953, 11.

148 Jean Whyte. 'Second Report to American Association of University Women', 1954. NLA: MS 9616.

149 This was the generally acknowledged view at the time. Osborn recommended Harrison Bryan as his successor, not Whyte. Jean did not apply for the position of Librarian at Macquarie University in 1971 following the death of Barry Scott, and Bryan records that he proposed Eoin Wilkinson for the position (Harrison Bryan. *No Gray Profession*, 1994, 68).

150 For example, Malvina E. Wood was Librarian of the University of Western Australia (1927–1959).

151 Monash University Council. 'Minute of Appreciation. Professor J.P. Whyte', 1989. NLA: MS 9616.

152 Brian McMullin. 'Yadlamalka girl shaped Australian librarianship'. *The Age,* April 18th–19th, 2003, 19.

153 'Doubling the number'. *Canberra Times,* September 28th, 1972.

154 Andrew Osborn to Jean Whyte, May 15th, 1973. SU: M 465.

155 Geoffrey Alley to Jean Whyte, July 25th, 1974. J. McEldowney Personal Collection, Dunedin, New Zealand.

156 Neil A. Radford. 'Harrison Bryan, Librarian', 1988, 2. Were all things equal? Jean had overseas qualifications but was still not appointed to positions gained by men with less experience and lesser qualifications.

157 Interview: Ross Harvey, 2005.

158 Jean Whyte and Neil A. Radford. 'Obituaries'. *The Australian,* May 7th, 1997, 14.

159 The others were Maureen Brunt in Economics, appointed in 1966, Enid Campbell in Law (1967), Mollie Holman in a personal chair in Physiology (1970), and Marie Neale who was a research professor in Education (1970) (Simon Marginson. *Remaking the University,* 2000, 34).

160 'Woman takes new chair at Monash'. *Standard Times* [Carnegie, Victoria], January 15th, 1975.

161 Jean Whyte to the Editor, *Canberra Times,* January 10th, 1975.

162 G. H. Pitt to Jean Whyte, July 24th, 1948. SLSA: PRG 1335/3-4.

163 G. H. Pitt to Jean Whyte, June 2nd, 1968. SLSA: PRG 1335/3-4.

164 Susan Magarey and Kerrie Round. *Roma the first,* 2007, 21.

165 'Mitchell, Roma Flinders'. In Graeme Davison, John Hirst and Stuart Macintyre, eds. *Oxford Companion to Australian history,* 1998, 432–433.

166. Interview: Grecian and Ross Day, 2008.
167. Ibid.
168. Transcript of a conversation between Jean Whyte and Geoffrey Alley, 1981. MON 1059: 2000/68/5.
169. Andrew Osborn to Jean Whyte, October 15th, 1961. SU: M 465.
170. Jean Whyte. 'The librarian's task, 1962: an editorial'. *ALJ* 11 (2) 1962, 55–60.
171. Transcript of a conversation between Jean Whyte and Geoffrey Alley, 1981. MON 1059: 2000/68/5.
172. Jean Whyte. 'Some Reminiscences of Geoffrey Alley', 1995, 1. J. McEldowney Personal Collection, Dunedin, New Zealand.
173. Jean Whyte and Neil A. Radford. 'Obituaries'. *The Australian*, May 7th, 1997, 14.
174. G.R. Manton. [Notes for a speech prepared for the retirement of Hector Monro], 1976. MON 1059: 2000/68. 82.
175. *Community Library Matters*, 2004.
176. Ibid.
177. Interview: John Legge, 2008.
178. Interview: Jane and Gordon Monro, 2005.
179. Harrison Bryan. 'Jean Primrose Whyte'. *ALJ* 38 (1) 1989, 6.
180. 'Late start, but Jean Whyte has the last word'. *Monash Reporter*, 9–88, 1988.
181. Interview: Brian McMullin, 2008.
182. Interview: Douglas Muecke, 2005.
183. Ibid.
184. Jean Whyte. 'Qualifications necessary for joining the staff of the Public Library of S.A.'. *Foggy Dew* 1 (7) 1956.
185. 'Minute of Appreciation. Professor J.P. Whyte', 1989. NLA: MS 9616.
186. Jean Whyte to D. Bradley, September 10th, 1981. MON 1059: 2000/68. 42.
187. Transcript of a conversation between Jean Whyte and Geoffrey Alley, 1981. MON 1059: 2000/68/5.
188. Ibid.
189. The subject of Jean's Adelaide M.A. was to have been the Australian literary ballad ('Valuable grant for study in U.S.'. *Advertiser* [SA], March 18th, 1953, 11), which she had hoped to complete by June 1952 (Jean Whyte to the Secretary, American Association of University Women, 1952. NLA: MS 9616). I have been unable to ascertain the subject of Jean's planned Sydney Master's (Honours) thesis; it may have been the seventeenth-century author Katharine Phillips, perhaps as a result of the first part of the Macdonald collection arriving in Sydney (Brian McMullin. Personal communication, May 3rd, 2006).
190. *Australian Literature in Tertiary Libraries: Project Report*, 1987; Margaret Isaacs, Linda Emmett and Jean P. Whyte. *Libraries and Australian literature*, 1988.
191. Interview: Sara Miranda, 2008.
192. Interview: Grecian and Ross Day, 2008.
193. Interview: Elizabeth Morrison, 2008.
194. Brian McMullin. 'Yadlamalka girl shaped Australian librarianship'. *The Age*, April 18th–19th, 2003, 19.
195. Interview: Harrison Bryan, 2005.

196 Brian McMullin. 'Yadlamalka girl shaped Australian librarianship'. *The Age*, April 18th–19th, 2003, 19.
197 Jean Whyte to Andrew Osborn, January 28th, 1959; SU: M 465.
198 Jean Whyte to Andrew Osborn, February 15th, 1959. SU: M 465.
199 Jean Whyte to Andrew Osborn, February 21st, 1959. SU: M 465.
200 Interview: Joan Barry, 2005.
201 Interview: Douglas Muecke, 2005.
202 Interview: Grecian and Ross Day, 2008.
203 G. H. Pitt to Jean Whyte, April 15th, 1969. SLSA: PRG 1335/3-4.
204 B.J. Zerman. [Medical report], 1981. NLA: MS 9616.
205 Jean Whyte to Andrew Osborn, February 18th, 1959. SU: M 465.
206 B.J. Zerman. [Medical report], 1981. NLA: MS 9616.; Interview: Douglas Muecke, 2005.
207 Interview: Brian McMullin, 2008.
208 Interview: Ray Olding, 2008.
209 Interview: Douglas Muecke, 2005.
210 Jean Whyte. 'Position application and curriculum vitae', 1959. NLA: MS 9616.
211 Jean Whyte. 'The Accreditation of Courses in Librarianship', 1974, 593 (quoting Matthew 18:20).
212 Jean Whyte. 'Direct service to readers', 1977, 312 (quoting John 10:10).
213 Jean Whyte. 'Doubts at midnight'. *Foggy Dew* 1 (1) 1956 (quoting Mark 12:17).
214 Jean Whyte. 'Position application and curriculum vitae', 1959. NLA: MS 9616.
215 Neil A. Radford. 'Obituaries. Jean Primrose Whyte AM', [2003].
216 Interview: Grecian and Ross Day, 2008.
217 Jean Whyte. 'Head not heart'. *ALJ* 26 (10) 18, 1977, 326.
218 David J. Jones. Personal communication, April 3rd, 2006.
219 Ibid.
220 Roma Mitchell. 'To whom it may concern', May 11th, 1956. NLA: MS 9616. I wonder whether this was written for Jean's unsuccessful application for a position at Melbourne University.
221 Interview: Neil Radford, 2005.
222 Brian McMullin. Personal communication, May 3rd, 2006.
223 Neil A. Radford. 'Notes for talk at Jean Whyte's funeral', 2003.
224 Interview: Michael Talbot, 2005.
225 Jean Whyte to Andrew Osborn, February 21st, 1959. SU: M 465.
226 ['From "One of his many friends"']. [Newspaper clipping], [1921]. SLSA: PRG 1335/10.
227 'Obituaries. Rev. Alexander Macully, M.A., LL.B.'. *The Observer* [SA], January 15th, 1921, 34b.
228 Interview: Wallace Kirsop, 2008.
229 John Levett. 'In conclusion'. *ALJ* 36 (4) 1987, 292–295.
230 'Lectures for Institutes'. *South Australian Institutes' Journal*, June–July 1915, 674.
231 Susan Magarey and Kerrie Round. *Roma the first*, 2007, 152.
232 *Community Library Matters*, 2004.
233 Interview: Elizabeth Morrison, 2008.

234 Harrison Bryan. 'Jean Primrose Whyte'. *ALJ* 38 (1) 1989, 14.

235 Jean Whyte to Andrew Osborn, January 14th, 1959. SU: M 465.

236 Ibid.

237 Prim did not have an easy life: he lived most of his life in lonely, remote areas; he was widowed shockingly and suddenly; he had experienced the horrors of World War I; he had brought up children alone in the bush; and he found retirement to the suburbs difficult (Interview: Mavis Crawford, 2008). Some of these experiences may have contributed to mental illness in later life. He is buried in the Macully family plot at St Jude's Cemetery, Brighton, with his wives Kitty and Eileen, their sister Norah and their parents Maria Julia and Alexander, with a plaque to remember Arnold, who died in France.

Billie died in September 2005 – although she was still alive while this book was being written it was not possible to interview her.

The information on Prim's medical condition came from his case notes, which are held on microfiche in the Medical Records Department, Glenside Campus of the Royal Adelaide Hospital.

238 Rachel Salmond. Personal communication, September 13th, 2008.

239 Interview: John Legge, 2008; Interview: Grecian and Ross Day, 2008.

240 Interview: Douglas Muecke, 2005.

241 John Levett. *Obituary. Remembering Jean Whyte*, 2003.

242 Mavis Crawford. 'Emeritus Professor Jean Primrose Whyte, AM'.

243 'The unknown anniversary'. In A.D. Hope's *Orpheus*. North Ryde, NSW: Angus and Robertson, 1991, 36–37. Reproduced courtesy of Curtis Brown Literary Agents on behalf of the Estate of A.D. Hope.

⭕ EPILOGUE

who in his senses would live the same life over, if he had to live again? And yet
– I'd still be a librarian[1]

The last time I saw Jean she was with Hector. We met, by chance, on a train. We talked, we said goodbye.

ENDNOTE

[1] Jean Whyte to Andrew Osborn, February 8th, 1959. SU: M 465.

APPENDIX 1

A WORD FROM CALLIMACHUS

This Presidential Address was delivered to the South Australian Branch of the Library Association of Australia on 28th November 1956. Reproduced from 'A word from Callimachus'. *Australian Library Journal* 6 (3) 1957, 95–100. Courtesy Australian Library and Information Association.

A Word from Callimachus[1]

By Jean P. Whyte, B.A., A.M.

Before Friday, 16th November, if you had asked me who Callimachus was, I would have said that he was the librarian of the Alexandrian Library, that he was a Greek poet and scholar, and that he was one of the first librarians whose name we know (and, incidentally, the first "literary gent" to run a library), and all of these things are true, but they are by no means the whole story. For Callimachus is like Merlin, or Peter Pan, or Rip Van Winkle. He is not dead—he has lived as long as the world has had libraries, and he lives today. I saw him last night in the stacks. I regret that he could not come to our meeting tonight; in fact I fear that I shall not see him again, but some of you who are younger than I am may be here to greet him when he returns.

If only I could read and speak Greek! For much of Callimachus's story can only be told in that language and I could not even listen with understanding. Some of his life as a librarian in Rome I did understand, but my Latin and yours is not good enough to enable me to tell you. So I have skipped the early part of his life until I come to that part of his story which can be told in English—to the days when this poet was a librarian in the English Monastery of York. He was the librarian in the monastery from A.D. 600 (he was absent on a journey to Italy for a few years, when Alcuin took over the library; but as you know, Alcuin left the monastery in A.D. 796 to journey to Tours and set up his school of calligraphy). At first, Callimachus wrote his poems almost entirely in Latin, and indeed he told me that the Anglo-Saxon which the native English were speaking at the time seemed a barbarous language to him—until he met an English monk called Caedmon. Caedmon was a poet, and he admired some hexameters which Callimachus had written, so Callimachus asked to read some of Caedmon's own verse. This verse was a revelation to Callimachus. He liked the strongly accented Anglo-Saxon lines and towards the end of the eighth century he wrote a number of poems in Anglo-Saxon under the pseudonym of Cynewulf.

The monastic library was not, as I had expected, entirely devoted to religious works and canon law. Perhaps because Callimachus was a poet, he collected poems and stories written not only in Latin but also in French and Anglo-Saxon. Among these manuscripts were those of Gawain and the Green Knight, Pearl, and Piers the Plowman. We have not been able to prove the authorship of Piers the Plowman and I have a theory that Callimachus knew more about the author than he cared to admit. Certainly he used the same verse rhythms with ease:

To him who beareth the book: behold we are bounden
For that wight hath wisdome: well favoured is he
Who hereth high mystery: and in his herte keepeth.
And loveth to lerne: and for men illumine
The sayings of the Savior: and Son of the Highest.

But derkely the devil: deleth with the dremer
Privately promising: power over all men.
Grete care must he carry: the Keeper of Knowledge,
That servants of Satan: sit not in scriptorum.
He checketh the cheater: with chains on his volumes.
Lest wicked wights steleth: the wordes of wisdome.

In about 1400, Callimachus set off for China and the East. He returned to Europe in the middle of the fifteenth century to find the monasteries and the universities which were springing up everywhere buzzing with the news of the invention of printing. Callimachus was a scholar, and a poet, and a librarian. He loved books and believed in

[1] This Presidential Address was delivered to the South Australian Branch of the Library Association of Australia on 28th November, 1956.

their value as preservers of the records upon which his world was based. And he loved the beauty of the volumes in the monastic libraries — the old Irish half-uncials and the clear rounded script of the Carolingian Minuscule — with their ornate illuminations. But he had been in the universities, and had seen the poorly written, ugly books, which the students hired from the stationarii, and he had regretted the lack of texts for study. So he greeted the advent of printing with mixed feelings:

> Johannes Gutenberg,
> Goldsmith of Mainz,
> John Fust, the Master
> And Peter Schoeffer
> Have lightened our travail
> And given us volumes,
> Not written with labour,
> By Scribe at his carrel,
> But printed in numbers
> A hundred together,
> So all men here-after,
> May buy books and read them.
> Ah, woe that the beauty,
> Of hand-written volumes,
> Has vanished forever!
> And those who would question
> Their rulers and betters,
> Can send through the Kingdom,
> Their treasonous pamphlets,
> And heretics scatter
> Their lies to the four winds.
> For books are no longer
> The precious possessions,
> Of priest and of prelate,
> Of statesman and student.
> And soon like the sea-sand
> They'll grow beyond number:
> And though the King's axes,
> And all the Queen's tortures
> Do battle against it,
> The press and the printer
> Shall never stop working.

The days of the monastic libraries were numbered in England, and the next hundred years were turbulent ones — and not good for such inflammable objects as books. In the British Isles the spirit of nationalism grew ever more violent.

Callimachus was in the Library of the University of Aberdeen when it was founded in 1494. The country was awake to the importance of books — in the towns of Edinburgh and Aberdeen the townspeople were admitted to the University libraries. The principal towns of Scotland had lecture schools in which reading in the vernacular was taught.

In 1496 Scotland's first compulsory Education Act was passed. This Act bade "all freeholders that are of substance put their eldest sons and heirs to schools from the age of six to nine years". And "thereafter to spend three years at schools of arts or law".

Throughout the fifteenth and early sixteenth centuries, Scotland was the home of the greatest poets writing in English, and Callimachus contributed something to that literature. His greatest friend in Scotland was Gavin Douglas, Bishop of Dunkeld, who first translated Virgil into the Scottish tongue, and truly did Douglas express the growing pride in the vernacular literature when he finished his twelve-year labour with the hope:

> Now salt though with every gentil Scot be kend,
> And to onletterit folk be red on hycht,
> That erst was bot with clerkis comprehend.
> . . . . .
> Sen Virgyll beys wydguar in Latyn sung,
> Thus beys my labour red in owr vulgar tung.

Around about 1600, Callimachus was putting away books in the Guild-Hall Library in London when in walked a gentleman in the doublet and hose of the day. He had a small pointed beard, and his forehead was high and wide, but the librarian remembered his eyes most vividly — brown and very bright and intelligent.

He asked for Holinshed's "Chronicles". Callimachus gave him the book and left him seated at a table. As he passed the reader's chair an hour later he glanced at the paper on which the man was writing and saw:

> . . . . Remember,
> First to possess his books; for without them
> He's but a sot as I am.

The Bodleian Library was opened at Oxford in 1602. We have many letters written by Bodley to his Librarian James, or as we know, Callimachus. The librarian's life was not always a happy one, and in fact some of Bodley's advice and conditions of employment seem a little impertinent:

> Sir, Concerning your letter of the 8. of this moneth, I haue not nowe the leasure, so to answear it all, as ether I am desirous, or some pointes thereof require. But yet if yow please, to weigh that little that I write, with a ballance

of a staied and untroubled judgement, I doe not doubt but I shall giue yow very good satisfaction. And first where yow wonder at my suddaine flatte denial of your continuance in that place, if so be yow should be maried: I did wonder as muche, to see yow come upon the suddaine, when I was ready to depart, and require to be resolved, what yerely stipend yow might trust to: because yow meant, as yow said, to resign your felowship very shortly, and might determine withall, to take a wife: for whiche your state would haue neede, of 40li stipend at the lest. This your abrupt and untimely demaund, with unusual termes and wordes, did seeme to me so very strange, as I complained unto yow, of your ouer late proposal, of a mater of that weight, when I was ready to begonne. Howbeit mine answear I am sure, was frindly and considerat. That yow should alwaies be assured of 20li from me, and that in time I made no question of raising it further to 20 or 30 more: whereof notwithstanding, I could not as yet giue any assurance. But for the point of your marriage, I might by no means yelde unto it: holding it absurd in yow or in any, for sundrie great respectes: neither did I, as I signified, see any necessitie of giuing ouer your fellowship . . . . Thus wishing to that humour which bredde the subject of this letter, all the purging that may be, and yourself all the good that you hart can desire, I betake both yow and all your actions, to God's good direction.

your unchangeable frind
Tho. Bodley.[1]

Nevertheless, Callimachus believed that his library would one day be the pride not only of Oxford but of the world:

Where the sweet Thames meanders on her way,
The gentle towers of Thomas Bodley rise,
Here shall the eager scholar spend his day,
On volumes that the world shall ever prize.
Here calm and peace dwell with neglected time,
While scholars study dream and history,
To give the world back some forgotten rime,
Or find some clue to nature's mystery.
Here shall the men of nations yet to be,
Pore over volumes by their world un-read,
And in the peace of Bodley's Library,
Shall keep the scholar's bargain with the dead.
And though his eyes see not those later days,
All men who enter shall speak Bodley's praise.

For Callimachus the seventeenth century was on the whole not very exciting. Of course, as a man of letters he found the company of Pepys and Milton exhilarating, and that of Congreve and Wycherley and the other dramatists of the Restoration disturbing. In fact, to a man who remembered the glories of the Elizabethan stage, the light-hearted frippery of the Restoration seemed very insignificant.

He seems to have spent most of his time in the Bodleian Library, with a few journeys, such as his trip to Scotland to the opening of the Advocates Library, and his voyage to France to see his friend Gustave Naude, Librarian of Mazarin's Library. Naude's influence on Callimachus was considerable. He insisted that a library should contain not only the accepted classics, but also the works of contemporary authors: not only works written in support of the true religion, but also the works of the principal "heretics or adherents of religions that are new and that differ from the one more commonly revered among ourselves as being more sound and true". And he also expressed in no uncertain terms his belief that the library should be open to all who wished to use it:

Nothing now lacks to complete these instructions except to grasp their object and chief application: for to suppose that after all this trouble and expense these lights should be hidden under a bushel and so many great minds condemned to everlasting silence and solitude is to understand ill the purpose of a library, which, no more or less than Nature herself, is doomed to lose all profit of itself, should it exhibit to solitude things so great, so noteworthy, so subtly formed, so resplendent, so beautiful (and beautiful not in one regard alone); it would, as you know, prefer to be examined, not merely looked at. Therefore I shall tell you, Monseigneur, with as much freedom as I have affection for your service, that in vain does he go to any great expense for books who does not intend to devote them to the public use and never to withhold them from the humblest of those who may reap any benefit thereby.

Callimachus made his first visit to the American continent in 1699, when he went with Dr. Thomas Bray, who was busily founding parochial libraries in Maryland.

Callimachus told me that he considered that the most important happening for libraries in the seventeenth century was the founding of the Royal Society in 1660 and the beginning of the publication of newspapers and periodicals. And, of course, the most important publication of the century from the librarian's viewpoint was Milton's "Areopagitica".

When Callimachus told me that he considered Allan Ramsay's Edinburgh Cir-

---

[1] Bodley, Thomas: Letter 14. To James. From Burnham, Sept. 11, 1601. In Thornton, J., Mirror for Librarians, p. 28.

culating Library, founded in 1725, to be a great step forward in the provision of libraries I was amazed. But he laughed at me.

"Remember", he said, "I speak of the eighteenth century, not the twentieth! Before the world could produce the free public library it had to learn the value of books, and these libraries helped."

But the great event of the eighteenth century was the founding of the British Museum. You remember the story of its foundation: Sir Hans Sloane left his collection for purchase by the nation and the British Museum Trustees decided to hold a lottery and to raise the money with which to buy a building, and to house not only Sloane's collection, but also the collection of Robert Cotton and the Harleian Manuscripts.

Here are Callimachus's verses on its opening in 1759:

This day we have opened the British Museum
All men of good will now should sing the Te Deum.
And rejoice that our London and not the Bodleian
Holds not and forever manuscripts Harliean,
May the labours of Sloane and collections of Cotton,
Be used by the student and never forgotten.
Because the Archbishop frowned not upon chance
Our Britain no longer will lag behind France.
For here will historians gather to read
The works which the present and future should heed.
And here will the students of politics write
The books that will alter our world overnight.
And we shall preserve while the paper shall last,
The hopes of the present, the dreams of the past.

I detected in these verses a growing interest in the unrestricted use of libraries, so I was not in the least surprised when Callimachus told me that his term as librarian of the Glasgow Mechanics' Institute convinced him that all citizens should have free access to books. It seems that he helped Edward Edwards and William Ewart in their fight for free rate-supported libraries throughout the United Kingdom, and he certainly rejoiced when the Act was passed in 1850:

No bells ring out in church or street,
 No village echoes with men's cheers
But in my ever listening ears—
 I hear a million hurrying feet,

And in my dreams I see them tread,
 The steps of buildings yet to be,
 And entering their library,
They prove the wisdom of the dead.

For long has knowledge kept her tower
 From days when priests and Kings ruled all,
 Until today the ramparts fall
And to the common man comes power.

No longer tied by class or fee,
 The poorest student now may read,
 For Britain here hath done a deed,
Which sets men's brains and spirits free.

May wisdom walk with knowledge still,
 May those who read find truth and light,
 Librarians defend the right
Of man to read what 'ere he will.

After the passing of this Act, Callimachus felt that he would like a holiday, so he set out for the United States, arriving in 1870 (and I wondered whether his arrival had anything to do with the excitement of the American librarians at that time). The first man that he met was a young student at Amherst College. This dark-eyed young man was full of what seemed to Callimachus rather crazy ideas (and remember that Callimachus had lived long enough to know the value of crazy ideas), so he listened to the young man, and, incidentally, the Decimal Classification owes a great deal of its acceptance to the fact that Callimachus managed to dissuade its author from putting Metaphysics next to Witchcraft under the general heading of Humbugs and Quackery, and that he insisted that Literature should not be made a subdivision of the Social Sciences.

Callimachus was present at the meeting in 1876 at which the American Library Association was formed. Here is his description of the proceedings:

Up rose Melvil Kossuth Dewey,
He was young and he was eager.
At his side Charles Ami Cutter
Not so young, but just as eager,
And they spoke unto the meeting
Spoke as prophets of the future,
And the others heard the message
Of these leaders in their wisdom:
"We will talk of cataloging
Till the last moon wanes forever,
Many rules will prove no stronger
Than the reed beside the river.
Above all we shall make whoopee
At our annual bigtime pow-wow."

From the United States Callimachus paid his first visit to the southern hemisphere.

He arrived in Adelaide in 1884—just in time to see the opening of the Public Library of South Australia. One of the impressive things about Callimachus is the way in which he picks up the current verse techniques of the day. And he did confess that he had been reading the *Bulletin* before writing this verse:

> In a distant Southern country
> Far from London's smoke and steam,
> The South Australian Company
> Tried Edward Wakefield's dream.
>
> They were gentlemen of substance,
> Freely did they come and stay,
> And they didn't look with favour
> On the folk of Botany Bay.
>
> When the ships sailed out from Plymouth,
> "Tam-o'-shanter", "Buffalo",
> With the Governor and surveyor,
> There were books stored up below.
>
> Through the years of drought and heat-wave,
> Never beaten, oft dismayed—
> Still the gentlemen of England,
> And the German peasants stayed.
>
> And their newspapers waxed fatter
> Till in 1884
> The men of South Australia
> Recalled 1834.
>
> They remembered Robert Gouger,
> And the hundred books that he
> Had gathered in Old England,
> For their public library.
>
> Most were lost but in their places,
> They had 13,000 more,
> So they thought they'd get some culture
> In 1884.
>
> Samuel Way and Richard Benham,
> (May their glory never fade)
> And a dozen other gentlemen,
> Of prosperous Adelaide.
>
> Founded, and then wisely governed,
> A State Public Library.
> So the men of South Australia
> Could get light and culture free!

I do not really know very much about Callimachus's wanderings in Australia, but he did leave this comment on the Mitchell Library. As you remember, David Scott Mitchell, who owned a property in the Hunter River district, N.S.W., and who spent his early life collecting books on English literature, turned to the collection of Australiana, and left to the Public Library of New South Wales the greatest collection of Australiana that this country possesses.

> 'Twas the man from Hunter River,
> Who struck the Sydney Town
> And he soon began to quiver
> As he wandered up and down.
> He wandered here, he wandered there till he was like to drop,
> Until at last he came upon a second-hand book shop.
>
> "No more for me the labour great,
> Of choosing English manna,
> A fallow field for me doth wait
> In this Australiana.
> I here declare that naught on earth can force me now to stop,
> I'll be the favoured customer of every good book shop.
>
> And when my book collecting's done
> And I from hope and sin am free,
> I shall bequeath them, every one,
> To New South Wales State Library.
> I'll leave no dead collection, to be a certain flop,
> But I shall leave them cash to spend in every good book shop."
>
> So Mitchell left the books that he
> Collected with such skill,
> To New South Wales State Library,
> And stated in his will
> That ever in the library the volumes had to stop,
> And gave them cash galore to spend in every good book shop.

As I mentioned at the beginning of my talk, I saw Callimachus in the stacks last night. On seeing him I hoped that I would be able to find out a good deal more about his impressions of Australian librarianship and in fact of librarianship in general. I would like, for instance, to know what he thinks of documentation. Whether he thinks that librarians ought to go to charm schools. What he thinks of Enid Blyton. But, alas, I didn't have a chance to ask him any of these questions. His first words to me were:

"Well, I must go now, but I hope that I shall be back."

"Why the hope? Why do you doubt? What could prevent you from coming back?" I asked.

He looked at me quizzically.

"I live only as long as libraries live", he said.

"And how long do you think that will be?" I asked. "Have you not powers to see into the future?"

JULY, 1957

Like a flash came his answer.

"There is no predetermined future to see into. It depends on you. But I know a great deal about the past, and I rather think that if libraries disappear from the earth the past and the present will also perish. However", he said, "I must be going. Here is my message to yourself and and your colleagues. I have had considerable trouble with it. The language has deteriorated since 1600 and I am afraid I can't write in the style of Eliot or Auden."

I took the piece of paper and read it. And I shall now read it to you:

To you who toil in stacks and fetch and carry
The books the world holds cheap, but loses dear.
I speak to you, librarians, and ask
That you should hearken to my words, for I
Am a librarian — I too have felt
The shaking ladder underneath my feet,
I have stamped dates upon a million cards
And staggered 'neath the weight of newspapers.
My friends, like yours, have envied me because
They think that all I do is read the books.
(And even as I'm angrily denying
The charge, I've known that I do not read
Enough — and wondered how I ever can?)
More than two thousand years have passed since I
First sorted rolls in Alexandria,
And I have seen the fires of chance and hate
Burn through more volumes than your world
    possesses.
And I have heard men twist the written word
To serve their dream of power. Have seen men
    change
The truth of history for a tyrant's end.
It is not long, as I can measure time,
Since books were not the right of every man.
And even now I see they are denied
To more than half the men who live on earth.
Ah yes! I know that knowledge walks with
    power,
And, without Wisdom, is a dangerous gift.
I know that books are bad as well as good.
But hear me — I am no hot headed youth —
I say there is no future for this world
I say that there is but little time,
Unless men learn the lessons that are held
In books and libraries. These lessons are
The *truth* that all we have and all we are,
We are, because each age, each creed, each
    nation,
Has given us something that we would not lose.
The *joy* that comes from literature, and from
The growing of a bigger, better rose.
The *faith* that comes from history and religion;
The *love* that comes from knowledge of mankind.
And you, who keep the libraries of the world,
Your task is harder than it's ever been.
The world is flooded with the written word —
You must preserve, select, and see that men
Can find and use the books, the magazines
The pamphlets, maps and microfilms, on which
The present and the future both depend.
More loud and strident grows the radio,
The newspaper, the T.V. and the film,
More urgent is your task to cater for
The individual — not "the audience".
So to your task, and know the task you do
Requires more knowledge than you'll ever have,
Needs more devotion than you'll ever give,
Gives few rewards — that other men respect.
Only the satisfaction that you serve
The cause of human happiness. That you
Preserve and put into the hands of others
The bricks and mortar that we need to make
The world in which we live: the precious stones
Of Truth and Beauty that do make us men.

JEAN P. WHYTE.

NEW SOUTH WALES BRANCH CONFERENCE

It has been pointed out to the Editor that there were some omissions from our account in the April issue of the New South Wales Branch Conference: "Reading and Research in a Technological Age", held in October last year. Our account mentioned two papers given to General Sessions at the Conference but we omitted that Miss Jean F. Arnot gave a paper entitled "Library Methods" and that Miss Barbara Johnston, B.Sc., gave a paper entitled "Library Equipment and Materials".

We also omitted to mention that the University Libraries Section had a discussion on "University Library Building Plans" and at a joint session with the Special Libraries Section heard addresses by Miss E. G. Stanley, B.A., and Mr. E. H. Wilkinson, B.A., entitled "Periodicals — their Acquisition, Circulation, Research, Use and Preservation". An address on "Literature of the Visual Fine Arts in New South Wales" was also given by Mr. H. G. Kaplan.

Regulations Under the New South Wales
    Library Act, 1939-1952 —— 10pt. Bl. Caps

Members will be interested to know that in February of this year, at the request of the Library Board of New South Wales, the New South Wales Government introduced regulations which provide for the issue of Certificates of Competency as Librarians and as Library Assistants by the Library Board of New South Wales, and also prescribe the circumstances under which Councils operating public library services are required to employ librarians holding Certificates of Competency.

APPENDIX 2
'SUCH A MIXTURE OF CONTRADICTIONS': ALEXANDER MACULLY

Alexander Macully was a Professor of Elocution, an Anglican priest, a poet, and, for a short time, a bankrupt.[1] He was renowned in his time as a great interpreter of Shakespeare. The mansions built for him still stand: 'Cullymont' in Canterbury, Victoria, and 'Dunluce' in Brighton, South Australia. He was an interesting old codger, worthy of memory. Here his story is told using his obituary from the Adelaide *Observer* as a framework.[2]

> Rev. Alexander Macully, M.A., LL.B.
>
> The death occurred on Saturday of the Rev. Alexander Macully, M.A., LL.B., at his residence, Dunluce, Brighton, at the age of 74 years. Mr. Macully was widely known.
>
> He was born in the cathedral city of Armagh, Ireland.

Alexander Macully claimed to have been born in Armagh, Ireland, in 1847. His father, noted in many documents, was G. John James Macully (sometimes without the initial G). His mother's name is never mentioned. This omission drew me initially to find out more about Alexander Macully: I am working on the biography of his granddaughter, Jean Primrose Whyte, foundation professor in the Monash University Graduate School of Librarianship, and, having taken notes on her family history, found that Macully's mother was not named in family records, nor anywhere else. I began looking for, but was unable to trace, Macully's birth record. He may have been born in Ireland, but, as his obituaries are selective in the material they use – perhaps because Macully was likewise selective – and his Irish connections important to him, I wondered whether the Irish birthplace may have been a romantic fabrication. This concern led eventually to the discovery of early newspaper articles which referred to Macully being 'an Australian native', who, after studying in Ireland, returned to Australia 'the land of his birth'.[3]

> When he was a child his parents emigrated to Melbourne, and there his father occupied an important position in the Civil Service for about 35 years.

John James had a civil-service career and was wealthy. A poster for the auction of 'Cullymont' at 2 Molesworth Street, Canterbury:

> 'Cullymont' was built as two adjoining residences as a 'Country Retreat' for John James McCully and his son Reverend Alexander McCully. Built in 1889, it was first occupied by them in 1890, and bears the McCully coat of arms with the clan motto 'Vi et Animo' (by strength and courage) ... possibly Victoria's largest semi-detached pair of mansion houses ... listed by the National Trust ... 'Cullymont' features intricately detailed stained glass roundels in the sidelights and transom of the front door depicting Shakespearian characters, reflecting the younger McCully's love of, and considerable talent for the theatre ... one of the finest grand family residences.[4]

Cullymont remains an impressive building, with the family's coat of arms mounted on the eastern wall of the house. The name 'Cullymont' begins with 'Cully' from Macully, perhaps 'mont' is from 'Rosemont', Alexander's wife's family home.

> He was educated at Scotch College, Melbourne, and distinguished himself in English literature, and obtained the first prize in elocution. He played cricket well, and occupied a place in the college eleven. Desiring to read for holy orders, he entered the famous Irish University, Trinity College, Dublin, and gained honours and took the degrees of M.A. and LL.B. During his college course he gained a host of friends, and was acknowledged as the first interpreter of literature, particularly Shakespeare, in Dublin. He gave several recitals in the hall of Trinity College, at the request of the Provost and Fellows. Edward Dowden, LL.D., Professor of English Literature, spoke of Mr. Macully in the following terms:- 'His naturally fine gifts of voice and expression were united with the gains which come from careful study. His rendering of the Hamlet scene was highly dramatic without ever over-stepping, I thought, the limits of right taste. Without attempting detailed criticism, I may sum up my impression by stating that Mr. Macully's second recital gave me an assurance of his remarkable power as a reader and reciter, and I believe made by appreciation of the portion of Shakespeare he rendered more full and accurate'.

He became one of Australia's most accomplished reciters of classic English literature, especially of Shakespeare: 'Mr. McCully is known amongst our *literati* as one of the ablest and most refined interpreters of our English classics'.[5] Macully composed and published poetry and wrote *The art of reading*, which was published in 1887.[6]

> In 1880, at Meath, Mr. Macully was ordained deacon by the Most Rev. Lord Plunket, of Meath, afterwards Archbishop of Dublin, and admitted to the order of priest by the Right Rev. William Alexander, Bishop of Derry, who was subsequently Primate of all Ireland [Church of Ireland, in the Anglican communion]. During his residence in Ireland he married a daughter of the Hon. Alexander Campbell, of Rosemont, Sydney.

'A daughter of the Hon. Alexander Campbell'. She was Maria (Minnie) Julia Campbell. Her father was the Honourable Alexander Campbell, MLC, JP, born in Scotland, who sailed to Sydney 'to seek his fortune'. He found it. He became a director, and, several times, the Chairman, of the Sydney Stock Exchange and a director of the Australian Mutual Provident Society; he founded the Mercantile Bank of Sydney, was manager of Agra and Masterman's Bank, a member of the Chamber of Commerce, and had various pastoral interests. He was a member of the Legislative Assembly of New South Wales and later of the Legislative Council, Postmaster-General and associate of Sir Henry Parkes. Campbell 'was prepared to give the working classes such liberties as did not affect the revenue. He was a vital member of Sydney's mercantile world and a shrewd businessman whose main concern both in private and in public was the advancement of the colony's commerce and trade'.[7] Like the Macullys, the Campbells were wealthy – from surviving photographs it is difficult to pick out the grandest mansion: the Campbells' 'Rosemont' in Sydney (which later became the home of Sir Charles and Lady Lloyd Jones), 'Cullymont' or Alexander and Minnie's 'Dunluce' in Adelaide.

The marriage of Minnie Campbell to Alexander Macully took place in Armagh and is described in a newspaper clipping headed 'Fashionable wedding in Armagh'.[8] Macully, who made a financial arrangement with his prospective father-in-law prior to the marriage, received an ample dowry.[9] Macully, at the time of his marriage, was Rector of Muff, County Donegal.

> For some years Mr. Macully took up the role of teaching in the colleges.

Macully combined his careers of elocution teacher and priest, sometimes doing one, most of the time both. He taught the Culture of the Speaking Voice and the Art of Reading at Trinity College and later in studios in Melbourne, Brisbane and Adelaide, teaching privately and in classes. He gave recitals in Ireland and in Australia and later was to lecture in poetry at various South Australian Institutes.

He was known as 'Professor Macully' from the time when, early in his career, he taught 'Elocution and Aesthetics of English Literature' at two ladies' colleges in Dublin – Alexandra College and the Rutland Square Institute. He was elected an Honorary Fellow of The Society of Science, Letters, and Art in London in 1885.

> In 1897 [sic] he returned to his work as a clergyman. In 1885 he was a curate at Bendigo, Victoria. During a brief sojourn in the Diocese of Brisbane, he built one of the most beautiful of its churches, at Clayfield, a suburb of the Queensland capital.

A small omission from the obituary is that for about three years (1888–1891?) he left the Anglicans to minister at the Unitarian Church, East Melbourne. There his 'aspirations toward religious freedom were not supported by any very strong convictions … he was only an enquirer in theological matters, and hence was not enthusiastically followed as a leader … Within a year a very serious falling off in attendance was manifested and before the term of his engagement was completed the congregation was fast approaching vanishing point'.[10]

While he was in Brisbane Macully also taught elocution and (another omission) was bankrupted. The insolvency case[11] is surprising, given the wealth of both Minnie and Alexander's families. It appears that Macully was caught up in the 1890s depression, having built 'Cullymont', living well and having bought land for his father to begin a nursery business; but his father could not repay him. Why did Macully need to lend money to his wealthy father? Why did his father-in-law not bail him out? Perhaps other family or friends were also caught up in the depression.

> After his return to Adelaide he acted as assistant priest at Hindmarsh and Bowden, also priest in charge of Penola, and assistant priest at the Semaphore. From 1905 until 1908 he was in charge of St. Jude's, Brighton.

I am unsure of the phrase 'his return to Adelaide', as this appears to be his first move there, although there were many moves, and Adelaide is given as an earlier address for his wife.

His final position was as the incumbent at St Jude's, Brighton, South Australia, built with funds donated by local people, in 1855, but not consecrated until over a century later, in 1977, because £100 was owed to the builders![12] He continued to teach elocution and to lecture at the South Australian Institutes.

Minnie and Alexander Macully built a grand home in Brighton in 1912, named 'Dunluce', as it was modelled on a wing of the Northern Irish castle 'Dunluce'. In the history of Brighton Dunluce is referred to as a castle with 12 acres of land, coach house and stables. It is still a handsome building. Bankruptcy was evidently short-lived.

> Mrs. Macully is well known for her kindness and practical sympathy. She has always evinced an ardent interest in parish work. The family comprises three daughters – Misses Eileen and Norah Macully and Mrs E.P. Whyte. The only son was killed in the war.[13]

The Macully children were born between 1885 and 1894. There appears to have been another omission: a son, Oscar Campbell Macully, who died in 1887, aged 7 months.[14] Their oldest daughter was Eileen, followed by Norah, who married but appears to have died childless, and their youngest child, Arnold Alexander, an A.I.F. gunner, who died in 1918, aged 24, at St. Sopelt, France. The youngest daughter was Kathleen ('Kitty') Duncan Campbell Macully, who married Ernest Primrose ('Prim') Whyte a year prior to Macully's death. Kitty and Prim had two daughters – Jean Primrose and Phyllis Primrose Whyte, Macully's only grandchildren, born after his death, both of whom inherited their grandfather's love of literature and neither of whom had children. Macully's only public memorial is his tombstone, but his daughter, Kitty Whyte, killed by a shark at Brighton, in 1926, is memorialized by a fountain next to the pier. Several years after Kitty's death Prim married her older sister, Eileen.

In later life Macully developed dementia, becoming a 'wanderer' who would stand in the middle of the road and shout 'Macully's lost!' until rescued.[15] He died in 1921 and is buried at St Jude's with Minnie, their three daughters and Prim, and there is a plaque for Arnold.

'So dear old Professor Macully has joined the angels! A most lovable man, and such a mixture of contradictions! Believed all things, hoped all things; to him nothing was impossible but what was impracticable'.[16]

ENDNOTES

1. 'Such a mixture of contradictions': ['From "One of his many friends"']. [Newspaper clipping], [1921]. SLSA: PRG 1335/10.

   The surname is variously spelled M'Cully, McCully or Macully.

   The State Library of South Australia holds a Macully scrapbook with newspaper clippings relating to recitals, poetry, etc.

2. 'Obituaries. Rev. Alexander Macully, M.A., LL.B.'. *The Observer* [SA], January 15th, 1921, 34b.

3. Joseph Fraser. 'Pen and ink sketches of prominent persons'. [Newspaper clipping], [1888?]. SLSA: PRG1288.

4. [Estate agent's promotional pamphlet], [1999?]. SLSA: PRG 1335/10/2-9.

   The grand mansion remains; the large coat of arms, painted in bright colours in contrast to the white walls, is attached to an exterior wall.

5. 'Rev. Alexander McCully'. [Newspaper clipping], n.d. SLSA: PRG 1335/10.

6   Alexander Macully. *The art of reading*. Melbourne: Mason, Firth & M'Cutcheon, 1887.

7   Douglas Pike, ed. *Australian Dictionary of Biography. Volume 3: 1851–1890*, 1969, 341–342.

8   'Fashionable wedding in Armagh'. [Newspaper clipping], n.d. SLSA: PRG 1335/10. Her parents are named, his are not.

9   *Copy of disposition of Trust Capital Clause in Settlement*. G.R. Campbell 24/5/27. SLSA: PRG 1335/10.

10 Dorothy Scott. *The Halfway House to Infidelity*, 1980, 38.

11 MACULLY, Alexander. Canterbury and Queensland. Insolvent, professor of elocution. Melbourne Court of Insolvency Index 1884–1900. Ref: 90/3273.

12 *Brighton: a walk through history*, 2001.

13 'Obituaries. Rev. Alexander Macully, M.A., LL.B.'. *The Observer* [SA], January 15th, 1921, 34b.

14 *Pioneer Index. Victoria 1836–1888* records the death of an Oscar Campbell Macully, aged 7 months, son of 'AlexR' and 'Minnie' Campbell Macully in 1887. Although this name does not appear in family records I assume that Oscar was Minnie and Alexander's child (could 'Oscar' have been in honour of Oscar Wilde, the Irish writer who was a contemporary of Macully at Trinity College, Dublin?). Minnie and Alexander appear not to have registered the births of any of their children except Arnold.

The Macully daughters were born between 1885 and 1891. The explorer Sir Douglas Mawson was born in 1882 and lived nearby in Brighton from 1904. I wonder whether the Misses Macully in the 'castle' were friendly with Mawson? The handsome Mawson was 'being pursued by Adelaide's society matrons' (Nancy Robinson Flannery, ed. *This everlasting silence*, 2000, 2). The woman Mawson was to marry, Paquita, was born in the same year as Kitty Macully and, like Kitty, had wealthy parents who lived in Brighton (on a five-acre estate). Mawson is buried in St Jude's Cemetery, Brighton.

15 Interview: Douglas Muecke, 2005. Both granddaughters, Jean (1923–2003) and Phyllis (1925–2005) Whyte, suffered from dementia which may have been inherited through the Macully family.

16 ['From "One of his many friends"']. [Newspaper clipping], [1921]. SLSA: PRG 1335/10.

APPENDIX 3

LETTER FROM K.A. (AXEL) LODEWYCKS TO R. SELBY SMITH, JUNE 15th, 1967

Dear Professor Smith

I understand that you have recently become involved in the long-standing proposal to establish a post-graduate school of librarianship at a Victorian university. Since I originated this proposal in 1958, I take the liberty of communicating to you the facts of my own involvement in the matter.

In 1958 the Murray Report appeared to herald a new era in Australian university development and the time seemed opportune to meet a long-felt need by proposing a scheme for the training of professional librarians at a level comparable with that provided for teachers in the University of Melbourne's Faculty of Education. My proposal for such a scheme was approved in principle by the Professorial Board of the University and a chair in librarianship was included in a list of deferred chairs. Since lack of finance was stated to be the obstacle in the way of implementing the scheme, I made certain approaches which resulted in an offer of finance from the Myer Foundation.

In 1961, the Library Association of Australia, having set up a committee to promote the establishment of schools of librarianship at universities, supported my proposal by appointing a deputation to the Vice-Chancellor of the University of Melbourne. As a result of this move the request that a detailed scheme for a school should be drawn up. The preparation of this scheme devolved on me and was carried out in practically every detail including estimates of staffing and accommodation, regulations, syllabus and reading lists. The scheme was supported in all essentials by the Library committee and the Faculty of Education, which agreed to the suggestion that it might take the school under its wing, and was recommended by the Professorial Board. However, it was foreseen in the light of past experience that the University would be committed at least partially to the cost of the scheme in spite of the offer of private financial assistance and it was decided that the University could not undertake this commitment in the triennium 1964–66.

Accordingly, the University in its submission to the Australian Universities Commission for the triennium 1967–69 highlighted the scheme for a post-graduate school of librarianship as an academic development together with the expansion of the Faculty of Medicine. The A.U.C. endorsed the scheme in its Third Report. However, the failure of the Commonwealth and State governments to implement the A.U.C.'s financial recommendations in full was caused by the deferment of the scheme by the University in favour of the expansion of the Faculty of Medicine.

Presumably, the A.U.C.'s endorsement of the scheme as an academic development in the University of Melbourne still stands and must again be considered in the light of the University finance in the triennium 1970–72. It is still my opinion that the University of Melbourne, in view of its central situation in the metropolitan area and the extent and variety of its Library collection, which includes the strongest Victorian holdings in the field of library science, remains the proper location for a post-graduate school of librarianship.

K.A. Lodewycks[1]

ENDNOTE

[1] K.A. Lodewycks to R. Selby Smith, June 15th, 1967. MON 1059: 2000/68. 93.

APPENDIX 4
BRIEF HISTORY OF THE GRADUATE SCHOOL OF LIBRARIANSHIP, MONASH UNIVERSITY

The Graduate School of Librarianship was established in 1975,[1] with Jean P. Whyte taking up appointment in July as Professor and Director of the School. Subsequent lecturing staff appointments in 1975 and early 1976 were Brian McMullin, Elizabeth Morrison, Radha Rasmussen and Richard Stayner. Michael Manning joined the GSL in 1980. Jeannette Rosengren was tutor from 1980 to 1984, followed by Jane Turner. The first students enrolled for the 1976 academic year.

1976

Master of Librarianship program commences.
Professor C. West Churchman of the University of California, Berkeley, conducts seminar 'The Future of Large Information Systems'.

1977

Continuing Education program of workshops and seminars offered to practising librarians.
GSL becomes founding member of AUSINET.
Herman Fussler of the University of Chicago is Visiting Professor at GSL from June to November.

1978

Diploma of Librarianship program commences, with initial support from the Myer Foundation.
Radha Rasmussen leads study tour to Denmark, June–July.

1979

First MLib graduates: Maureen Keane and Sylvia Ransom, 6 June.

1980

Master of Arts program commences.
ARGC-funded Early Imprints Project begins, with Brian McMullin as chief investigator.

1981

CTEC-funded 'Storage' study commences under direction of Jean Whyte; carried out by Richard Stayner and Research Fellow, Valerie Richardson.
The Sonneteer's History of Philosophy by Hector Monro printed at the Ancora Press by members of the GSL; launched 14 October.

1982

MA students Sandra Penny and Brian Hubber in UK on first GSL/Blackwell's Study Tour.

1983

GSL publishes Stayner/Richardson report, The Cost-Effectiveness of Alternative Library Storage Programs.
Brian McMullin Munby Fellow in Bibliography at Cambridge University, 1983/84.

1984

Forum on Australian Colonial Library History held in June, organized by Elizabeth Morrison.
Jeanette Rosengren, Jane Turner and GSL students take part in ABN Online Data Input Library School Pilot Project.

1985

Harrison Bryan visits GSL 5 June, the occasion of the conferring on him by Monash University of the degree of LLD.
First PhD graduate: Michael Talbot, 4 December.
Michael Manning consultant to ASCIS on specifications for school library automation.
Richard Stayner resigns.

1986

Elizabeth Morrison resigns.
First GSL Seminar for graduates and students held at Monash University in August.

1987

Xalid Abd-Ul-Wahid, tutor part-time.
Judith Ellis and Frank Upward present report on the introduction of a program in archives and records management.
Jean Whyte awarded the Library Association of Australia's H.C.L. Anderson Award.
Report on Australian Literature in Tertiary Libraries presented to the Committee to Review Australian Studies in Tertiary Education by Jean Whyte.
Arrival of Ross Harvey, Mary Ronnie and Brian Haratsis (part-time) as lecturers.
GSL Alumni Association formed: Mari Davis elected President.
Second GSL Alumni Association Seminar held at the Australian Institute of Family Studies in September.

1988

Courses in archives and records management introduced.
Jean Whyte awarded AM in Australia Day honours.
Rachel Salmond, tutor part-time.
Third GSL Alumni Association Seminar dedicated to Professor Jean Whyte, held at Monash City Premises, in November.

ENDNOTE

[1] *Librarianship in Australia*, 1988, 27–28.

APPENDIX 5

JEAN PRIMROSE WHYTE: A BIBLIOGRAPHY

Note: I have not listed Jean's published poetry except those poems which are quoted in the text.

PUBLICATIONS

1941

'Editorial'. *Chronicles of St Peter's Girls* 54, 1941, 5.
'The greater things'. *Chronicles of St Peter's Girls* 54, 1941, 23–24.
'Old Scholars' Association Essay'. *Chronicles of St Peter's Girls* 54, 1941, 43.

1949

'Presidential message'. Australian Institute of Librarians. South Australian Branch. *Quarterly Bulletin* 10, Winter 1949.

1953

'You want first prize in the flower show?' *Australian Library Journal* 2 (4) 1953, 126.

1956

'In-service training or library schools'. *Australian Library Journal* 5 (1) 1956, 1–5.
Review of *Books: libraries: librarians*: contributions to library literature. Selected by John David Marshall, Wayne Shirley, and Louis Shores, edited by John David Marshall. *Australian Library Journal* 5 (2) 1956, 87.
'Doubts at midnight'. *Foggy Dew* 1 (1) 1956.
'Qualifications necessary for joining the staff of the Public Library of S.A.'. *Foggy Dew* 1 (7) 1956.

1957

[Whyte, Jean?] 'Know your department – Staff Training Officer'. *Foggy Dew* 2 (3) 1957, 8.
'A word from Callimachus'. *Australian Library Journal* 6 (3) 1957, 95–100.
Review of *Information indexing and subject cataloging, alphabetical: classified, coordinate: mechanical* by John Metcalfe. *Australian Library Journal* 6 (4) 1957, 186–188.
'How far in seventeen years?'. *Foggy Dew* 2 (4) 1957, 1–2.

1959

Editorship of *Australian Library Journal* including authorship of unsigned editorial contributions from 8 (1) 1959 to 19 (11) 1970.
'Editorial'. *Australian Library Journal* 8 (1) 1959, 1–2.
'Editorial'. *Australian Library Journal* 8 (2) 1959, 57.
[Whyte, Jean?]. 'The Fisher Library, University of Sydney'. *Australian Library Journal* 8 (2) 1959, 62–64.
'Editorial'. *Australian Library Journal* 8 (3) 1959, 113.
'Editorial'. *Australian Library Journal* 8 (4) 1959, 169.

'The Recruitment of librarians'. In *Proceedings of the 10th Conference*. [Sydney?]: [Library Association of Australia], [1959?].

1960

'Editorial'. *Australian Library Journal* 9 (1) 1960, 1.
'Editorial'. *Australian Library Journal* 9 (2) 1960, 55.
'Editorial'. *Australian Library Journal* 9 (3) 1960, 109.
Review of *Union list of higher degree theses in Australian University Libraries* by Mary J. Marshall. *Australian Library Journal* 9 (3) 1960, 150.
Review of *Library Research in Progress, Nos. 1, 2, October 1959, January, 1960. Australian Library Journal* 9 (3) 1960, 150–151.
'Editorial'. *Australian Library Journal* 9 (4) 1960, 163–164.

1961

'Editorial'. *Australian Library Journal* 10 (1) 1961, 1–2.
'Editorial'. *Australian Library Journal* 10 (3) 1961, 109.

1962

'The librarian's task, 1962: an editorial'. *Australian Library Journal* 11 (2) 1962, 55–60.
Review of *India's National Library* by B.S. Kesavan. *Australian Library Journal* 11 (2) 1962, 105–106.
'Wing books held in Australian libraries: Supplement No. 1'. *Australian Library Journal* 11 (3) 1962, 153–162.
'New houses: an editorial'. *Australian Library Journal* 11 (4) 1962, 163.
Review of *Canadian index to periodicals and documentary films: an author and subject index. January 1948 – December 1959* edited by Margaret E. Wodehouse and Ruth Mulholland. *Australian Library Journal* 11 (4) 1962, 212–213.

1963

'A sense of proportion: Sir Frank Francis comments on the Australian library scene'. *Australian Library Journal* 12 (1) 1963, 1–2.
'Education for Librarianship Abroad: Australia'. *Library Trends* 12 (2) 1963, 295–305.
'The *Australian Library Journal* in 1963: an editorial'. *Australian Library Journal* 12 (4) 1963, 163–164.

1964

'After the conference: an editorial'. *Australian Library Journal* 13 (1) 1964, 1–2.
'Namoi Regional Library bans "The thin red line"'. *Australian Library Journal* 13 (1) 1964, 17.
'A policy for the Library Association of Australia? An editorial'. *Australian Library Journal* 13 (2) 1964, 55–57.
Review of *Australian little magazines, 1923–1954: their role in formation and reflecting literary trends* by John Tregenza. *Australian Library Journal* 13 (2) 1964, 85–90.
Review of Index of Australian and New Zealand poetry by Eleanora Isabel Cuthbert. *Australian Library Journal* 13 (2) 1964, 86–87.

'The importance of the edition: an editorial'. *Australian Library Journal* 13 (3) 1964, 109–110.
[Introduction to] 'Correspondence'. *Australian Library Journal* 13 (3) 1964, 129.
MJWL [Jean Whyte and Margaret Lundie]. 'The journal of Abel Jansz Tasman 1642'. *Australian Library Journal* 13 (4) 1964, 177.
'The Library's role in helping the undergraduate'. In *The University of Sydney, Office of Advisory Services, Notes on University Education*, Bulletin No. 6, Teaching and Learning in the Faculty of Science, December 1964, 45–48.

1965

'Heard in a corridor'. *Australian Library Journal* 14 (1) 1965, 23.
'Copyright Law in Australia'. *Vestes* 8 (1) 1965, 3–9.
'The thirteenth Biennial Conference, Canberra. 1965'. *Australian Library Journal* 14 (3) 1965, 109–110.
'Changes in the *Australian Library Journal*, 1966'. *Australian Library Journal* 14 (4) 1965, 215.

1966

'National book resources: an editorial'. *Australian Library Journal* 15 (1) 1966, 1–6.
'Are we failing our public?'. *Australian Library Journal* 15 (1) 1966, 19.
'A question of space'. *Australian Library Journal* 15 (5) 1966, 183.
Hine, Janet D., Jean P. Whyte and Jean M. Murray. *The Australian Library Journal Index. Volumes 1–14 1951–1965*. Sydney [New South Wales]: Library Association of Australia, 1966.

1967

'The Queensland Conference: editorial'. *Australian Library Journal* 16 (5) 1967, 187.
'A man's world: the library profession and library education in Australia'. *Library Journal* 92 (20) 1967, 4120–4122.

1968

'Editorial Committee'. *Australian Library Journal* 17 (1) 1968, [i].
'The *Australian Library Journal* in 1968'. *Australian Library Journal* 17 (1) 1968, 1–2.
'Editor goes to America'. *Australian Library Journal* 17 (7) 1968, 234.
'The National Library'. *Australian Library Journal* 17 (8) 1968, 257–258.

1969

'Editor returns from North America'. *Australian Library Journal* 18 (3) 1969, 84.
'The Adelaide Conference'. *Australian Library Journal* 18 (9) 1969, 263–264.
Reference books on English literature. Sydney: University of Sydney, 1969.

1970

'David Barry Scott'. *Australian Library Journal* 19 (1) 1970, 21.
'An editor signs off'. *Australian Library Journal* 19 (11) 1970, 470.
Review of *Interlibrary loan involving academic libraries* by Sarah K. Thomson. *Australian Library Journal* 19 (11) 1970, 445–446.

Review of *National Library of Australia, Acquisitions Newsletter, No 1* and *Short title catalogue of books printed in the British Isles, the British Colonies and the United States of America and of English books printed elsewhere, 1701–1800*. *Australian Library Journal* 19 (11) 1970, 446–447.

'Trends abroad: Australia'. *Library Trends* 19 (1) 1970, 122–130 [also cited as 'Intellectual freedom: trends abroad: Australia'].

1971

'John Metcalfe and the Library Association of Australia'. *Australian Library Journal* 20 (4) 1971, 5–13.

Review of *Libraries in France* by J. Ferguson. *Australian Library Journal* 20 (6) 1971, 47.

Review of *Library issues: the sixties* edited by E. Moon and K. Nyren. *Australian Library Journal* 20 (7) 1971, 40–41.

'Professionalism defined'. *Australian Library Journal* 20 (10) 1971, 35–36.

'The Library Association of Australia: structure, nature, role'. In *Proceedings of the 15th Biennial Conference*. Sydney: Library Association of Australia, 1971, 382–386.

1972

'Library euphemisms'. *Australian Library Journal* 21 (1) 1972, 34.

'Obituaries' [George Pitt.] *Australian Library Journal* 21 (4) 1972, 176–177.

'Twenty-one years of the *Australian Library Journal*: Jean Whyte'. *Australian Library Journal* 21 (6) 1972, 234–236.

Review of *Heritage of the graphic arts* edited by C.B. Grannis. *Australian Library Journal* 21 (10) 1972, 448–449.

'Who uses a university library, why and to what effect?'. In *Proceedings of the 16th Biennial Conference*. Sydney: Library Association of Australia, Conference Committee, 1972, 527–537. Also in Eric J. Wainwright. *Readings in Australian librarianship II: Australian library surveys: a selection of readings from the publications of the Library Association of Australia*. Surry Hills, NSW: Library Association of Australia, 1979, 1–11.

[Whyte, Jean, ed.]. *Proceedings of the 16th Biennial Conference held in Sydney, August 1971*. Sydney: Library Association of Australia, Conference Committee, 1972.

1973

'Professor of English'. *Australian Library Journal* 22 (2) 1973, 35.

Review of *International cooperation in Orientalist librarianship* edited by E. Bishop and J.M. Waller. *Australian Library Journal* 22 (4) 1973, 165–166.

'And now the videotape'. *Australian Library Journal* 22 (10) 1973, 400.

1974

'The Accreditation of Courses in Librarianship'. In *Proceedings of the 17th Biennial Conference*. Sydney: Library Association of Australia, 1974, 593–608.

[Whyte, Jean, ed.] *Librarianship in Australia*. 2nd ed. Canberra: Australian Government Publishing Service, 1974.

'The Curriculum in Australian Library Schools'. In Edward A. Parr and Eric J. Wainwright, eds. *Curriculum Design in Librarianship: Proceedings of the Colloquium on Education for Librarianship*. Perth: WAIT Aid Inc., 1974, 123–138.

1975

Review of Library Association of Australia. *Proceedings [of the] 18th Biennial Conference., Melbourne, August 1975.* Melbourne: Conference Committee, 1976. *Australian Academic and Research Libraries* 8 (1) 1975, 51–55.

1976

'In the mainstream: the Graduate School of Librarianship at Monash University'. *Australian Library Journal* 25 (2) 1976, 51–58.
Review of *Guide to the research collections of the New York Public Library* compiled by S.P. Williams. *Australian Library Journal* 25 (14) 1976, 352.
'Silver or lead: the *Australian Library Journal* after 25 years'. *Australian Library Journal* 25 (16) 1976, 398–399.
'Issues in Australian librarianship'. In Boyd W. Rayward, ed. *The variety of librarianship: essays in honour of John Wallace Metcalfe.* Sydney: Library Association of Australia, 1976, 190–217.

1977

'New service for Wombat Beach'. *Australian Library Journal* 26 (1) 1977, 9.
'Glare-free history'. *Australian Library Journal* 26 (2) 1977, 43.
'Head not heart: why I am against Library Workers Against Uranium Mining'. *Australian Library Journal* 26 (19), 1977, 326–328.
'Direct service to readers'. In Harrison Bryan and Gordon Greenward, eds. *Design for diversity*. St Lucia, Queensland: University of Queensland, 1977, 271–312.

1978

'No gold stars'. *Australian Library Journal* 27 (2) 1978, 19.
'Higher degrees in librarianship'. *Australian Library Journal* 27 (3) 1978, 39–42.
'Introduction'. In *Reflections on the future of research libraries: two essays*, by Herman H. Fussler and Harrison Bryan. [Clayton, Victoria]: Graduate School of Librarianship, Monash University, 1978.

1979

'Touching condition'. *Australian Library Journal* 28 (1) 1979, 3.
[Obituary for Arthur Brown]. *Australian Library Journal* 28 (15) 1979, 288.
Review of *Australian and New Zealand library resources*, by Robert B. Downs. London: Mansell; Melbourne: D.W. Thorpe, 1979. *Australian Academic and Research Libraries* 12 (1) 1979, 62.

1980

Review of *Outlines of modern librarianship* by James G. Ollé. *Australian Library Journal* 29 (1) 1980, 41.

1981

'Australia'. In Miles M. Jackson, ed. *International handbook of contemporary developments in librarianship*. Westport, Connecticut: Greenwood, 1981, 325–347 [also cited as 'Contemporary development in librarianship in Australia'].

'Random remarks from a long-time librarian, short-time teacher of librarians'. In *Library education under siege: proceedings of a seminar*. Sydney: Library Association of Australia, 1981, 57–61.

'Walter Stone: Obituary'. *Incite* 2 (17) 1981, 7.

1982

'Professional discourse among university librarians in Australia 1926–1937'. In M. Burns and C. Palmer, eds. *Innovation no stranger: essays in Australian librarianship in honour of Ira Raymond*. Adelaide: Investigator Press for the Barr Smith Library, 1982, 69–82.

Review of *Library Literature II – The best of 1980* edited by William Katz. The Scarecrow Press, Metuchen, New Jersey, 1981. *Information Processing & Management* 18 (6) 1982, 323.

1983

Review of *Australian libraries*. 3rd edition. Edited by Peter Biskup and Doreen M. Goodman. *Australian Library Journal* 32 (2) 1983, 61–62.

'Introduction'. In Richard A. Stayner and Valerie E. Richardson. *The cost-effectiveness of alternative library storage programmes*. Clayton, Victoria: Graduate School of Librarianship, Monash University, 1983, iii–iv.

1984

'Librarians and scholars'. In *Australian academic libraries in the seventies: essays in honour of Dietrich Borchardt*, edited by Harrison Bryan and John Horacek. St Lucia: University of Queensland Press, 1984, 243–262.

Review of Neil A. Radford and John Fletcher. *'In establishing and maintaining a Library.' Two essays on the University of Sydney Library*. Sydney: University of Sydney Library, 1984. *Australian Academic and Research Libraries* 3 (3) 1984, 175–176.

1985

'Making history'. In Elizabeth Morrison and Michael Talbot, eds. *Books, libraries and readers in Colonial Australia*. Clayton: Graduate School of Librarianship, Monash University, 1985, 135–140.

'Control and diversity: a short history of course recognition in Australia'. *Education for Librarianship*. 2 Summer 1985, 5–25.

'From ALA to LAA – the Australian Institute of Librarians'. In P. Biskup and M. Rochester, eds. *Australian Library History: papers from the Second forum on Library History, Canberra, 19–20 July 1985*. Canberra: Canberra CAE, 1985, 122–133.

1986

'Some thoughts on the *Australian Library Journal*'. *Australian Library Journal* 35 (4) 1986, 185–186.

1987

'"To unite persons engaged in library work": the Australian Institute of Librarians'. *Australian Library Journal* 36 (4) 1987, 193–207.

Margaret Isaacs, Linda Emmett and Jean Whyte. *Australian literature in tertiary libraries: project report*. Canberra: Committee to Review Australian Studies in Tertiary Education, 1987.

'Australian content in tertiary libraries'. *The Australian Author*, 19 (3) 1987, 7–11.

1988

Review of *Readings in Canadian library history* edited by Peter F. McNally. *Australian Library Journal* 37 (1) 1988, 72–73.

[Entries in] Harrison Bryan, ed. *ALIAS. Australia's library, information and archives services – an encyclopaedia of practice and practitioners*. 3 vols. Canberra: ALIA, 1988–1991:

- Australian Institute of Librarians (AIL), I, 73–76.
- Australian Library Association (ALA), I, 79–80.
- Bryan, Harrison (1923–[2009]), I, 125–126.
- Horton, Warren Michael (1938–[2003]), II, 32.
- Library Association of Australia (LAA), II, 80–83.
- Metcalf, Keyes Dewitt (1889–1983), II, 124–125.
- Paltridge, Cynthia (1922–), II, 174.
- Pitt, George Henry (1891–1972), II, 186–187.
- Purnell, Herbert Rutherford (1883–1944), II, 210–211.
- Ramsay, Margery Campbell (1923–[1998]), III, 6.
- Scott, Leigh (1888–1963), III, 35–36.
- Stone, Walter (1910–81), III, 81.
- Wood, Malvina Evalyn (1893–1976), III, 154.

'Fifth ceremony: Professor Jean Whyte: For the record' [Commemoration Address. University of Adelaide]. *Lumen: the University of Adelaide News Magazine* 17 (6) 1988, 8.

'Harrison Bryan and the making of Australian library history'. In *An enthusiasm for libraries: essays in honour of Harrison Bryan*, edited by Jean P. Whyte and Neil A. Radford. Melbourne: Ancora, 1988, 35–56.

Isaacs, Margaret, Linda Emmett and Jean P. Whyte. *Libraries and Australian literature: a report on the representation of Australian creative writing in Australian libraries*. Melbourne, Ancora, 1988.

Review of *The Book in Australia: Essays towards a cultural and social history*. Edited by D.H. Borchardt and W. Kirsop. Australian Reference Publications in association with Centre for Bibliographical and Textural (sic) Studies Monash University 1988 (Historical Bibliography Monograph 16). *Australian Academic and Research Libraries* 21 (2) 1988, 131–132.

'Waltzing with Matilda – Australian libraries 1788–1988'. In Janet Robinson, ed. *Proceedings of the 25th LAA Conference Sydney 1988*. Sydney: Library Association of Australia, 1988, 75–88.

Whyte, Jean and Neil A. Radford, eds. *An enthusiasm for libraries: essays in honour of Harrison Bryan*. Melbourne: Ancora, 1988.

1991

Upward, Frank and Jean P. Whyte, eds. *Peopling a profession: papers from the Fourth Forum on Australian Library History Monash University 25 and 26 September 1989*. Melbourne: Ancora, 1991.

1993

'Tending the sacred flame: John Metcalfe's contribution to professional librarianship in Australia'. In W. Boyd Rayward, ed. *Libraries and life in a changing world: the Metcalfe years, 1920–1970: papers from Australian Library History Forum V at the University of New South Wales, 6–7th November, 1992.* Sydney: School of Information, Library and Archive Studies, University of New South Wales, 1993, 30–46.

1996

'From papyrus scrolls to the Internet'. *Savant*, June 1996, 15–16.

1997

Whyte, Jean and Neil Radford. 'Obituaries. Librarian built up uni collection' [Andrew Osborn.] *The Australian*, May 7th, 1997, 14.

'John Bray and the Libraries Board of South Australia'. In Wilfrid Prest, ed. *A portrait of John Bray: law, letters, life*. Adelaide: Wakefield, 1997, 115–127.

1998

'Mitchell, Roma Flinders'. In Graeme Davison, John Hirst and Stuart Macintyre, eds. *Oxford companion to Australian history*. Melbourne: Oxford University, 1998, 432–433.

2000

The poems of Callimachus. [Melbourne]: Ancora, 2000.

2007

Whyte, Jean and David J. Jones. *Uniting a profession: the Australian Institute of Librarians 1937–1949*. Kingston, ACT: Australian Library and Information Association, 2007.

CORRESPONDENCE

Jean Whyte to:

- Acutt, S. October 28th, 1981, and October 6th 1982. MON 1059: 2000/68. 46.
- Alley, Geoffrey. October 16, 1981. MON 1059: 2000/68. 5.
- Asheim, Lester. August 9th, 1956 and January 3rd, 1975. NLA: MS 9616.

- Asheim, Lester. September 12th, 1975. MON 1059: 2000/68. 6.
- [Bald], Jane. September 6th, 1976. MON 1059: 2000/68. 42.
- Bradley, D. September 10th, 1981. MON 1059: 2000/68. 42.
- Brown, Cecily. August 12th, 1976. MON 1059: 2000/68. 42.
- Butchart, J.D. December 17th, 1974. MON: SLO 72330.
- Cathie, Ian. May 5th, 1988. NLA: MS 9616.
- Datar, C. January 14th, 1976. MON 1059: 2000/68. 47.
- Dean, Graduate Library School University of Chicago, Illinois. June 18th, 1952. NLA: MS 9616.
- Decker, Lindy. July 25th, 1975. MON 1059: 2000/68. 37.
- Eddowes, D. December 12th, 1972. NLA: MS 9616.
- Editor, *Canberra Times*. January 10th, 1975.
- Enderby, K. June 15th, 1973. NLA: MS 9616.
- Fleming, Alan. 1973–1974. NLA: MS 9862
- Foley, Karen. November 14th, 1972. NLA: MS 9616.
- Knaus, E.L. August 2nd, 1973. NLA: MS 9616.
- Manton, G.R. 24th July, 1974. NLA: MS 9616.
- Manton, G.R. October 10th, 1974. MON: SLO 72330.
- Manton, G.R. [1977?]. MON 1059: 2000/68. 13.
- Osborn, Andrew. Correspondence, 1958–1993. SU: Acc 1542. M 465.
- Overy, Malvina. August 14th, 1973. NLA: MS 9616.
- Pargetter, R.J. January 3rd, 1995. NLA: MS 9616.
- Pitt, G. H. Correspondence, 1948–1972. SLSA: PRG 1335.
- Ramsay, Margery. September 17th, 1973. NLA: MS 9616.
- Ramsden, M.J. November 5th, 1974. NLA: MS 9616.
- Secretary, American Association of University Women, 1952. NLA: MS 9616.

CURRICULA VITAE

Curriculum vitae, 1958. NLA: MS 9616.
Position application and curriculum vitae, 1959. NLA: MS 9616.
Curriculum vitae, [1962?] NLA: MS 9616.
Curriculum vitae, [1964?]. NLA: MS 9616.
Curriculum vitae, [1972?]. NLA: MS 9616.
Curriculum vitae, 1974. NLA: MS 9616.

UNPUBLISHED WORKS

1954–1959

'A proposal for a Master's Thesis. 1954'. NLA: MS 9616.
'Second Report to American Association of University Women', 1954. NLA: MS 9616.
'Education for librarianship in the United States and in Australia: a comparison: a dissertation submitted to the Faculty of the Graduate Library School in candidacy for the degree of Master of Arts'. Chicago, Illinois: August, 1956. NLA: MS 9616.

1960–1969

'The Availability of Scientific Information in Australia: working paper presented to the Conference of Directors of Scientific Information Centres in the Asian-Pacific Region, June 10–14, 1963, Hong Kong'. NLA: MS 9616.

1970–1979

'A report on the administration of public libraries in South Australia. Jean P. Whyte'. Sent to D. Dunstan, Premier, SA, 9.5.1974. NLA: MS 9616.
[Memorandum], January 7th, 1974. NLA: MS 9616.
'Preliminary notes on the School of Librarianship at Monash University', [1975]. NLA: MS 9616.

1980–1989

Whyte, Jean and L.J. Sussex. 'A statistical study of the unique monographic holdings of research libraries in Australia'. (Monash University Special Research Grant). [1982]. MON 1059: 2000/68. 27.
[Notes for a speech prepared for a celebration of the conferring of the award of Order of Australia for Harrison Bryan], [1984]. NLA: MS 9616.
Personal notes, [1987?]. NLA: MS 9616.
Retirement reminiscences. 1988. NLA: MS 9616.

1990–

'The T.H. Woodrow Award', 1990. NLA: MS 9616.
'The library in the twentieth century' [Address to Alumni Seminar, Monash University, 27 July 1991].
'Some reminiscences of Geoffrey Alley, the University of Western Ontario and Upper Hutt (sent to Jock McEldowney, in the hope that these will be useful)'. Held by J. McEldowney, Dunedin, New Zealand.
'Graduation address Monash University, 1996. For Faculty of Arts Graduands 15/5/96'. NLA: MS 9616.
Book Design Awards, 1970–1: Judges' report. Australian Book Publishers Association. NLA: MS 9616.
'Towards a history of the Australian Institute of Librarians'. Held by David J. Jones, Sydney.

BIBLIOGRAPHY

'250 at library party'. [Newspaper clipping], n.d. SLSA: PRG 1335/1.

[Advertisement]. *Australian Library Journal* 6 (1) 1957, 11.

American Library Association. *American Library Association membership directory 1979. Members as of August, 1979*. Chicago, Illinois: American Library Association, 1979.

Andrea, Brian. [Medical certificate], October 4th, 1973. NLA: MS 9616.

Asheim, Lester. 'Education for librarianship in the United States: some problems and challenges'. *Australian Library Journal* 18 (11) 1969, 401–406.

'Australia Day honours'. *Advertiser* [SA], January 26th, 1988.

'Australian Imperial Force. Nominal Roll. 4th Light Horse Brigade Train, 14th A.S.C.'. National Archives of Australia. Defence Service Records. [NAA:B2455, Whyte, Ernest Primrose].

Australian Institute of Librarians. *Annual reports*, 1944–1945.

Australian Institute of Librarians. South Australian Branch. *Minute Book*. October 8, 1937 – December 17, 1952. SLSA: SRG 109 Series 2, Vols. 1–7.

Australian Institute of Librarians. South Australian Branch. 'Congratulations'. *Quarterly Bulletin* 1, 1944, [14].

Australian Institute of Librarians. South Australian Branch. *Quarterly Bulletin* 7, 1946, [1].

Balnaves, John. 'A leader in cooperation: the Australian National Library'. *Library Journal* 92 (20) 1967, 4117–4119.

Bennet, Imelda. 'Uranium worry'. *Australian Library Journal* 27 (2) 1978, 19.

Biskup, Peter. *Libraries in Australia. Topics in Australasian library and information studies, Number 19*. Wagga Wagga, NSW: Centre for Information Studies, 1994.

Biskup, Peter and Maxine K. Rochester, eds. *Australian Library History: Papers from the Second forum on Australian Library History, Canberra, 19–20 July, 1985*. Canberra: Canberra CAE, 1985.

Biskup, Peter and Margaret Henty, eds. *Library for the nation*. Canberra: *Australian Academic and Research Libraries* and the National Library of Australia, 1991.

'The "Bizarre" Mayor'. *Australian Library Journal* 16 (2) 1967, 75.

Blum, Rudolf. *Kallimachos: the Alexandrian library and the origins of bibliography*. Madison, Wisconsin: University of Wisconsin, 1991.

[Board of Examination]. 'Executive Officers, representative councillors, Board of Examination'. *Australian Library Journal* 5 (1) 1956, 22.

Board of Examination. 'Board of Examination'. *Australian Library Journal* 9 (4) 1960, 184.

Board of Examination. 'Board of Examination'. *Australian Library Journal* 10 (4) 1961, 181–182.

[Board of Examination]. 'Graduate qualifications for librarianship'. *Australian Library Journal* 11 (2) 1962, 65–66.

Board of Examiners. 'Minimum standards for the recognition of courses in librarianship'. *Australian Library Journal* 13 (3) 1964, 153–154.

Board of Examiners. 'News Release'. *Australian Library Journal* 15 (4) 1966, 161–162.

'Books – all types – are exhibits at show'. [Newspaper clipping], n.d. SLSA: PRG 1335/2.

Borchardt, Dietrich H. 'Journals for the Profession – comments on their role and function'. *Australian Library Journal* 38 (3) 1989, 219–226.

'Branches'. *Australian Library Journal* 1 (4) 1952, 90–92.
'Branches'. *Australian Library Journal* 1 (6) 1952, 139.
'Branches'. *Australian Library Journal* 2 (2) 1953, 38–42.
'Branches'. *Australian Library Journal* 2 (3) 1953, 70–73.
'Branches'. *Australian Library Journal* 2 (4) 1953, 104–108.
'Branches and Sections'. *Australian Library Journal* 4 (3) 1955, 115–117.
'Branches and Sections'. *Australian Library Journal* 5 (4) 1956, 147.
Bray, J.J. 'Censorship'. *Australian Library Journal* 13 (2) 1964, 60–70.
Brewer, Joan. 'Education for librarianship'. In *An enthusiasm for libraries*. See Jean P. Whyte and Neil A. Radford, eds., 1988, 57–80.
Brideson, H.C. [Reference for Jean Whyte]. May 8th, 1956. NLA: MS 9616.
Brideson, H.C. 'The Public Library of South Australia'. *Australian Library Journal* 6 (2) 1957, 61–64.
Bridge, Carl. *A trunk full of books: history of the State Library of South Australia and its forerunners*. Netley, South Australia: Wakefield in association with the State Library of South Australia, 1986.
Brighton: a walk through history. Adelaide: City of Holdfast Bay, 2001. www.holdfast.sa.gov.au/webdata/resources/files/Brighton_a_walk_through_history_brochure 1.pdf.
Brown, W.L. 'Correspondence'. *Australian Library Journal* 19 (10) 1970, 386.
Brown, W.L. 'Editorial'. *Australian Library Journal* 21 (6) 1972, 227–228.
[Bryan, Harrison]. 'Banana benders all'. *Australian Library Journal* 3 (2) 1954, 41.
[Bryan, Harrison]. 'Movement at the station'. *Australian Library Journal* 6 (1) 1957, 3–4.
Bryan, Harrison. *Annual Reports of the Librarian*, 1959–1972. SU Archives.
Bryan, Harrison. 'A hand press for the University of Queensland'. *Australian Library Journal* 10 (2) 1961, 65–67.
Bryan, Harrison. 'Scholars, teachers, students and librarians'. *Arts: The Proceedings of the Sydney University Arts Association* 2 (3) 1963, 169–183.
Bryan, Harrison. 'The new Fisher library at the University of Sydney: an inheritor's impressions'. *Australian Library Journal* 12 (2) 1963, 67–70.
Bryan, Harrison. 'Librarianship ... a profession without professors'. *Australian Library Journal* 12 (4) 1963, 190–197.
Bryan, Harrison. *Librarian's Information Bulletin*, 1963–1972.
Bryan, Harrison. *Australian university libraries: today and tomorrow*. Sydney: Bennett, 1965.
Bryan, Harrison. 'Automation in action'. *Australian Library Journal* 15 (4) 1966, 127–140.
Bryan, Harrison. 'A first computer-printed catalogue for N.U.'. *Australian Library Journal* 15 (5) 1966, 200–201.
Bryan, Harrison. 'L.A.A. Board of Examiners. News release No. 9'. *Australian Library Journal* 16 (3) 1967, 127–128.
Bryan, Harrison. 'Australian university libraries: A gloomy conclusion?'. *Library Journal* 92 (20) 15 1967, 4113–4116.
Bryan, Harrison. 'The Fisher "sit-ins" of April 1967'. *Vestes: the Australian Universities' review*. 11 (1) 1968, 153–159.
Bryan, Harrison. 'A profession with a professor'. *Australian Library Journal* 17 (9) 1968, 306–307.

Bryan, Harrison. 'The explosion in published information – myth or reality'. *Australian Library Journal* 17 (11) 1968, 389–401.

Bryan, Harrison. 'An Australian library in the AM: earlier years of the University of Sydney Library'. *Journal of the Royal Australian Historical Society* 55 (3) 1969, 205–227.

Bryan, Harrison. 'David Barry Scott, O.B.E., B.A., A.L.A.A.: a personal appreciation'. *Australian Library Journal* 19 (1) 1970, 19–21.

Bryan, Harrison. 'A decade of change: the Library Association of Australia and education for librarianship 1961–1971'. *Australian Library Journal* 20 (1) 1971, 14–20.

Bryan, Harrison. 'Rationalization of Australian library holdings in history'. *The Australian University* 9 (3) 1971, 222–236.

Bryan, Harrison. 'Twenty-one years of the *Australian Library Journal*: Harrison Bryan'. *Australian Library Journal* 21 (6) 1972, 231–233.

Bryan, Harrison. 'University of Sydney Library. Library Automation Programme'. *Report to Library Advisory Committee*. April 8th, 1972. SU Archives.

Bryan, Harrison. 'Obituary' [Beatrice Pilcher Wines]. *Australian Library Journal* 21 (10) 1972, 451–452.

Bryan, Harrison. 'Editorial: The *Australian Library Journal* Mark V'. *Australian Library Journal* 29 (1) 1980, 3–4.

Bryan, Harrison. Review of *Innovation no stranger*. *Australian Library Journal* 32 (2) 1983, 60–61.

Bryan, Harrison. 'The Metcalf seminar – 25 years on'. *Australian Library Journal* 33 (1) 1984, 32–35.

Bryan, Harrison. 'Collection development in Australian University Libraries, 1949 to 1980'. In H. Bryan and J. Horacek, eds. *Australian Academic Libraries in the Seventies. Essays in Honour of Dietrich Borchardt*. St Lucia: University of Queensland, 1984, 33–63.

Bryan, Harrison. 'Jean Primrose Whyte AM, BA, AM, FLAA: summing up a career'. *Australian Library Journal* 38 (1) 1989, 5–14.

Bryan, Harrison. 'Librarianship in Australia – Lion, Lamb or Lemming?' *Australian Library Journal* 38 (3) 1989, 227–240.

Bryan, Harrison. 'The achievement of the LAA (and the AIL) over the first fifty years'. *Australian Library Journal* 36 (4) 1987, 244–246.

Bryan, Harrison. 'Some comments and an occasional rejoinder'. In *An enthusiasm for libraries*. See Jean P. Whyte and Neil A. Radford, eds., 1988, 215–254.

Bryan, Harrison , ed. *ALIAS. Australia's library, information and archives services – an encyclopaedia of practice and practitioners*. 3 vols. Canberra: ALIA, 1988–1991.

Bryan, Harrison. 'Osborn, Andrew Delbridge (1902–[1997])'. In Harrison Bryan, ed., *ALIAS*, 1988–1991, Vol. 2, 171–172.

Bryan, Harrison. 'Whyte, Jean Primrose (1923–[2003])'. In Harrison Bryan, ed., *ALIAS*, 1988–1991, Vol. 3, 150–151.

Bryan, Harrison. *No gray profession: reminiscences of a career in Australian libraries*. Adelaide: Auslib, 1994.

Buick, W.G. 'Correspondence'. *Australian Library Journal* 6 (5) 1958, 210–211.

Burge, Elizabeth. 'Too elitist for comfort'. *Australian Library Journal* 26 (1) 18, 1977, 5.

Cameron, Alan. *Callimachus and his critics*. Princeton, N.J.: Princeton University, 1995.

Cameron, Margaret A. 'We were not "dragooned into membership" ... we simply never found out there was a choice'. *Australian Library Journal* 36 (4) 1987, 286–290.
'Censorship in Sandringham'. *Australian Library Journal* 18 (11) 1969, 394.
'Chandler, George (1915–[1992])'. In Harrison Bryan, ed., *ALIAS*, 1988–1991, Vol. 1, 144–145.
'Change of editor'. *Australian Library Journal* 19 (9) 1970, 340.
Cleary, Jim. 'Freedom is just a word'. *Australian Library Journal* 27 (4) 1978, 84–85.
'Clever woman'. [Newspaper clipping], n.d. SLSA: PRG 1335/1.
Connell, W.F.N., G.E. Sherington, B.H. Fletcher, C. Turney, U. Bygott. *Australia's first: a history of the University of Sydney*. 2 vols. Sydney: University of Sydney in association with Hale & Iremonger, 1991–1995.
Cochrane, Peter, ed. *Remarkable occurrences: the National Library of Australia's first 100 years 1901–2001*. Canberra: National Library of Australia, 2001.
Community Library Matters, 2004. www.monash.edu.au/pubs/monmag/issue14-2004 /community/library.html.
Cope, R.L. 'A profession with a professor'. *Australian Library Journal* 17 (9) 1968, 307.
Cope, R.L. 'The Library Keeper's business: its impact and relevance today'. *Australian Academic and Research Libraries* 33 (2) 2002, 97–112.
Corr, Graham P. 'Education for librarianship'. *Australian Library Journal* 32 (1) 1983, 61–62.
'Correspondence'. *Australian Library Journal* 13 (3) 1964, 129–135.
'Courses in librarianship'. *Australian Library Journal* 24 (4) 1975, 178–179.
Crawford, Mavis. 'Emeritus Professor Jean Primrose Whyte, AM'. Copy in possession of C.E.J. Jenkin.
Cummings, John. *A birthday ode for Miss Whyte, in ottava rima*, n.d. NLA: MS 9616.
Darling, Keith. 'Correspondence'. *Australian Library Journal* 12 (3) 1963, 144–145.
'Doubling the number'. *Canberra Times*, September 28th, 1972. NLA: MS 9616.
Doust, R.F. 'Report of General Council meeting, Sydney, August 1964'. *Australian Library Journal* 13 (3) 1964, 151–153.
Duncan, W.G.K. 'A librarian's first loyalty'. *Australian Library Journal* 10 (4) 1961, 163–174. Reprinted in *Australian Library Journal* 21 (6) 1972, 237–245.
'Editorship of the journal'. *Australian Library Journal* 7 (4) 1958, 118.
[Estate agent's promotional pamphlet], [1999?]. SLSA: PRG 1335/10/2-9.
Farmer, Geoffrey A.J. 'The South Australian Collection in the Public Library of South Australia'. *Australian Library Journal* 14 (4) 1965, 200–205.
'Fashionable wedding in Armagh'. [Newspaper clipping], n.d. SLSA: PRG 1335/10.
Fielding, Derek. 'Censorship'. In Harrison Bryan, ed., *ALIAS*, 1988–1991, Vol. 1, 142–144.
Fisher History: A Brief History of the University of Sydney Library [Compiled from published texts and articles], [2002?]. http//:setis.library.usyd.edu.au/uslhistory/uslhistory02.html.
'The Fisher Library, University of Sydney'. *Australian Library Journal* 8 (2) 1959, 62–64.
Flannery, Nancy Robinson, ed. *This everlasting silence: the love letters of Paquita Delprat and Douglas Mawson 1911–1914*. Carlton South, Victoria: Melbourne University, 2000.
Flowers, E. 'Objectives of training for library service'. *Australian Library Journal* 12 (1) 1963, 3–10.
Flowers, E. 'To the Association's credit, 1938–1987'. *Australian Library Journal* 36 (4) 1987, 226–228.

Flowers, E. 'Library Schools'. In Harrison Bryan, ed., *ALIAS*, 1988–1991, Vol. 2, 94–97.

Forshaw, Joseph M. *Parrots of the world*. Melbourne: Lansdowne, 1973.

Foskett, A.C. 'Education for librarianship: some thoughts on developments in the United Kingdom'. *Australian Library Journal* 24 (4) 1975, 163–173.

Fraser, Joseph. 'Pen and ink sketches of prominent persons'. [Newspaper clipping], [1888?]. SLSA: PRG1288.

['From "One of his many friends"']. [Newspaper clipping], [1921]. SLSA: PRG 1335/10.

'Future administration of the Library Association of Australia'. *Australian Library Journal* 9 (4) 1960, 177–178.

Gamble, Allan. *University of Sydney: pen sketches*. [Sydney]: University of Sydney, 1968.

Garner, Imogen. 'A tribute to our past leaders'. Biennial Conference speech, 2004. www.alia.org.au/publishing/speeches/garner.html.

'Gets high post'. *Advertiser* [SA], February 6th, 1959, 20.

Gregory, Agnes. 'Correspondence'. *Australian Library Journal* 18 (11) 1969, 416–417.

Hagger, Jean. 'Education for librarianship in the United Kingdom'. *Australian Library Journal* 13 (3) 1964, 123–128.

Hagger, Jean. 'Principles into practice: the new course in librarianship at R.M.I.T.' *Australian Library Journal* 18 (11) 1969, 413–416.

Hankel, Valmai. 'Pages of life an inspirational read'. *Advertiser* [SA], April 26th, 2003, 72.

Harvey, Ross. 'Monash University's Graduate School of Librarianship, Records and Information Management and "Traditional" Librarianship'. *Education for Librarianship Australia* 7 (1) Autumn 1990, 8–9.

Harvey, Ross. 'Losing the quality battle in Australian education for librarianship', [2004]. www.alia.org.au/publishing/alj/50.1/full.text/quality.battle.html.

'H.C.L. Anderson Award. Citation for Jean Primrose Whyte, BA, MA, FLAA', [1987]. NLA: MS 9616.

'H.C.L. Anderson Award'. In Harrison Bryan, ed., *ALIAS*, 1988–1991, Vol. 1, 16–17.

Hine, Janet D. *Index to conference proceedings 1938 to 1971 of the Australian Institute of Librarians and its successor the Library Association of Australia including their Annual Reports 1937/38 to 1953*. Sydney, New South Wales: [Library Association of Australia], 1975.

Hirst, John. 'Correspondence'. *Australian Library Journal* 11 (1) 1962, 49.

Hirst, John. 'Correspondence'. *Australian Library Journal* 11 (3) 1962, 151–152.

Hirst, John. 'Correspondence'. *Australian Library Journal* 12 (2) 1963, 103–104.

Hirst, John. 'Correspondence'. *Australian Library Journal* 17 (9) 1968, 292.

Hooks, Barbara. 'Advanced librarian course from Monash'. *The Age*, January 10th, 1975, 12.

Hope, A.D. 'The unknown anniversary'. In *Orpheus*. North Ryde, NSW: Angus and Robertson, 1991, 36–37.

Horrocks, Norman. 'Down under: opportunity beckons'. *Library Journal* 92 (20) 1967, 4107–4109.

Horton, Alan. 'Censorship – a report'. *Australian Library Journal* 15 (4) 1966, 171–172.

Inter-library Loan Committee. 'Inter-library Loan Committee'. *Australian Library Journal* 9 (4) 1960, 211.

Inter-library Loan Committee. 'Report of the Inter-Library Loan Committee, 1960–1961'. *Australian Library Journal* 10 (4) 1961, 214–216.
['It is with sincere regret']. [Newspaper clipping], [1926]. SLSA: PRG 1335/1.
Jean Primrose Whyte 27 June 1923–18 March 2003. Funeral Service. Monash University. 24 March 2003. Copy in possession of C.E.J. Jenkin.
Jenkin, Coralie E.J. 'I was a librarian by accident. Jean Primrose Whyte: A biography in progress', [2006]. www.csu.edu.au/faculty/educat/sis/CIS/epubs/LibEduc/Fschrift_Primrose_Whyte.pdf.
Johnson, Athol. 'The Royal Charter and its implications'. *Australian Library Journal* 12 (4) 1963, 182–186.
Johnson, Athol and R.F. Doust. 'The Library Association of Australia: statement of history, objects, activities and achievements: prepared in 1961 in connexion with the application for a royal Charter by A.L. Johnson, General Treasurer; revised and with a postscript by R.F. Doust, General Secretary, 1965'. *Australian Library Journal* 14 (1) 1965, 1–11.
Jones, Barry. *Barry Jones' dictionary of world biography*. Melbourne: Information Australia, 1994.
Jones, David J., ed. *The Australian librarian's manual. Volume 1. Documents*. Sydney: Library Association of Australia, 1982.
Jones, Philip. 'Philosopher of integrity practised his preachings'. *The Australian*, July 24th, 2001, 16.
Keane, M.V. 'The development of education for librarianship in Australia between 1896 and 1976, with special emphasis upon the role of the Library Association of Australia'. *Australian Library Journal* 31 (2) 1982, 12–23.
Keane, M.V. 'Chronology of education for librarianship in Australia, 1896–1976'. *Australian Library Journal* 31 (3) 1982, 16–24.
Keane, M.V. 'To everything there is a season … a time to plant and a time to pluck up that which is planted – a life-cycle analysis of education for librarianship in South Australia, 1944–1994'. In B.J. McMullin, ed. *Instruction and amusement: papers from the Sixth Australian Library History Forum*. Monash Occasional Papers in Librarianship, Recordkeeping and Bibliography, No. 8. Melbourne: Ancora, 1996.
Kenny, Janice. *National Library of Australia: history and collections*. Canberra: National Library of Australia, 1984.
'Know your department. 8. School of mines library'. *Foggy Dew* 2 (1) 1957, 3.
Knox, Jeanette. 'Education for librarianship; a decade in perspective'. *Australian Library Journal* 38 (2) 1989, 125–132.
Kosa, Gézá A., ed. *Who's who in Australian Libraries*. Surry Hills, NSW: Library Association of Australia, 1968.
Kosa, Gézá A., ed. *Biographical dictionary of Australian Librarians (formerly Who's Who in Australian libraries*. 2nd ed. Melbourne: Burwood State College, 1979.
Kosa, Gézá A., ed. *Biographical dictionary of Australian librarians*. 3rd ed. Melbourne: Academia, 1984.
Kosa, Gézá A., ed. *Biographical dictionary of Australian librarians*. 4th ed. Melbourne: Academia, 1990.
'LAA 50 – National Committee'. *Australian Library Journal* 36 (4) 1987, 192.

[LAA Certificate], September 17th, 1952. NLA: MS 9616.

La Scala, Jane. 'Major achievements of the LAA'. *Australian Library Journal*. 36 (4) 1987, 229–232.

'Late start, but Jean Whyte has the last word'. *Monash Reporter*, 9–88, 1988. NLA: MS 9616.

'Lectures for Institutes'. *South Australian Institutes Journal*, June–July 1915, 674.

Lenan, Robin. 'Letters'. *Australian Library Journal* 38 (3) 1989, 171–174.

Levett, John. 'In conclusion'. *Australian Library Journal* 36 (4) 1987, 292–295.

Levett, John. *Obituary. Remembering Jean Whyte*. www.alia.org.au/publishing/incite/2003/07/jean.whyte.html.

Librarianship in Australia: a seminar to honour Jean P. Whyte Foundation Professor and Chairman of the Graduate School of Librarianship. [Clayton, Victoria]: Graduate School of Librarianship Alumni, 1988.

Libraries Board of South Australia. *Annual Reports*, 1949–60.

Library Association of Australia. *Annual Reports*, 1952–1971.

'Library Association of Australia 1961 Conference Programme, August 21st-August 25th'. *Australian Library Journal* 10 (2) 1961, 110–113.

'Library Association of Australia 1959 Conference. Tentative programme'. *Australian Library Journal* 8 (2) 1959, 57–58.

'Library Association of Australia. Ninth Annual Conference'. *Australian Library Journal* 6 (4) 1957, 150.

[Lodewycks, K.A.] 'University of Melbourne. Proposed post-graduate school of librarianship. Specimen Scheme'. May 25th, 1962. MON 1059: 2000/68. 93.

Lodewycks, K.A. 'A proposed university school of librarianship'. *Australian Library Journal* 17 (1) 1968, 32–33.

Lodewycks, K.A. 'Letters'. *Australian Library Journal* 20 (5) 1971, 41.

Lodewycks, K.A. *The Funding of Wisdom: Revelations of a Library's quarter century*. Melbourne: Spectrum, 1982.

Lodewycks, K.A., ed. *The Campaign for a new State Library of Victoria*. Box Hill South, Victoria: [The Author], [1990].

Logan, M.I. 'Citation for Emeritus Professor Jean Primrose Whyte AM for the degree of Doctor of Letters *honoris causa*'. MON 1059: 2000/68/5.

Lundie, Margaret. 'Correspondence'. *Australian Library Journal* 14 (2) 1965, 84–85.

Lundie, Margaret. 'University of Sydney Library since the War'. *Australian Library Journal* 20 (6) 1971, 5–9.

Lundie, Margaret. 'What Jean Whyte meant to the Sydney University Library'. *FIB [Fisher Library Officers' Association Information Bulletin]* 8 (2) 1971, 1–2.

Macully, Alexander. *The art of reading*. Melbourne: Mason, Firth & M'Cutcheon, 1887.

Magarey, Susan, ed. *Dame Roma: glimpses of a glorious life*. [Adelaide]: Axiom Publishing in association with the John Bray Law Chapter of the Alumni Association of the University of Adelaide, 2002.

Magarey, Susan and Kerrie Round. *Roma the first: a biography of Dame Roma Mitchell*. Kent Town, South Australia: Wakefield, 2007.

Maguire, Carmel. 'Courses in librarianship available in Australia'. *Australian Library Journal* 20 (4) 1971, 22–24.

Manning, Geoffrey H. *From Aaron Creek to Zion Hill: the place names of South Australia.* [Adelaide]: 2000.

Manning, Geoffrey H. *Manning's place names of South Australia: From Aaron Creek to Zion Hill: an extension and revision of Manning's place names of South Australia* (1990). Modbury, South Australia: Gould Books, 2006.

Manton, G.R. 'Preliminary proposals for a Graduate School of Librarianship', [1972]. MON 1059: 2000/68. 93.

Manton, G.R. [Notes for a speech prepared for the retirement of Hector Monro], 1976. MON 1059: 2000/68. 82.

Marginson, Simon. *Remaking the University.* St Leonard's, NSW: Allen & Unwin, 2000.

Masterman, L.C. 'Correspondence'. *Australian Library Journal* 7 (3) 1958, 82–83.

Masterman, L.C. 'Correspondence'. *Australian Library Journal* 11 (3) 1962, 150–151.

May, Frederick. 'The concupiscence of the oppressor'. *Australian Library Journal* 13 (2) 1964, 73–84.

McEldowney, W.J. *Geoffrey Alley, librarian: his life and work.* Wellington, New Zealand: Victoria University, 2006.

McKinlay, John. 'A mess of ephemera'. *Australian Library Journal* 26 (1) 18, 1977, 6.

McMullin, Brian. 'Harrison Bryan, bibliographer and hand-printer'. In *An enthusiasm for libraries. See* Jean P. Whyte and Neil A. Radford, eds., 1988, 20–34.

McMullin, Brian. 'The School within the Institution'. *Education for Librarianship: Australia* 6 (2–3) Winter/Spring 1989, 10–13.

McMullin, Brian. 'Yadlamalka girl shaped Australian librarianship: Jean Primrose Whyte, Emeritus Professor, Graduate School of Librarianship, Monash University 27 June 1923–18 March 2003'. *The Age*, April 18th, 2003, 19. Reprinted in *Australian Library Journal* 52 (5) 2003, 105–107.

Metcalfe, John. 'A comment on our history'. *Australian Library Journal* 5 (4) 1956, 142–144.

Metcalfe, John. 'The standards of librarianship and the status of the library profession'. *Australian Library Journal* 8 (4) 1959, 171–180.

Metcalfe, John. 'Courses and qualifications in librarianship ... Additions and adumbrations'. *Australian Library Journal* 12 (2) 1963, 96–102.

Metcalfe, John. 'The true story'. *Australian Library Journal* 20 (4) 1971, 44–47.

Metcalfe, John. 'Twenty-one years of the *Australian Library Journal*: John Metcalfe'. *Australian Library Journal* 21 (6) 1972, 229–231.

Miller, L. 'Realism in training for librarianship'. *Australian Library Journal* 6 (2) 1957, 54–57.

'Master's Degree in Librarianship'. [Advertisement]. *Australian Library Journal* 24 (13) 1975, 370.

Modra, Helen M. 'The short march: social responsibility in Australian librarianship 1970–1983'. Master of Education thesis, unpublished, Monash University, 1986.

Monash University. Council. 'Minute of Appreciation. Professor J.P. Whyte, 1989'. NLA: MS 9616.

Monash University. Council. 'Minutes of Council'. Item 4.1.1. December 9th, 1974. MON EA/195/1.

Monash University. Council Committee for an appointment to a Chair of Librarianship. 'Minutes. Meeting No. 1', [early 1974?]. MON 1059: EA/195/1.

Monash University. Faculty Board. 'Minutes', January, 1970. MON 1059: 2000/68. 93.
Monash University. Graduate School of Librarianship, [1974?]. MON 1059: 2000/68. 47.
Monash University. Graduate School of Librarianship. *Annual Reports*, 1975–1976.
Monash University. [Internal debit/credit note], 1974. MON: SLO 72330.
Monash University. 'Monash University Graduation Ceremony', [1996], 5. NLA: MS 9616.
Monash University. *Vera Moore Fund Committee*. MON 1059: 2000/68. 1.
[Monro, Hector?]. 'JPW – A panegyric'. *Australian Library Journal* 38 (2) 1989, 191.
Monro, Hector. *Fortunate catastrophes: an anecdotal autobiography*. Melbourne: Quokka, 1991.
Morrison, Elizabeth. 'The Graduate School of librarianship at Monash University: The Beginnings'. *Education for Librarianship: Australia* 6 (2–3) Winter/Spring 1989, 5–9.
Morrison, Elizabeth and Michael Talbot, eds. *Books, libraries and readers in Colonial Australia: papers from the forum on Australian Colonial Library History held at Monash University, 1–2 June, 1984*. Clayton, Victoria: Graduate School of Librarianship, Monash University, 1985.
Murray, Jean M. 'Fourteen years on'. *Australian Library Journal* 16 (1) 1967, 3–5.
Murray, Jean M. 'Harrison Bryan: a bibliography, 1950–1987'. In *An enthusiasm for libraries*. See Jean P. Whyte and Neil A. Radford, eds., 1988, 255–276.
'National Library of Australia. Senior professional vacancies'. *Australian Library Journal* 21 (4) 1972, 180.
'New committees'. *Australian Library Journal* 15 (3) 1966, 136.
'News. Millionth book for Sydney University Library'. *Australian Library Journal* 15 (6) 1966, 235–238.
Northam, W.F. [Memo]. December 12th, 1974. MON: SLO 72330.
'Notices and News'. *Australian Library Journal* 5 (3) 1956, 121–122.
'Obituaries. Rev. Alexander Macully, M.A., LL.B.'. *The Observer* [SA], January 15th, 1921, 34b.
'Officers and councillors, 1953'. *Australian Library Journal* 2 (1) 1953, 2.
Osborn, Andrew D. 'The crisis in cataloging: a paper read before the American Library Institute at the Harvard Faculty Club, June 21, 1941'. *Library Quarterly* 11 (4) 1941, 393–411.
Osborn, Andrew D. 'The Library Keeper's Business'. *Arts* 1 (3) 1959, 176.
Osborn, Andrew D. *Goldfields settlers: the story of Andrew and Susan Osborn in Beechworth*. Cape Cod [Massachusetts]: Orana, 1983.
Our nation's album: the library's first 100 years: a history of the National Library of Australia. Canberra: National Library of Australia, 2001. www.nla.gov.au/nla.arc-33961.
Page, Ivan. 'Correspondence'. *Australian Library Journal* 15 (2) 1966, 49–51.
Pastoral pioneers of South Australia. Adelaide: Publishers Limited, 1925–1927.
Peake, Dorothy and Marea Terry. 'Computer printed union list of serials in branch and department libraries in the University of Sydney Library'. *Australian Library Journal* 19 (4) 1970, 149–153.
Penfold, Dulcie. Review of *Libraries in the east; an international and comparative study* by G. Chandler. *Australian Library Journal* 21 (3) 1972, 128–129.
Persis, Sister. [Reference for Jean Whyte], 1942. NLA: MS 9616.

Pike, Douglas, ed. *Australian Dictionary of Biography. Volume 3: 1851–1890*. Carlton, Victoria: Melbourne University, 1969.

Pioneer index. Victoria 1836–1888. Index to births, deaths and marriages in Victoria. Melbourne: Registry of Births, Deaths and Marriages, Victoria, 1998.

Radford, Neil A. 'Student borrowing from a university library'. *Australian Library Journal* 15 (4) 1966, 154–160.

Radford, Neil A. 'Borrowing for research from a university library'. *Australian Library Journal* 16 (2) 1967, 77–81.

Radford, Neil A. 'Intra-mural use of a university library'. *Australian Library Journal* 16 (5) 1967, 209–216.

Radford, Neil A. 'Re-defining the L.A.A.'s role in education for librarianship'. *Library Association of Australia. Proceedings of the 19th biennial conference held in Tasmania, August 1977. Libraries in Society*. Hobart: Conference Committee, 1977, 139–150.

Radford, Neil A. 'Recognition of courses in librarianship'. *Australian Library Journal* 27 (2) 1978, 22.

Radford, Neil A. 'Education for librarianship: the changing role'. *Australian Library Journal* 27 (5) 1978, 102–106.

Radford, Neil A. 'Education for librarianship and the manpower problem'. *Australian Library Journal* 26 (8) 1978, 197–202.

Radford, Neil A. 'Harrison Bryan, Librarian'. In *An enthusiasm for libraries*. See Jean P. Whyte and Neil A. Radford, eds., 1988, 1–19.

Radford, Neil A. 'Notes for talk at Jean Whyte's funeral', 2003. Copy in possession of C.E.J. Jenkin. [Photocopy].

Radford, Neil A. 'Obituaries. Jean Primrose Whyte AM', [2003]. www.alia.org.au/publishing/aarl/34.3/obituaries.html.

Radford, Neil A. and Joan E. Barry. 'I.B.M. punched card circulation at Sydney University Library'. *Australian Library Journal* 15 (6) 1966, 228–234.

Radford, Wilma. 'Correspondence'. *Australian Library Journal* 11 (3) 1962, 147–150.

Radford, Wilma. 'Formal training for library service'. *Australian Library Journal* 12 (1) 1963, 11–14.

Radford, Wilma. 'Correspondence'. *Australian Library Journal* 13 (4) 1964, 193.

Radford, Wilma. 'Education for librarianship'. *Australian Library Journal* 18 (11) 1969, 407–412.

Radford, Wilma. 'The School of Librarianship, University of New South Wales'. *Australian Library Journal* 19 (11) 1970, 417–419.

Radford, Wilma. 'Higher degrees for Australian librarians'. *Australian Library Journal* 20 (3) 1971, 9–13.

Ramsay, Margery. 'Solutions in search of a problem'. *Australian Library Journal* 12 (1) 1963, 15–20.

Ramsay, Margery. 'Librarianship as a field for academic study', [1972?]. MON 1059: 2000/68. 93.

Ramsay, Margery. [Untitled note], [1974]. MON 1059: EA/195/1.

Ramsay, Margery. 'From LAA headquarters: education for the new librarianship'. *Australian Library Journal* 24 (2) 1975, 66–67.

Raymond, I.D. 'The pattern of Australian education for librarianship: a critical comment'. *Australian Library Journal* 20 (3) 1971, 5–8.

Rayward, W. Boyd. 'The future of library education in Australia – and its past'. *Australian Library Journal* 38 (2) 1989, 115–123.

Rayward, W. Boyd, ed. *Libraries and life in a changing world: the Metcalfe years, 1920–1970: papers from Australian Library history forum V at the University of New South Wales, 6–7th November, 1992*. Sydney: School of Information, Library and Archive Studies, University of New South Wales, 1993.

Reid, Barrett. 'Books in Australia: publishing, selling, acquiring, and a word about censorship'. *Library Journal* 92 (20) 1967, 4123–4126.

Reid-Smith, Edward, compiler. *A directory of library schools and lecturers in librarianship in Australia, 1978*. Wagga Wagga, NSW: Department of Library and Information Science, Riverina, 1978.

Resuscitator. 'Mrs Whyte's death'. *The Register* [SA], March 20th, 1926.

'Rev. Alexander McCully'. [Newspaper clipping], n.d. SLSA: PRG 1335/10.

Richardson, Norman A. *The pioneers of the north-west of South Australia 1856–1914*. Adelaide: W.K. Thomas & Co., 1925. Facsimile edition: Adelaide: Libraries Board of South Australia, 1969.

Routh, Spencer. Review of *How to find out, a guide to sources of information for all, arranged by the Dewey Decimal Classification* by G. Chandler. *Australian Library Journal* 13 (2) 1964, 85.

[Rylah, Arthur]. http://adbonline.anu.edu.au/biogs/A16090b.htm.

'S.A. librarian studies training in American library schools'. *Advertiser* [SA], May 31st, 1955, 16.

St. Peter's Collegiate Girls' School 1894–1968: A history of the Sisters' School in Adelaide during 74 years. Stonyfell, South Australia: St. Peter's Girls' School, 1972.

Saunders, W.L. 'Education for librarianship in Great Britian' [sic]. *Australian Library Journal* 18 (11) 1969, 386–392.

'School officers'. *Chronicles of St. Peter's Girls* 54, 1941, [1].

Scott, Barry. 'Library associations in Australia, past and present'. *Australian Library Journal* 5 (3) 1956, 102–108.

Scott, Dorothy. *The halfway house to infidelity: a history of the Melbourne Unitarian Church, 1853–1973*. [Melbourne]: Unitarian Fellowship of Australia and the Melbourne Unitarian Peace Memorial Church, 1980.

'Secretarial notes'. Australian Institute of Librarians. South Australian Branch, *Quarterly Bulletin*. 8, 1946, 4.

Sharr, F.A. 'Like an ambitious young man: Australian public libraries'. *Library Journal* 92 (20) 1967, 4110–4112.

Slight, Owen E. 'Sydney University Library moves its research collections'. *Australian Library Journal* 16 (6) 1967, 240–244.

Smith, J.S. 'Correspondence'. *Australian Library Journal* 14 (2) 1965, 85.

State Records Office of South Australia. Page 34/79 GRG 26 Series List 10/11 page 25. *Monthly and annual reports of Adelaide Lending Service 1946–69*. Series 11, No. 9.

'Statement of Principles on Freedom to Read'. *Australian Library Journal* 13 (3) 1964, 136.

Statton, Jill, ed. *Biographical index of South Australians 1836–1885*. 4 vols. Marden, SA: South Australian Genealogy and Heraldry Society, 1986.
Stout, A.K. 'Correspondence'. *Australian Library Journal* 14 (2) 1965, 84.
Thorn, W.D. 'Building library collections for research'. In *An enthusiasm for libraries. See* Jean P. Whyte and Neil A. Radford, eds., 1988, 99–113.
Tierney, Jean Hume. 'Correspondence'. *Australian Library Journal* 19 (10) 1970, 386.
'To help New Australians'. [Newspaper clipping], n.d. SLSA: PRG 1335/1.
Transcript of a conversation between Jean Whyte and Geoffrey Alley, 1981. MON 1059: 2000/68/5.
Trask, Margaret. 'Judgement, energy, intellectual capacity, and vision; the role of the Board of Examiners and the Board of Education'. *Australian Library Journal* 36 (4) 1987, 232–235.
'University appointments. The University of New South Wales'. [advertisement]. *Australian Library Journal* 17 (1) 1968, vi.
'The University of Adelaide'. [Newspaper clipping], n.d. NLA: MS 9616.
University of Chicago. *Fellowship appointments for the academic year 1954–55*. NLA: MS 9616.
University of Sydney. Library. 'Australian University Libraries – Reader Services Unit output – Main Library only 1971', 1972. SU Archives.
University of Sydney. Library Committee [and predecessors]. *Minute books*. SU Archives.
University of Sydney. Library. *Report on the collections, 1959–1960*. Sydney: 1961.
University of Sydney. Senate. *Minute books*. SU Archives.
'University of Sydney Library staff reorganization'. *Australian Library Journal* 15 (3) 1966, 104–105.
Vago, Judy, ed. *Library Interlending Conference 1983. Proceedings of the Library Association of Australia National Interlending Conference 31 August–2 September 1983*. Sydney, New South Wales: Library Association of Australia, New South Wales Branch, 1984.
'Valuable grant for study in U.S.'. *Advertiser* [SA], March 18th, 1953, 11.
Vanslambrouck, Paula. 'Library managers'. *Australian Library Journal* 21 (1) 1972, 34.
Victorian Universities Committee. Item '46.2'. *Victorian Universities Committee. AUC Fifth report – collaboration between universities*, April 1972. 2000/68. 93 MON 1059.
Wainwright, Eric J. *Readings in Australian librarianship II: Australian library surveys: a selection of readings from the publications of the Library Association of Australia*. Surry Hills, NSW: Library Association of Australia, 1979.
Ward, Jack. [Correspondence]. *Australian Library Journal* 13 (3) 1964, 133.
'Warm tributes at farewell'. *FIB [Fisher Library Officers' Association Information Bulletin]* 8 (2) September 1971, 3.
Waters, David. 'The education explosion: some problems for Australian university libraries'. *Australian Library Journal* 14 (3) 1965, 126–129.
Whackers Up. 'Our great northerner'. *Northern Sportsman*, n.d. SLSA: PRG 1335/1.
Whalan, R.E. 'Correspondence'. *Australian Library Journal* 11 (4) 1962, 197–198.
Whalan, R.E. 'Correspondence'. *Australian Library Journal* 12 (3) 1963, 144.
Whitehead, Derek. 'AM and PM: the Munn-Pitt report'. *Australian Library Journal* 30 (1) 1981, 4–10.
Who's Who in Australia. Melbourne: Herald and Weekly Times, 1996.

Whyte, Jean P. – see Appendix 5, a bibliography of publications by Jean Primrose Whyte, which includes works co-authored by her.

'Whyte' [Birth notice]. *The Register* [SA], June 30th, 1923.

'Woman killed by shark'. *The Register* [SA], March 19th, 1926, 9.

'Woman takes new chair at Monash'. *Standard Times* [Carnegie, Victoria], January 15th, 1975.

Wilde, William. *Australian poets & their works: a reader's guide*. Melbourne: Oxford University, 1996.

Wilkinson, E.H. 'Education for librarianship in Britain: a visitor's impressions'. *Australian Library Journal* 17 (7) 1968, 243–248.

Wilkinson, E.H. 'From the monumental to the modular and beyond'. In *An enthusiasm for libraries*. See Jean P. Whyte and Neil A. Radford, eds., 1988, 127–143.

Wroblewski, J.H. 'Correspondence'. *Australian Library Journal* 15 (4) 1966, 141–142.

Zerman, B.J. [Medical report], 1981. NLA: MS 9616.

CORRESPONDENCE

Alley, Geoffrey T. to Jean Whyte. Correspondence, 1968–1980. Held by J. McEldowney, Dunedin, New Zealand.

Butchart, J.D. to Jean Whyte, December 11th, 1974. MON: SLO 72330.

Cox, James R. to Jean Whyte, November 18th, 1988. NLA: MS 9616.

Fleming, Alan to Jean Whyte, 1972–1974. NLA: MS 9616.

Gregory, Agnes to Jean Whyte, February 4th, 1988. NLA: MS 9616.

Lodewycks, K.A. to R. Selby Smith, June 15th, 1967. MON 1059: 2000/68. 93.

Logan, M.I. to Jean Whyte, December 14th, 1988. NLA: MS 9616.

Manton, G.R. to Jean Whyte, September 25th, 1974. MON 1059: EA/195/1.

Manton, G.R. to I.B. Tate, [1975]. MON: SLO 72330.

Mitchell, Roma. 'To American Association of University Women', October 31st, 1952. NLA: MS 9616.

Mitchell, Roma. 'To whom it may concern', May 11th, 1956. NLA: MS 9616.

Othams, H.R. to Jean Whyte, October 28th, 1952. SLSA: PRG 1335.

Pitt, G.H. to Committee on Fellowships and Scholarships, University of Chicago. September 5th, 1952. NLA: MS 9616.

Ramsay, A.M. to American Association of University Women, November 3rd, 1952. NLA: MS 9616.

Selby Smith, R. to K.A. Lodewycks, June 20th, 1967. MON 1059: 2000/68. 93.

Whyte, E.P. to Messrs T.H. Doman & Co. Ltd, November 9th, 1943. SLSA: PRG 1335/8.

INTERVIEWS BY AUTHOR / PERSONAL COMMUNICATION

Adamson, Peter. October 1st, 2005. Adelaide, South Australia.

Barry, Joan. January 7th, 2005. Sydney, New South Wales.

Brewer, Joan. August 4th, 2008. Adelaide, South Australia.

Bryan, Harrison. January 6th, 2005. Sydney, New South Wales.

Crawford, Mavis. December 17th, 2008. By telephone.

Crossley, John. July 22nd, 2008. Clayton, Victoria.

Day, Grecian and Ross. June 20th, 2008. Clayton, Victoria.
Fanning, Pauline. October 28th, 2008. Canberra, ACT.
Fox, Lorraine. March 7th, 2005. Canberra, ACT.
Harvey, Ross. January 3rd, 2005. Chiltern, Victoria.
Jones, David. April 3rd, 2006, personal communication; September 17th, 2008, personal communication.
Kafkarisos, Steven. June 22nd, 2005. Melbourne, Victoria.
Kirsop, Wallace. June 27th, 2008. Melbourne, Victoria.
Lange, Joan. July 12th, 2005. Adelaide, South Australia.
Legge, John. July 22nd, 2008. Clayton, Victoria.
Lowe, John. January 1st, 2005. Falls Creek, Victoria.
McEldowney, W.J. April 17th, 2006, personal communication.
McMullin, Brian. May 26th, 2008. Melbourne, Victoria; May 3rd, 2006, personal communication.
Miranda, Sara. July 22nd, 2008. Clayton, Victoria.
Morrison, Elizabeth. October 29th, 2008. Canberra, ACT.
Muecke, Douglas. July 14th, 2005. Adelaide, South Australia.
Monro, Jane and Gordon. January 7th, 2005. Sydney, New South Wales.
Olding, Ray. August 4th, 2008. Adelaide, South Australia. August 8th, 2008, personal communication.
Powell, Graeme. October 28th, 2008. Canberra, ACT.
Radford, Neil. January 7th, 2005. Sydney, New South Wales. January 17th, 2005, personal communication. June 29th, 2009, personal communication.
Richardson, Denis. June 21st, 2006. Kew, Victoria.
Salmond, Rachel. January 3rd, 2005. Chiltern, Victoria. September 13th, 2008, personal communication.
Talbot, Michael. July 13th, 2005; August 5th, 2008. Adelaide, South Australia.
Upward, Frank. June 27th, 2008. Melbourne, Victoria.

ARCHIVES

Monash University Archives. MON 1059 and SLO.
National Library of Australia. MS9616.
State Library of South Australia. PRG 1335.
State Records of South Australia. GRG 26.
University of Sydney Archives. M. 465.

INDEX

Abd-Ul-Wahid, Xalid, 12.2
Adelaide Lending Service, 02.1, 02.3-02.4, 02.7, 07.7, 07.15
Alexander, William, 10.2
Alexandra College, Dublin, 01.2, 10.3
Alley, Geoffrey, 03.10, 03.11, 05.3, 06.3, 06.16, 07.10, 07.15, 07.17, 07.21
American Association of University Women, 02.8, 02.9, 07.15
American Library Association, 02.9, 07.5, 07.6, 07.9
Ancora Press, Monash University, 06.12, 07.2, 12.1
Anderson Award, HCL, 07.1, 12.2
Archives, 02.1, 02.3, 02.5, 06.6, 06.12, 07.2, 07.3, 12.2
Art Advisory Committee, Monash University, 07.21
Art Gallery of South Australia, 02.11, 07.24,
Association of College and Research Libraries, 07.6
Australia-China Society, 07.6
Australian Institute of International Affairs, 07.6
Australian Institute of Librarians, xii, 02.2, 02.3, 02.5, 02.6, 02.7, 05.1, 05.3, 06.6, 07.3, 07.4, 07.5, 07.8
Australian Library Journal, 02.7-02.8, 03.1, 03.9, 03.11, 04.1-04.3, 07.7, 06.13, 07.5, 07.8-07.11, 07.13, 07.14, 07.15, 07.17, 07.18, 07.19
Australian literature, *see* Poetry
Australian Universities Commission, 06.1, 11.1
Baggins, 03.2, 03.11, 05.1, 05.2, 06.3, 07.16-07.17, 07.19
Banquo Club, *see* Monash University Banquo Club
Barry, Joan, 03.11
Behymer, EH, 02.8
Beta Phi Mu Honour Society in Librarianship, 07.6
Bethany College, West Virginia, 02.8
Bibliographical Society of Australia and New Zealand, 07.6
Board of Examination, 02.7, 03.9-03.10, 06.5, 06.11, 06.13, 07.4, 07.5, 07.6, 07.13
Book Collectors Society, 07.6

Bookshop Board, Monash University, 06.12
Borchardt, DH, 04.2, 06.1
Botanic Gardens Library, Adelaide, 02.3
Bouette, Irene, 06.8
Bradley, David, 06.18
Bray, John, 07.9, 07.17, 07.19
Brereton, J. Le Gay, 03.7
Brewer, Joan, 07.1
Brideson, Hedley, 02.6, 02.10, 02.11, 03.2, 06.13, 07.12, 07.13, 07.16
Bridge, Carl, 02.6
Brown, Arthur, 07.2
Brown, Laurie, 04.3, 06.2,
Brunt, Maureen, 07.31
Bryan, Harrison, xii, 01.5, 02.2, 02.10, 03.2, 03.4, 03.5, 03.8, 03.9, 03.10, 03.11, 03.14, 04.1, 04.2, 04.3, 05.1, 05.2, 06.2, 06.4, 06.8, 06.10, 06.12, 06.13, 06.16, 06.18, 07.2, 07.5-07.6, 07.7, 07.12, 07.14, 07.16, 07.17, 07.21, 07.31, 12.2, *Fig. 7*
Bryant, Phillip, 06.18
Buick, George, 02.6, 07.13
Butler, R, 07.8
Callimachus, 02.8, 07.1-07.2, 07.11, 07.25
Campbell, Alexander, 01.2, 10.2
Campbell, Enid, 07.31
Campbell family, Sydney, 01.3
Campbell, Minnie, *see* Macully, Minnie
Canadian Library Association, 07.6
Canberra College of Advanced Education, 06.17
Canberra Times, 07.15
Carey, Elaine, *see* Cure, Elaine de
Censorship, 02.7, 04.3, 07.8-07.11
Chandler, George, 05.1, 05.2-05.3, 05.4, 06.4, 06.11, 06.13, 07.5, 07.12, 07.15-07.16, *Fig. 7*
Charles, Prince of Wales, 07.2
Children's libraries, 07.14
Churchman, C. West, 06.18, 12.1

Clark, Ernest, 06.1, 06.2
Committee on Overseas Professional Qualifications, 06.13, 07.6
Commonwealth National Library, see National Library of Australia
Conference of Directors of Scientific Information Centres in the Asian-Pacific Region, Hong Kong, 03.10, 07.11
Cope, Russell, 04.2, 04.3
Counsell, James, 01.3
Cowan, WA, 03.2
Crawford, Bruce, 01.5
Crawford, Mavis, 01.5, 07.25, 07.17
'Cullymont', Melbourne, 01.2-01.3, 10.1-10.4
Cure, Elaine de, 07.19-07.20
Davis, Mari, 12.2
Day, Grecian and Ross, 07.21
Dervish, Bejah, 01.4
Doman, TH & Co, 01.4
Dowden, Edward, 10.2
Duncan, WGK, 03.2, 07.9
'Dunluce', Adelaide, 01.3, 10.4
'Dunluce', Northern Ireland, 01.3, 10.4
Education for librarianship, 02.4-02.6, 02.7, 02.8-02.9, 03.9, 03.11, 04.3, 06.1-06.20, 07.4-07.5, 07.7
Elizabeth, Queen Mother, 05.2
Elizabeth Public Library, 02.6
Ellis, Judith, 12.2
Ellis, Lee, 07.10
English Association, 07.6
Faculty of Information Technology, Monash University, 07.24
Farmer, GAJ, 04.2, 04.3
Fellowship of Australian Writers, 07.6
Fergus and Tansie, 07.17
Fisher Library, University of Sydney, xii, 03.1-03.16, 04.2, 05.1, 05.2, 07.2, 07.6, 07.7, 07.9, 07.14–16, 07.17, 07.18, 07.21, 07.22, 07.23, 07.24
Fisher, Thomas, 03.2
Fleming, Alan, 05.1, 05.2, 05.3, 05.4, 06.3, 06.4, 06.16, 07.14, *Fig. 7*

Flinders University, Adelaide, 07.15
Freedom of information, see Censorship
Friends of Fisher Library, University of Sydney, 03.9, 07.2, 07.6
Friends of the Monash University Library, 06.12, 07.2
Friends of the Public Library of South Australia 07.2, 07.6
Fulbrighters Association, 07.6
Fulvius, Laurentius, see Brown, Laurie
Fussler, Herman, 02.9, 12.1
Gledhill, Miss, 07.8
Government Departmental Libraries, Adelaide, 02.3
Graduate Library School, University of Chicago, 02.8-02.9, 02.10, 06.11, 07.12,
Graduate School of Librarianship, Monash University, xii, 00.1, 06.1-06.20, 07.2, 07.3, 07.4, 07.5, 07.7, 07.11, 07.18, 07.24, 10.1
Gregory, Agnes, 07.1
GSL Alumni Association, Monash University, 06.13
Hall, DR 04.2
Hand-printing, 03.9, 06.12, 07.2, 07.18
Haratsis, Brian, 12.2
Harvey, Ross, 06.10, 06.11, 07.2, 12.2
Heath, Louisa, see Whyte, Louisa
Hine, Janet, 04.2, 04.3
Historical studies, 06.7
Hodge, Sarah, 01.3
Holman, Mollie, 07.31
Holt, Zara, 05.2
Honorary Doctor of Letters, 07.1
Hope, AD, 07.25
Hubber, Brian, 06.10, 12.1
Hudson, Hugh, 05.4
Humphries, Barry, 07.8
Jenkin, Coralie, xii–xiii, 00.1
Jenkins, GF and RK, 01.7
Jenkins, GK, 01.7
Jocelyn, Professor, 03.8
Jones, David, xii, 07.3, 07.22
Jury, Charles Rischbieth, 03.8, 07.19, 07.21

Kalliota Station, South Australia, 01.4
Kazlaukas, Edward, 06.18
Keane, Maureen, 12.1
Kirsop, Wallace, 03.7, 06.18
Lake Hut Station, SA, 01.4
Lange, Joan and Rudi, 01.7
Laughton, Miss, 07.8
Levett, John, 07.25
Library Advisory Committee, University of Sydney, 03.7, 03.8, 03.14
Library Association of Australia, xii, 02.3, 02.6, 02.7, 02.8, 02.10, 03.2, 03.9, 03.11, 04.1-04.3, 05.3, 06.1, 06.13, 07.1, 07.3, 07.4, 07.5, 07.6, 07.7, 07.9-07.11, 07.13, 07.15, 07.25
Library Council of Victoria, 07.6
Library history, 02.8, 02.9, 06.7, 06.9, 6.14, 07.1-07.4, 07.10
Library History Forums, 07.3, 07.5, 12.2
Library Workers Against Uranium Mining, 07.11
Lillecrap, Horace, 01.7
Lloyd Jones, Sir David and Lady, 01.3, 10.3
Lodewycks, Axel, 06.1, 07.29, 11.1
Lowe, John, 07.4
Lubetzky, Seymour, 07.13
Lundie, Margaret, 04.3, 07.17, 07.18
Macquarie University, 07.15, 07.31
Macully, Alexander, 01.1, 01.2, 01.3, 01.6, 02.1, 02.2, 07.19, 07.22, 07.23-07.24, 07.25, 07.34, 10.1-10.5, *Fig. 4*
Macully, Arnold, 01.3, 01.6, 07.34, 10.4
Macully, Jessie Eileen, *see* Whyte, Jessie Eileen
Macully, John James, 01.1-01.2, 10.1
Macully, Maria Julia (Minnie), 01.2-01.3, 01.6, 07.34, 10.2-10.5
Macully, Norah, 10.4
Macully, Oscar Campbell, 01.6, 10.4, 10.5
Manning, Michael, 12.1-12.2
Manton, Guy, 06.1-06.4, 06.12, 07.5, 07.15
Marachowie Station, South Australia, 01.4
Maroney, Mary Lou, 06.8
Martin, Angus, 06.18

Martin, Ray, 06.11
Matheson Library, *see* Monash University Library
Matheson, JA Louis, 06.12
Mawson, Douglas, 01.6, 10.5
Mawson, Paquita, 01.6, 10.5
May, Frederick, 07.9
McDonald, Eleanor May, *see* Whyte, Eleanor May
McEldowney, Jock, 03.10
McMullin, Brian, 06.8, 06.11, 06.17, 06.18, 07.17, 07.23, 12.1-12.
McMullin, Lisbeth, 07.17
Melbourne Theatre Company, 07.18
Metcalf Seminar, 02.10, 02.11, 03.1, 03.2, 06.13, 07.5, 07.12
Metcalf, Keyes, 02.10, 02.11
Metcalfe, John, xii, 04.2
Mines Library, *see* South Australian Department of Mines Library, Adelaide
Mitchell, Harold, 07.17
Mitchell, Dame Roma, 01.1, 02.8, 07.17, 07.21, 07.23, 07.24, 07.25, *Fig. 9*
Modra, Helen, 07.11
Monash Caulfield Campus, 07.2
Monash University, 05.3, 06.1-06.20, 07.1, 07.2, 07.5, 07.11, 07.13, 07.14, 07.15-07.16, 07.17, 07.18, 07.24
Monash University Banquo Club, 07.18
Monash University Council, 06.12, 06.13
Monash University Library, 06.1-06.2, 06.12, 07.2, 07.18, 07.24
Monash University Museum of Art, 06.12, 07.24
Monash University Professorial Board, 06.12
Monash, John, 06.1
Monro, Hector, 07.17, 07.18-07.19, 07.21, 07.25, 08.1, 12.1, *Fig. 8*
Monro, Joyce, 07.18
Moorabbin Library, Victoria, 07.8
Morrison, Elizabeth, 06.8-06.9, 6.11, 06.13, 06.18, 07.3, 07.17, 07.24, 12.1-12.2
Morrison, Perry, 06.18
Muecke, Audrey, 06.3

Muecke, Douglas, 06.3, 07.19, 07.25
Mundowdna Station, South Australia, 01.3
Myer Foundation, 06.11
Myer, Ken, 07.5, *Fig. 7*
Nadarajah, Radha, *see* Rasmussen, Radha
National Library of Australia, 02.10, 03.5, 03.11, 03.12, 05.1-05.5, 06.3, 06.13, 07.2, 07.5, 07.6, 07.7, 07.14, 07.15-07.16, 07.17, 07.21
National Library of Australia Advisory Committee in the Humanities, 07.6
National Library of Australia Council, 06.13, 07.5-07.6
Neale, Marie, 07.31
New South Wales Department of Technical Education, 06.17
Nuriootpa Pulic Library, 02.7
O'Brien, Edna, 07.10
Olding, Ray, 02.7, 05.4, 07.13, 07.17, 07.22
Osborn, Andrew, 02.11, 03.1-03.2, 03.4, 03.8, 03.9, 03.10, 03.11, 05.1, 05.3, 06.4, 06.13, 07.2, 07.11, 07.12, 07.14, 07.15-07.16, 07.17-07.18, 07.23, 07.24, 07.31, *Fig. 10*
Paltridge, Cynthia, 02.7
Parkes, Henry, 01.2, 10.2
Paterson, Banjo, 07.19
Penfold, Dulcie, 05.3
Penny, Sandra, 06.10, 12.1
Sister Persis, 01.6
Phoenix, 07.19
Piscator Press, University of Sydney, 03.9, 04.2, 07.2
Pitt, George, 02.3-02.4, 02.8, 02.6-02.7, 03.2, 06.12, 07.1, 07.2, 07.8, 07.10, 07.12, 07.14, 07.15, 07.16, 07.17, 07.21
Playford, Thomas, 02.6
Plunket, Lord, 10.2
Poetry, 01.2, 01.5, 02.7, 02.8, 03.1, 03.5-03.6, 03.7, 06.13-06.15, 07.1-07.2, 07.10, 07.16, 07.18, 07.19-07.21, 07.22, 07.23, 07.24, 07.25, 07.26, 09.1-09.6, 10.1, 10.2 10.3
The Poetry, Adelaide, 07.19, 07.25
Poetry Monash, 07.19
Prince Alfred College, Adelaide, 01.3

Public Library of New South Wales, Sydney, 03.8
Public Library of South Australia, xii, 02.1-2.14, 05.3, 07.2, 07.4, 07.6, 07.8, 07.12, 07.13, 07.14-07.16, 07.17, 07.24
Quambi Nursing Home, Adelaide, 01.4
Quingle, 07.17
Radford, Neil, [xii-xiii], xii, 02.11, 06.8-06.9, 06.10, 06.11, 06.13, 07.12, 07.17, 07.18, 07.22, 07.23
Radford, Wilma, 06.4, 06.17, 07.4, 07.9, 07.23
Ramsay, Alec, 02.8
Ramsay, Margery, 06.2, 06.10, 06.15, 06.16, 07.2, 07.17
Ranganathan's Colon Classification, 07.13, 07.14, 07.31
Ransom, Sylvia, 12.1
Rasmussen, Henning, 07.17
Rasmussen, Radha, 06.8, 06.18, 06.10, 07.17, 12.1
Rayward, Boyd, 06.11, 07.17
Reader education, 07.7
Registration, 02.2, 02.4-02.5, 03.9, 07.4-07.5, 07.13
Reid, Barrett, 06.18
Richardson, Denis, 06.2
Richardson, Valerie, 12.1
Robinson, William, 07.24
Rogers, Frank, 03.4
Ronnie, M, 12.2
'Rosemont', Sydney, 01.2, 01.3
Rosengren, Jeannette, 12.1-12.2
Rosenthal, Robert, 06.18
Royal Institute of Public Administration Regional Group, Canberra, 07.11
Royal Lifesaving Society, 01.1
Royal Melbourne Institute of Technology, 06.1, 06.17, 07.10
RSPCA, 07.24
Rutland Square Institute, Dublin, 01.2, 10.3
Ryder Cheshire, 07.24
Rylah, Sir Arthur, 07.8
St Jude's Church of England, Adelaide, 01.1, 01.3, 01.4, 01.6, 07.34, 10.3-10.4
St Peter's Collegiate Girls' School, 01.4-01.5, 07.23

Salmond, Rachel, 07.13, 07.25, 12.2
Sandringham Council, Victoria, 07.10
School of Library and Information Science, University of Western Ontario, 03.10, 03.11, 06.5, 06.6, 06.10, 06.11, 07.12, 07.23
School of Library Science, University of Pittsburgh, 03.10
Scotch College, Melbourne, 01.1, 10.2
Scott, Barry, 07.31
Scott, WAG, 06.2
Selby Smith, R, 11.1
Slight, Owen, 03.9
South Australian Department of Mines Library, Adelaide, 02.3, 02.12, 07.14
South Australian Institute of Technology, 06.17
South Australian Institutes, 01.3, 02.1, 10.3
South Australian Public Service Association, 07.11
Southwell, Brian, 06.2
Spring, John, 06.18
State Library of South Australia, *see* Public Library of South Australia
State Library of Victoria, Melbourne, 07.2, 07.6, 07.29
Statement on Freedom to Read, *see* Censorship
Stayner, Richard, 06.8, 12.1-12.2
Strout, Ruth, 02.14
Sydney Technical College, 06.17
Talbot, Michael, 07.3, 12.2
Tasmanian College of Advanced Education, 06.17
Tauber Report, 02.10
Townsend, Aubrey, 07.18
Trinity College, Dublin, 01.1-01.2, 01.6, 10.2-10.3
Turner, Jane, 12.1-12.2
Twaddle, Valda, 06.8
Unitarian Church, East Melbourne, 01.2, 10.3
United Nations Association, 07.6
University of Adelaide, 02.1, 02.2, 02.4, 02.11, 03.2, 03.8, 03.11, 06.8, 07.5, 07.9, 07.14, 07.19, *Fig. 3*
University of California, Los Angeles, 07.13
University of Melbourne, 06.1, 07.33, 11.1
University of Michigan, 03.15, 03.8
University of Minnesota at Minneapolis, Library School, 07.13
University of New South Wales, School of Librarianship, 06.17, 07.4-07.5, 07.15
University of Queensland Library, 07.16
Upward, Frank, 06.12, 07.3, 07.13, 12.2
Uranium debate, 07.11
Vera Moore Fund Committee, Monash University, 06.12, 07.21
Ward, Jack, 07.10
Watt, Robert, 07.23
Western Australian Institute of Technology, 06.17
White, Harold, 02.10, *Fig 7*
Whitlam, Gough, 05.3, 05.4, 06.11
Whyte, Counsell and Company, 01.3
Whyte, Eleanor May, 01.3
Whyte, Ernest Primrose (Prim), 01.1, 01.3, 01.4, 01.6, 01.7, 02.2, 03.2, 07.14, 07.17, 07.19, 07.22, 07.23, 07.25, 07.34, 10.4, *Fig. 6*
Whyte, Frank, 01.3
Whyte, Jean Primrose
    and animals, 03.2, 03.11, 05.1, 05.2, 06.3, 07.16-07.17, 07.19, *Fig. 2*
    and art, 07.21, 07.24
    and cataloguing, 02.2, 02.3, 02.4, 02.7, 02.10, 03.5, 03.6, 03.8, 03.9, 03.14, 04.3, 06.4, 06.6, 07.13, 07.14
    and information in languages other than English, 02.4, 06.8, 06.9, 07.7
    and library buildings, 03.5, 07.6
    and new and groundbreaking work, 07.7
    and politics, 07.22
    and religion, 07.22
    and sport, 07.22
    and technology, 03.3, 03.5-03.7, 04.3, 05.1, 06.4, 06.3, 06.5-6, 06.7, 06.8, 06.9, 06.10, 07.4, 07.7-07.8
    birth, 01.4
    death, 07.25, 07.27
    driving, 03.11, 07.21-07.22

head prefect, 01.5, 07.24
health concerns, 02.3, 03.2, 05.3, 06.3, 07.21, 01.4
intellect, 07.22-07.23, 07.24
library mania, xii, 03.2
overseas study, 02.8-02.9, 02.10
registration, 02.2
role of women, 07.14-07.16
schooling, 01.4-01.5
recruiting and mentoring, xii, 02.5, 02.6, 03.7, 05.3, 07.12-07.14
working hours, 02.2-02.3, 03.11, 07.12
world perspective, 07.11
Whyte, Jessie Eileen (Eileen), 01.4, 01.5, 01.7, 02.2, 07.25, 07.34, 10.4
Whyte, John, 01.3, 01.6
Whyte, Kathleen Duncan Campbell (Kitty), 01.1, 01.3, 01.4, 01.6, 01.7, 02.2, 07.7, 07.17, 07.19, 07.22, 07.25, 07.27, 07.34, 10.4, *Fig. 5*
Whyte, Louisa, 01.3
Whyte, Norah, 07.34
Whyte, Phyllis Primrose (Billie), 01.1, 01.4, 01.5, 02.2, 07.7, 07.14, 07.17, 07.19, 07.21, 07.25, 07.34, 10.4, *Fig. 1*
Whyte, William, 01.3
Wilde, Oscar, 01.6, 10.5
Wilkatana Station, South Australia, 01.4
Wilkinson, Eoin, 07.31
Williams, Bruce, 03.11
Williams, Christobel, 01.5
Wine, 02.7, 06.3, 07.19, 07.21, 07.24
Wines, Beatrice, 03.9, 03.15
Winston Churchill Memorial Trust, 07.24
Wintabatinyana, 01.4, 01.7
Wirraminna Station, South Australia, 01.4, 01.7
Wollaston, Pam, 07.19-07.20
Women, role of, 02.3, 02.6, 05.1, 07.14-07.16
Wood, Malvina E, 07.31
World Federal Union, 02.1, 07.6
Yadlamalka Station, South Australia, 01.4-01.5, 01.6, 01.7, 02.1, 07.14, 07.16, 07.19, 07.20, 07.21, 07.24